WHAT PEOPLE ARE SAYING ABOUT
Rethinking GOD with Tacos

Rethinking God with Tacos is a gateway invitation to a grand and bountiful feast, spread out for your delight and enjoyment—and perhaps a wee bit of consternation. The servants bearing the bread and wine are those whose lives are afire, marked by the transformative flames of the Good Gospel. Read and weep. Be filled and embraced by Relentless Affection.

—Paul Young,
Author of *The Shack*

I encourage anyone on a journey of rethinking and reconstructing the beliefs they were raised with or indoctrinated in to obtain Jason Clark's new book, *Rethinking God with Tacos*. Jason is a phenomenal storyteller and writer, weaving together the thoughts of his podcast guests into a beautiful tapestry of life-giving quotes, principles, wisdom, and, above all, a fresh unveiling of the Father, Son, and Spirit.

This book will edify and challenge you, and perhaps even anger you. Above all, it will cause you to think for yourself, and if you let it, transform you. Thank you, Jason, for who you are and all you do in the Kingdom of the dear Son.

—Jamie Englehart
Author/Overseer C.I.M. Network

I'm so thankful for people like Jason! He has helped me in a way that is so rich and deep on my own journey of rediscovering God and His goodness. We've had some amazing and challenging discussions that've ended in deeper respect, appreciation, and growth. I love that we can have relationships like this across the Body of Christ, regardless of any differing beliefs. Relationships are more important than being right!

In his new book, *Rethinking God with Tacos*, Jason has challenged and stretched me yet again, ultimately helping me grow and gain a much deeper understanding of God's love and goodness.

Our good Father is way better than we could ever think!

—Chris Gore
Author of *Release the Healers*, New Zealand

Processing our spiritual development requires listening to one another and re-evaluating our assumptions. *Rethinking God with Tacos* compiles some of the most fascinating conversations with people who may not have all the right answers but are certainly asking all the right questions.

—Keith Giles
Author of *The Quantum Sayings of Jesus: Decoding the Lost Gospel of Thomas*

Chatting with Jason and Derek was a delight. They didn't seem to be too interested in justifying themselves (the plague of our race) but were thrilled to "justify" the judgment of God, as Paul puts it. "Let God be true though everyone a liar" (Romans 3:4). I love the cast of characters in this book. I know some. I don't think they ever lied to me, but I know they delight in rethinking and rediscovering our God, who is "The Good" and whose Judgment is Jesus. May you read and fall in love all over again.

—Peter Hiett
Author of *The History of Time* and *the Genesis of You*

If Jason wove tapestries, his would hang in the most prestigious and opulent palaces of the world. *Rethinking God with Tacos* weaves together, not just notes and quotes from famous people, but storylines and wisdom from those whom Jason calls friends. This book will weave your story together with beautiful people and release you into more freedom on your journey with Jesus.

—Bob Switzer
Pastor/Author of The Epic Narrative
Podcast, thebobswitzer.com

Jason has again taken historically lifeless elements of theology and infused them with the compelling call of God's perfect love and union with Him. This time, his approach differs, examining the subject from all angles through the insights of thought leaders and practitioners. The goal isn't to agree with every point—far from it! Instead, it's to engage and be forged more deeply with the perfect love of the One, the author and perfecter of our faith. Read it. . . . I dare you!

—Mark Appleyard
Co-Founder, Anothen, anothen.co

It is time to rethink our picture of God. But we don't need to pursue this project in a stuffy, stale way. Who knew that tacos would bring us all to Jason's whimsical relational theological table for this much-needed, wide-ranging conversation? Buy the book. Rethink God. And eat some tacos!

—David Artman
Author of *Grace Saves All: The Necessity of Christian Universalism*

I first crossed paths with Jason Clark at a conference years back, both of us preaching our hearts out. Pretty sure they won't invite us back together unless they're desperate for a sequel to "How to Wreck an Event With Good News." And honestly, I'm fine with it. There's something about dropping gospel truth that makes folks clutch their theological pearls, rattles their religious cages, and rouses their rabble. Jason, though? He's the kindest kind of rabble-rouser, the guy who'll stir the pot with a grin, all while radiating greater love. It pours out of him toward Jesus, his family, and, of course, a perfectly crafted taco. This journey is a treasure, and this book documents the ride. I'm just honored to be part of this ragtag crew of love-drunk misfits, and grateful to call these troublemakers my friends.

—Bill Vanderbush
Author/Speaker, billvanderbush.com

Jason has a disarming humility, combined with a unique gift for bringing together a wide range of people who can shed light on the Beautiful Gospel, the Trinitarian understanding of a gospel rooted in a Person, who is the Word of God. His relaxed discussions in the Tacos podcasts draw out a treasure chest of gems, fascinating jewels of insight into the wonder of this grace message, emanating from the Community of Love. In this book, he has collected a precious summary from so many valuable conversations and presented them in a way that the reader can gain a helpful overview. I highly recommend it.

—David Hewitt
Leader of Wellsprings Community
Author of *Reconstructing Ecclesia* and *Ultimate Rest*

Rethinking God with Tacos is a masterful compilation of inspired and insightful voices—each of whom has had the honor of being a guest on the wildly beloved *Rethinking God with Tacos Podcast*, which has truly taken on a God-life of its own. What unites these diverse contributors is a shared, courageous grappling with a breathtaking God—One who defies boxes and formulas, and who lovingly invites all His children into the depths of His goodness, love, and beauty.

Woven between each guest's revelation, Jason shares his encounters and insights, drawing readers into a more expansive and transformative way of rethinking God. This is not a book to miss. So grab your favorite taco and feast at the table of wonder set before you. Stellar work, Jason!

—Catherine Toon, MD
Author/Speaker/Podcaster/Coach
Founder and CEO, Imprint and Catherine Toon Ministries

If it is "the Truth" that sets us free, then a search for truth should be paramount to our walk in faith and living as citizens of this invisible Kingdom. But in searching for a vast cosmic truth, certainty and exactitude are not the way; these processes are far too limiting to help find an unlimited God. Open-heartedness, humble discussion, and the joining together of seekers creates a path for opportunity to discover. Jason Clark, in his Rethinking God group, has created a forum for just such a searching conversation. Jason has shown us all a way to gather, to think together, and to find a path of grace and love.

—Bob Hamp
LMFT, Founder of Think Differently Academy

Humanity's current stage is desperate for a more expansive theology, something inclusive, gracious, and open-ended. Jason's *Rethinking God with Tacos* podcast, and now this book, is the kind of work we need. I hope you listen and read (and apply).

—Jonathan J. Foster
Author of *Theology of Consent: Mimetic Theory in an Open and Relational Universe*

There is no greater platform hosting conversations beneficial to those disentangling themselves from religion and stepping into the freedom of the Kingdom than the *Rethinking God with Tacos* podcast. This book distills and weaves together the truths unearthed in those conversations, offering a roadmap for those who have long sensed, deep in their hearts, the reality of the Trinity, our union, and the Kingdom—but have struggled to find the language to express it.

I highly recommend this resource for those who are committed to restructuring their belief systems around the foundational truth that "God is good and only good. He has only ever been good. And only ever been good in exactly the way that Jesus revealed."

—Dubb Alexander
Author of *Kingdom Theology: Volume 1*
& From the Cult to the Kingdom

Rethinking God With Tacos is a fresh, thought-provoking collection that invites readers to explore God's love and ways with curiosity and an open heart. Through unconventional but honest theology, this book gently dismantles common religious beliefs and offers a deeper, more grace-filled vision of God. It helps the reader grow in authentic love for God and others, not by fear or dogma, but by the wonder and spiritual freedom that only grace can bring.

—Steve McVey
Author of *Quantum Miracles: Unlocking Hidden Laws that Govern Miracles*, www.stevemcvey.com

Jason Clark has a gift—not just for powerful storytelling, but for inviting us to reimagine God through the lens of union, joy, and relentless love. *Rethinking God with Tacos* is not merely clever in title; it's profound in content. With every chapter, Jason dismantles the false scaffolding of fear-based theology and rebuilds our hearts on the secure foundation of a God who looks exactly like Jesus.

As a friend and fellow traveler in this grace-awakening journey, I've seen firsthand Jason's passion for Christ-centered revelation and his unflinching commitment to relational theology. His voice is needed now more than ever. This book is for the weary, the deconstructing, and the curious—those who've dared to hope that the good news might actually be . . . well, good. It turns out it is. And Jason serves it up with laughter, humility, deep theological insight—and yes, tacos.

—Matthew Hester
Founder of Present Truth Academy,
Author of *The Rorschach God*

Wow! Jason is such a gifted communicator and a strategic magnet in the Trinity economy, gathering global voices together in this symphony of conversation. His writing style is captivating. I just loved going through and touching sentences and pages in his Tacos Tapestry, celebrating the gifts in precious lives across the planet!

So beautifully articulated in John chapter 14 and mirrored in Jason's account of little Eva—Papa lifting troubled hearts to see the nearness of Who's been with us all along, "Hey, Phillip, I've been with you so long and you haven't seen the Father!?" Incarnate life exhibiting Father in the flesh of Sonship! To see the One is to see the other! And "NO," said Jesus, "I am not about to orphan or abandon you; I come to you! In Holy Spirit!"

The One does not diminish the other! JUST as I am in my Father, SO you are in me, And I in you! And ALL flesh shall see it TOGETHER!

—Francois du Toit
Author of *The Mirror Bible,* mirrorword.net

The work that Jason Clark has done in *Rethinking God with Tacos* is simply a beautiful cross-pollination of theological perspectives. A compilation and curation of conversations, I believe you will find that it reflects the truest essence of unity, which has always been diversity. In a church culture where there is so much polarization, Jason has courageously created a much-needed forum for the curious to question our answers. So many people today need guides like Jason and his colleagues who can compassionately assist them in finding their way out of the echo chambers of religious thought. Your response to reading this book will probably be "thank you for helping me to realize I'm not crazy or a heretic for questioning what I have always been taught."

—Randall Worley
Author of *Wandering and Wondering*
and *Brushstrokes of Grace*

A friend asked me the other day if Mary and I watch all the podcasts. I responded with. "Yes, of course, he's our kid."

Throughout my career in home construction and remodeling, I've had the privilege of working alongside some of the most talented and creative craftsmen and artists in their respective trades. The best, those who leave the biggest impression, are the ones who do it merely for love. I've often walked with these craftsmen to remind them that profit isn't a sin, that providing well for their families is honorable, and that a healthy respect for financial gain—for love's sake—is a good thing.

No other motivation.

Paul is clear about this motivation of love. I love how the Mirror Bible interpretation of 1 Corinthians 9:16 is a testimony to what we have seen up close in the life of Jason and Karen. "I live to preach; it consumes my total being. Your money is not going to make any difference since this Gospel has my arm twisted and locked behind my back. In fact, my life would be reduced to utter misery if it were not possible for me to preach the Good News."

Paul couldn't help himself. Neither can Jason.

Jason is a true artist. Over the years, we've watched his passion for quality and excellence in everything he touches. Karen is thankful he also has some carpentry skills because he could never afford to hire one. His music, writing, preaching, storytelling, podcast conversations, and team-building skills continue to amaze, as he gives hardly a moment's thought to whether it will pay his bills.

I am here to confirm that both he and Karen are motivated by love and love alone. This *Gospel has their arms twisted and locked behind their backs*. However, as Jason's parents, we are thankful that these days, when we look in his fridge, it's always full. It's refreshing to see a team coming around him to help fill in the gaps, and release him to "preach" with more freedom this Good News—to create with LOVE.

And now you all get to reap the benefits with us. Now we all can enjoy the read!

—Lloyd Clark
Pastor/Entrepreneur/Author, *The Life I Dreamed Of*

Jason has a rare gift—not just for writing or teaching, but for creating space where people feel seen, safe, and invited into something deeper. This book carries that same spirit. It's thoughtful, disarming, and full of the kind of good news that actually sounds like good news. Every chapter feels like a conversation that stays with you—because it's not just theology, it's story, it's heart, it's Jesus. If you're hungry to rethink God through the lens of love, this book is a beautiful place to start.

—Bryant Spratlin
Pastor, teacher, counselor, fellow traveler

Mix contagious childlike joy with a deep passion for Jesus and a genuine love for people, and you have Jason Clark, who brilliantly leads us into the eternal dance with the Lover of our souls that has already begun. Meandering through the pages of *Rethinking God with Tacos* will convince you that though the grace covenant seems almost too good to be true, it is in fact the very essence of the Good News. It sets us free to enjoy the sweet depth of intimate face-to-face relationship with the Trinity that has always been their dream and desire.

—Brent Lokker
Author of *Always Loved: You are God's Treasure, Not His Project*

Rethinking God with Tacos is a desperately needed re-presentation of who God truly is—a vision that breaks away from the shackles of retributive theology and reveals the heart of the Triune God: fully relational, unfailingly good, and fiercely loving. With the insight of a theologian and the compassion of a pastor, Jason gently dismantles harmful misconceptions and leads us into a healing, transformative encounter with the God who is Love—kind, close, and never vengeful. This book is a lifeline for anyone yearning to know a God who restores rather than condemns, looks just like Jesus, and who calls us to reflect that Love to others.

—Dr. Matt Pandel
Theologian, Behavioral Psychologist, Educator
President, Global Grace Seminary

Rethinking GOD with Tacos

Copyright © 2025 by Jason Clark

Published by UNORTHODOX Resources

All rights reserved. No portion of this book may be reproduced, stored in a retrieval system, or transmitted in any form or by any means—electronic, mechanical, photocopy, recording, scanning, or other—except for brief quotations in critical reviews or articles, without prior written permission of the author.

Unless otherwise noted, all Scripture quotations are taken from the Holy Bible, New International Version®, NIV®. Copyright © 1973, 1978, 1984, 2011 by Biblica, Inc.™ Used by permission of Zondervan. All rights reserved worldwide. www.zondervan.com. The "NIV" and "New International Version" are trademarks registered in the United States Patent and Trademark Office by Biblica, Inc.™ | Scripture quotations marked BSB are from The Holy Bible, Berean Study Bible, BSB, Copyright ©2016, 2020 by Bible Hub Used by Permission. All Rights Reserved Worldwide. | Scripture quotations marked KJV are taken from the King James Version of the Bible. Public domain. | Scripture quotations marked NKJV are taken from the New King James Version®. Copyright © 1982 by Thomas Nelson. Used by permission. All rights reserved.

For foreign and subsidiary rights, contact the author.

Cover design by: Todd Petelle
Cover photo by: Seth Snider

ISBN: 978-1-964794-00-6   1 2 3 4 5 6 7 8 9 10

Printed in the United States of America

Jason Clark
Foreword by C. Baxter Kruger, Ph.D.

Rethinking GOD with Tacos

Reclaiming the Gospel of Love

UNOXODO RESOURCES

*This book is dedicated to all those who have graced the podcast with their presence and revelation of God's always good love.
Thank you.*

CONTENTS

Foreword . . . . *xxiii*
Acknowledgments . . . . *xxxiii*
Introduction 35
CHAPTER 1. What Is the Gospel? 41
CHAPTER 2. The Cross 55
CHAPTER 3. Union 75
CHAPTER 4. A Christological Hermeneutic 89
CHAPTER 5. Relational Theology 113
CHAPTER 6. On Deconstruction 129
CHAPTER 7. Trinitarian Faith 145
CHAPTER 8. The Incarnation 155
CHAPTER 9. Identity 167
CHAPTER 10. A Path to Wholeness 189
CHAPTER 11. The Church 201
CHAPTER 12. The Kingdom 219
CHAPTER 13. Grace 237
CHAPTER 14. Inclusion 251
CHAPTER 15. Rethinking Universalism 271
CHAPTER 16. Rethinking Hell 287
CHAPTER 17. Justice 309
CHAPTER 18. The Long Arc of Love 323

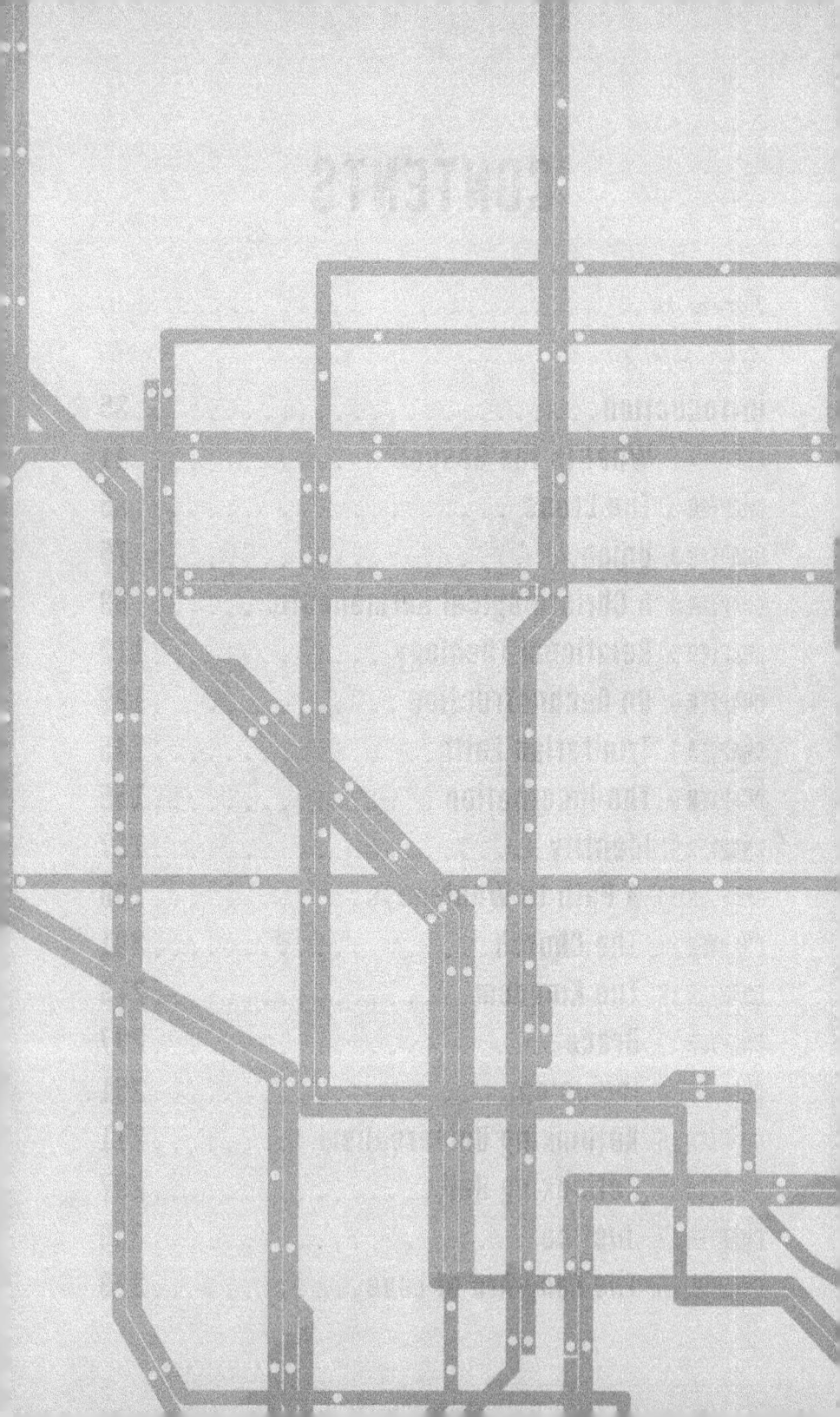

FOREWORD

What excites me about this book is that we get to overhear conversations between Jason and people from around the world with diverse backgrounds on the famous *Rethinking God with Tacos* Podcast. But groupthink is not necessarily a good thing. It could be a pooling of clever, dead-end ignorance with scripture verses. What makes these conversations exceptional is that they are about the real Jesus—the Jesus of the apostles and the early church, the Jesus who has been lost over the centuries in assumptions that have blinded us to His reality.

Jason likes to refer to himself as a *relational* theologian, which I suppose is his attempt to distance himself from what he really thinks about theologians! But the best theologians in history, the ones we still read, have always been relational. They have always been driven by the questions of the soul and the broken heart, and by astonishment at the love of the blessed Trinity to cross all the worlds of diabolical delusion and human pain to find us and give us eyes to see the eternal, everlasting, never-flinching, never-crossed-their-mind-to-abandon-us—covenant love of the Father, Son, and Holy Spirit.

Somewhere in the first chapter, Jason, speaking of a moment with his daughter when she was interrupted with fear, says, "I positioned myself in her pain, confusion, disappointment, and lack of understanding." Jason wrote these words, but Jesus said them first—incarnated them—and said them again through Jason's pen. This is the gospel.

Our relationship with the Father has been profoundly destroyed by fear. We have created a god in the image of this fear. We tarred the Father's face with the brush of our own darkness, and hand-crafted a religion, with scripture verses, to go with it. We have been running and playing church ever since. Our running and playing have left those we love, or want to, alone, as we chase one promising solution after another, only to be left shattered again and again, but still scanning the horizon for the next, latest rendition of religion.

This book is a collection of joyful conversations between Christian sisters and brothers who have met Jesus in their own broken lives. We have serious questions about what we have been taught in the Church in the West, and how it does not work in real life. We did not know that the "Western model of Christianity" with its angry and distant God, its assumption of human separation from God, the cross as the place where God poured out His wrath on Jesus that was aimed at us, and such nonsense, was not the early Church's vision at all. The Western model is an aberration. What many of us have grown up hearing is not the astonishing gospel, but a bizarre and, at times, pathetic mixture of Adam's fallen mind, Greek philosophy, Roman law, and Christian revelation.

The gospel is not the news that we can receive Jesus Christ into our lives. The gospel is the news that Jesus Christ, the Father's eternal and anointed Son incarnate, has received us into His life—exactly as it was planned before the creation of the world (Ephesians 1:3-5; 2 Timothy 1:9). According to John and Paul, all things without exception were created in and through and by and for Jesus Christ, and He holds all things together (John 1:3; Colossians 1:16-17). John Calvin wrote:

> *The Word of God was not only the fount of life to all creation, so that those which had not existed began to be, but that His life-giving power makes them remain in their state. For did not His continued inspiration quicken the world, whatsoever flourishes would without doubt immediately decay or be reduced to nothing.[1]*

The anointed Son did not become human in order to establish a relationship with the human race, for all things were created and are sustained in Him. He became human to recreate His relationship, His union with humanity inside the abyss of diabolical delusion and our broken humanity.

According to the apostles, each and every one of us has lost our minds (1 Corinthians 2:14; Ephesians 4:17ff; John 1:10ff, 18). So much so that Jesus says that we actually *love* the darkness and *hate* the light (John 3:19-20), and are

---

[1] Calvin, John. *Institutes of the Christian Religion.* Edited by John T. McNeill. Translated by Ford Lewis Battles. 2 vols. Louisville, KY: Westminster John Knox Press, 2006. Book 1, Chapter 16.

incapable and unwilling to come to Him (John 5:37-42). So, the Father's anointed Son *came to us.* According to Irenaeus, "Our Lord Jesus Christ, who did, through His transcendent love, become what we are, that He might bring us to be even what He is Himself." It is quite astonishing. All that the Son has with his Father in the fellowship of the Holy Spirit, the shared life, the fullness and joy, the righteousness and blessedness, the holiness and goodness, everything He is, Jesus has brought to us, in order that we may share in His own communion with His Father in the Holy Spirit. But what is the point of such an astonishing gift if we are not capable of receiving it? Why would the Father give to us His own Son when He knows we are unwilling and incapable of coming to Him? Irenaeus sees the logic of the real gospel. If the goal is to bring us to be what He is that we might share in His life with His Father, then He must meet us where we are. He must become what we are.

The Scriptures teach that the Father's Son did indeed become a human being, one of us. Such a sacrificial act of humble love is almost too beautiful to believe. But the incarnation is still more beautiful yet. To deliver us from evil, He must enter our delusion and bring His sanity to us. He must find a way to bring His faithfulness to His Father into our unfaithfulness, His determined will into our willful rejection of Him, His eyes into our blindness, His heart into ours, His holiness into our flesh, His goodness into our sin. This is why John tells us that Jesus not only became human, He became "flesh" (John 1:14), which is our humanity twisted in evil. And Paul is bold to say that Jesus who knew no sin, "became sin" (2 Corinthians 5:21). Only in this way could Jesus meet us, become what we are, so that He could give Himself and all that He is with His Father and the Holy Spirit *to us* as we are in the great delusion.

But how could the Son who lives face to face with His Father in undiluted fellowship in the Spirit possibly enter into our delusion and idolatry, where the Father is not known or honored at all, and we are broken souls? Here we stand a hair's breadth from the most astonishing love in the cosmos. Our Lord Jesus, the Father's eternal and beloved and faithful Son, the one anointed in the Holy Spirit without measure, the Creator and Sustainer of all things not only became human, He made His way inside our diabolical delusion down to the very bottom of its abyss where all is sorrow and pain and dead. How? In a single word, *submission*. He made His way inside the abyss of our delusion by submitting to us and our hatred and vile unfaithfulness to Him. It was not the Father's wrath that was poured out on Jesus on Calvary's hill. *It was ours.* We murdered him. We condemned Him. In an act of utter apostasy, the human race damned and cursed and crucified the Father's anointed Son.

The Father never abandoned Jesus. "Behold, an hour is coming, and has come, for you to be scattered, each to his own home, and to leave Me alone; and yet I am not alone, because the Father is with Me" (John 16:32; see 8:29). Paul declares that "God was in Christ reconciling the cosmos to himself" (2 Corinthians 5:19). And the Holy Spirit was not a spectator watching with a box of tissues from a distance. As always, the Father, Son, and Holy Spirit are together, indivisibly one. In Jesus, the life of the eternal and blessed Trinity, and nothing less, descended into the abyss of human delusion and rage and wrath. Jesus submitted Himself to be mocked, scourged, and murdered by human beings, while they were breathing Christological air. The story is not about sinners in the hands of an angry God. The story is about God in the hands of angry sinners. In Jesus's submission to us, He found His way into the flesh, into sin, into our insanity, where Satan had his hold, and into the place where the blackest darkness blinds us all to the Father's face. And there in Jesus's submission to us, He brought His indivisible oneness and at-oneness with His Father, and His own limitless anointing in the Holy Spirit into our insanity and idolatry, into our unfaithfulness and apostasy, into our flesh and sin. Our contribution to our salvation was to damn the eternal Word of God, and Jesus and His Father and the Holy Spirit took up our damning of the Son and transfigured it into the mercy seat where the human race is embraced at its apostate worst in everlasting divine mercy. This is the new covenant, the new creation, the recreation of all things in the very person of Jesus Christ, whereby He, in His shocking self-surrender to us, restored His union with us all by way of our unfaithful treachery.

The gospel is the news of what became of the Father's Son, and of what became of us and creation in Him. As Paul proclaims, when Jesus died, we died—Adam, the human race, you and me, all of us died with Him (2 Corinthians 5:14; Ephesians 2:4ff). In Jesus, God has not only done something *for* us, but *with* us and *to* us. As we murdered the Father's

Son, God took us into the grave with Jesus. And God raised us up with Jesus, quickening us with Holy Spirit life, and seated us with Jesus at His right hand, far above rule and authority, and every name that is named, not only in this age, but also in the one to come (Ephesians 2:4-6; 1:21).

And there is more. For Paul and John, the salvation of the human race in Jesus's incarnate life, death, resurrection, and ascension is also the *revelation* to us of the *mystery* of God hidden from the foundation of the world. Jesus and His recreated union with us is not plan B, or a half-time adjustment, quickly conceived after the failure of Adam. Jesus's union with us is the goal of our creation. Here in Jesus, and in His indivisible union with His Father and the Holy Spirit, and His indivisible union with broken humanity, we see the one, eternal will of the Triune God for the human race. And it has all become historical and personal fact—reality. This is what it means that Jesus is the *Light* of the world (John 8:12; 12:46). He is the source and the meaning of our existence. Standing before Him, we are looking at the eternal dream of the Triune God for us. All true Christian theology stands here in Jesus, in marvel and in wonder and worship.

As we encounter Jesus Himself in our delusion, a thousand questions emerge. How can this be? How could we have been so wrong about the Father? What is Jesus's life with his Father really like? What does it mean that we are all included in Jesus's anointing in the Holy Spirit? If Jesus is in His Father, and we are in Him, and He is in us (John 14:20), why is the world, and why is my life, such a mess? How is Jesus the answer to our relational bankruptcy, our addictions, and the myriad of "isms" that afflict His world? It is questions like these, heart questions about the reality and the meaning of Jesus's union with us, that the enlightening conversations in this book revolve around.

A few years ago, I was sitting in the car waiting to pick up two of my grandchildren. Leonard Cohen's famous song *Hallelujah*[2] played on the radio. It is a haunting, beautiful song, but there is not much gospel in it. As I listened, these words came to me.

The Sacred Word
  I heard there was a sacred Word
  That Abba spoke before the earth
  But you don't really care for gospel, do yah?
  Before the worlds came to be
  They dreamed a dream of you and me
  And pledged their faithful love for us forever.
  Hallelujah, Hallelujah, Hallelujah, Hallelujah.
  But Adam to the whisper fell
  He broke our minds and turned all to hell
  But Abba's Word abides forever faithful.
  Into the dark, the Memra came
  And Abraham believed His name
  But Israel, O Israel, hardly knew yah.
  Hallelujah, Hallelujah, Hallelujah, Hallelujah.
  I heard there was a little girl
  Yes, she said to Abba's Word
  And through her faith, the Word was born unto yah.

---
2 Leonard Cohen, vocalist, "Hallelujah" by Leonard Cohen and Mikael Wiehe, December 11, 1984, track 5 on *Various Positions*, D Angers Musique Inc.

As Abba's Word we cursed and damned
He bowed before us as the little Lamb
And made His way inside us all forever.
Hallelujah, Hallelujah, Hallelujah, Hallelujah.
I heard there was a sacred Word
That Abba spoke before the world
And now He speaks His sacred Word within yah.
Listen now, and listen soft
Abba's Word sings in your heart
And it's not a cold or broken hallelujah.
Hallelujah, Hallelujah, Hallelujah, Hallelujah.

—C. Baxter Kruger, Ph.D.
Author of the international bestsellers,
The Shack Revisited and *Patmos*

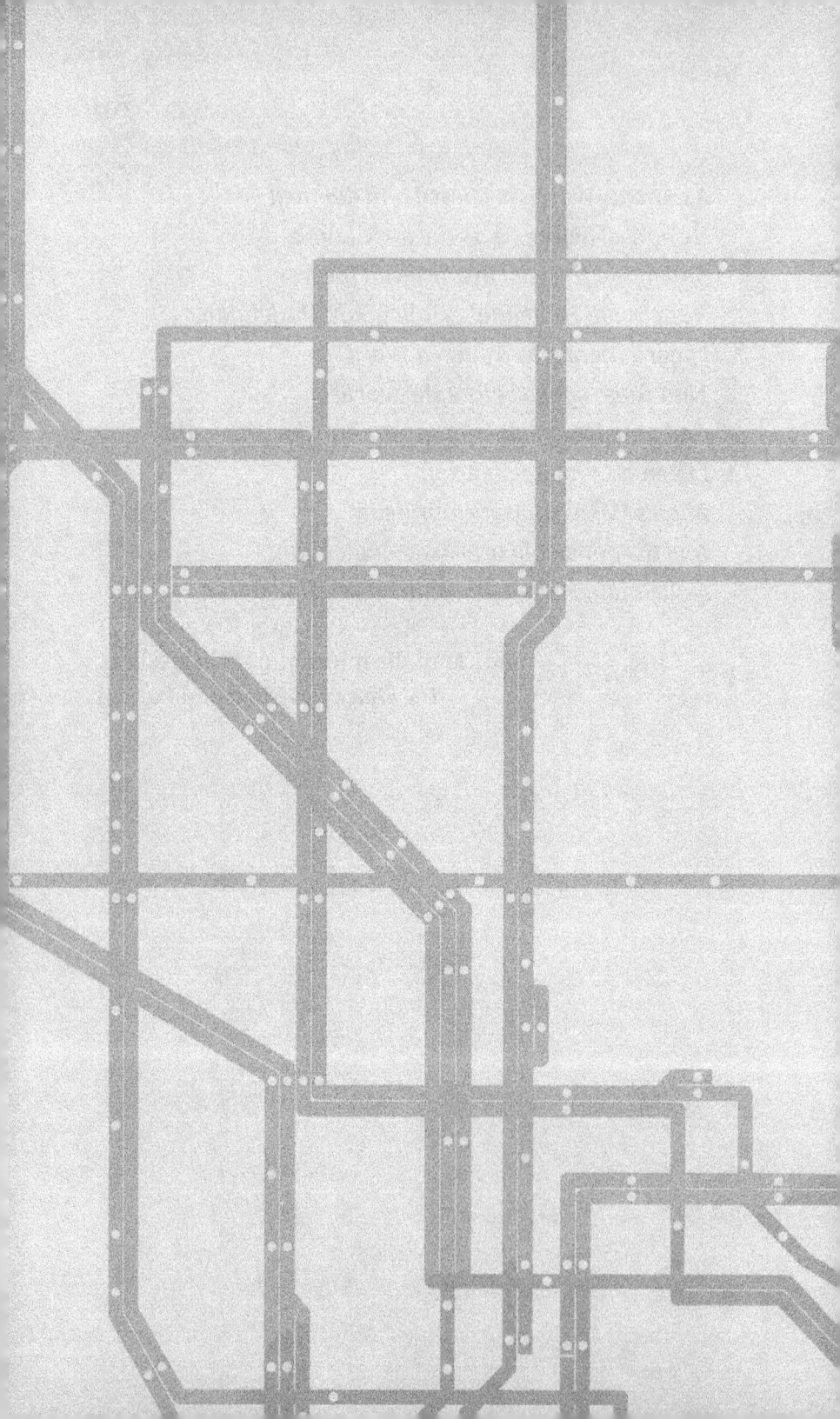

ACKNOWLEDGMENTS

I want to thank:

Our podcast guests and co-hosts—specifically my friend Derek Turner. I'm honored to be on this Good News journey together.

The podcast community—your kindness, connection, and encouragement are life-giving.

My bride, Karen, and my kids—Madeleine and Joseph, Ethan and Eva—my mom and dad on both sides of the family, and all the rest of my family and friends. I love you.

Those who walk with us to carry this Family Story: Jeremy and Kathryn Cole, Mark and Julie Appleyard, Brooke and Danl Waters, Bryant and Libby Spratlin, Baxter Kruger, and David Peck. There is exponential life around you all.

Thanks to our home church, we love doing life together.

I want to thank Martijn van Tilborgh, who has championed this union message, and everyone at Four Rivers Media—notably, Megan Adelson, a brilliant editor and a pleasure to work with, and Allison van Tilborgh-Martinous, who developed and kept everything flowing. This book wouldn't have happened without the whole team.

And thanks to Seth Snider for the incredible photography. And Father. And Son. And Holy Spirit.

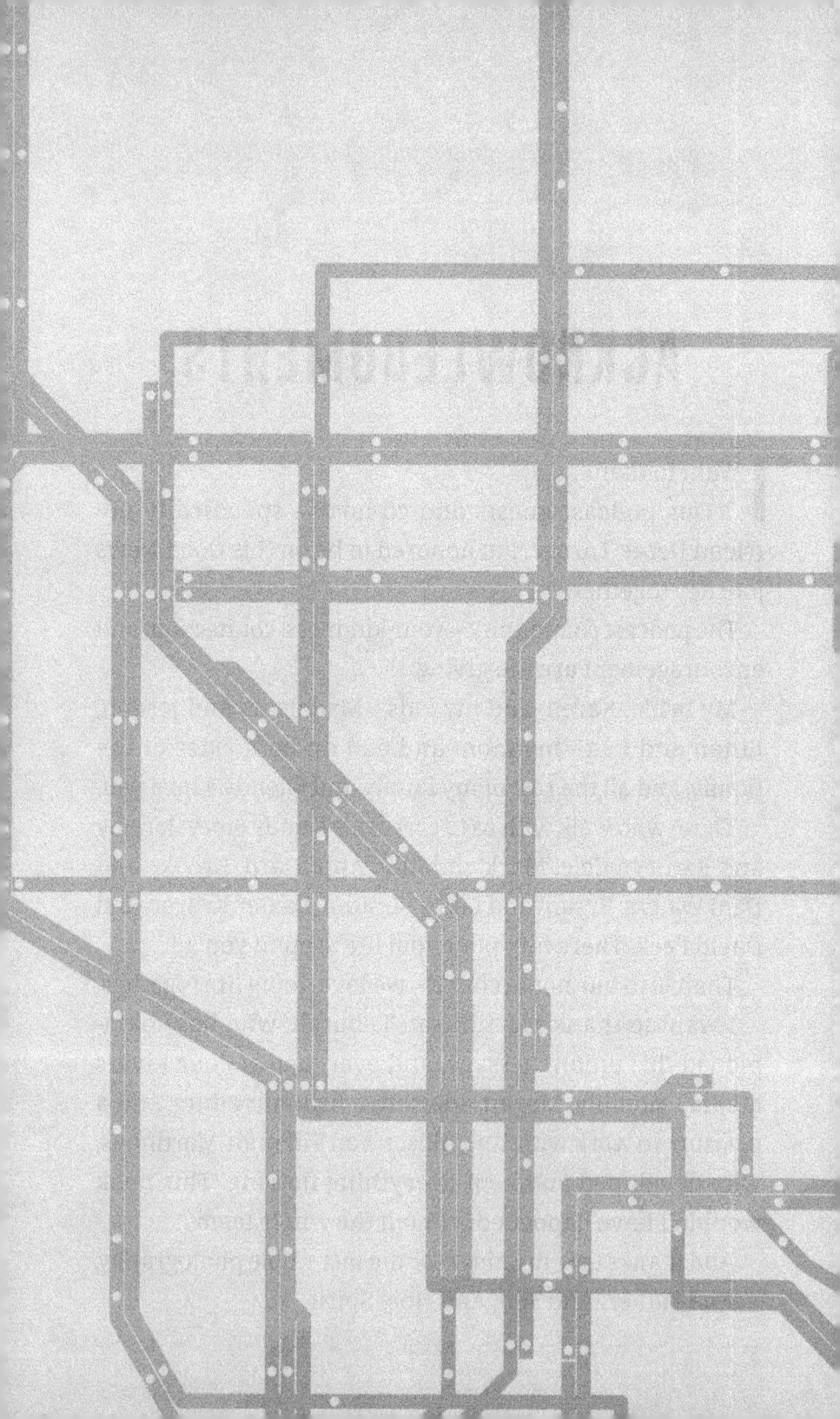

INTRODUCTION
An Invitation to the Table

Jesus constantly revealed God as better than we imagined. He did things at odds with how God was expected to behave. And it was often confusing—even offensive. He healed on the Sabbath. He elevated children, honored women, and embraced the outcast. He refused to call down fire on His enemies. He forgave the adulterous woman. And in every act, He shattered expectations of what God was like.

Jesus even did things that were better than how the Bible seemed to describe Him. He offended people simply by believing, acting, and teaching that God was better than their best thoughts about Him.

Time and again, Jesus revealed a God who was more compassionate, forgiving, and generous than anyone anticipated. His every act of kindness, lavish mercy, and radical grace upended people's assumptions. Especially those who thought they knew God best.

Humanity had "God-boxes." And Jesus kept blowing them up. He was better than we could think.

And nothing has changed.

Even today, Jesus confronts our narrow interpretations and challenges our best theological constructs with one unshakable reality: the relentless, unchanging, always good, never-ending love of God.

We all have God-boxes. They're shaped by culture, tradition, or personal experience. They're crafted from well-intentioned but limited approaches to Scripture and transactional atonement theories. But God, in His kindness, refuses to stay in those boxes.

Paul writes that it's God's goodness that leads us to repentance—to rethink. This journey of rethinking isn't a one-time event; it's an ongoing transformation. It's a life-long journey. As we awaken to union, as our minds are renewed, we begin to see clearly. And the clearer we see, the more amazed we are by how good He is in light of how small our boxes are.

This journey is stunning. It's marked by righteousness, peace, joy.

And sometimes, it's lonely.

A few years ago, a friend prayed over Karen and me. He shared a word that named the season we were in with the promise of a future we are now experiencing.

"Jason, I see you guys on an island."

We felt that. We were deep in the process of rethinking. Jesus was blowing up our God boxes with a revelation of His love that was too good for most of the folks around us.

He continued. "You've explored, discovered, and stewarded the resources of this island, even though it has been lonely. You've awakened to measureless love—the answer to every question that aches in the heart of humanity."

Then the picture shifted.

"But you're not alone," he continued, smiling. "Your island is part of an archipelago—a whole chain of islands. Each one unique. Each one stewarded by people equally convinced of the goodness of God. And I see a day coming when bridges will be built between these islands, where once you felt alone, you will know connection, and the resources of the islands will flow."

That word gave language to our story.

We were living in a world that preached separation, but we were learning to live in union. And though it was lonely, those years were sacred. They anchored us in presence, in trust, and in the deep, unshakable reality of God's always-good love.

And then . . . the bridges started appearing.

Conversations. Friendships. Podcasts. People who had navigated their island seasons and discovered, like we had, that God is better than our last best thought about Him. That there is no shadow of turning with Thee.

This book is a collection of those bridges.

Rethinking God with Tacos is a record of conversations with friends—pastors, poets, philosophers, and prophets—who have dared to be offended by the goodness of a God who won't stay in the box. They have been willing to rethink. This book recognizes the moments of holy curiosity and delicious offense, where God is better than the last time we checked. The book highlights friends who have helped me rethink not just what I believe, but how I belong. They've given language to a gospel of union.

These podcast years have been bridge years, connecting years. And this book explores the vast archipelago rethinking that has been going on since before the beginning. It's an invitation to rediscover the always-good love of God. I couldn't include every voice from the podcast, but I'm thankful for every person who has dared to step beyond the box and into the mystery of our union with the Father, Son, and Holy Spirit.

So, bring your questions. Your doubts. Your God-boxes.

Together, we're part of something breathtaking: an awakening to grace, love, and union. The revelation that God is better than we thought, and oneness with Him, has always been the point.

Let's rethink God together.

With tacos, of course.

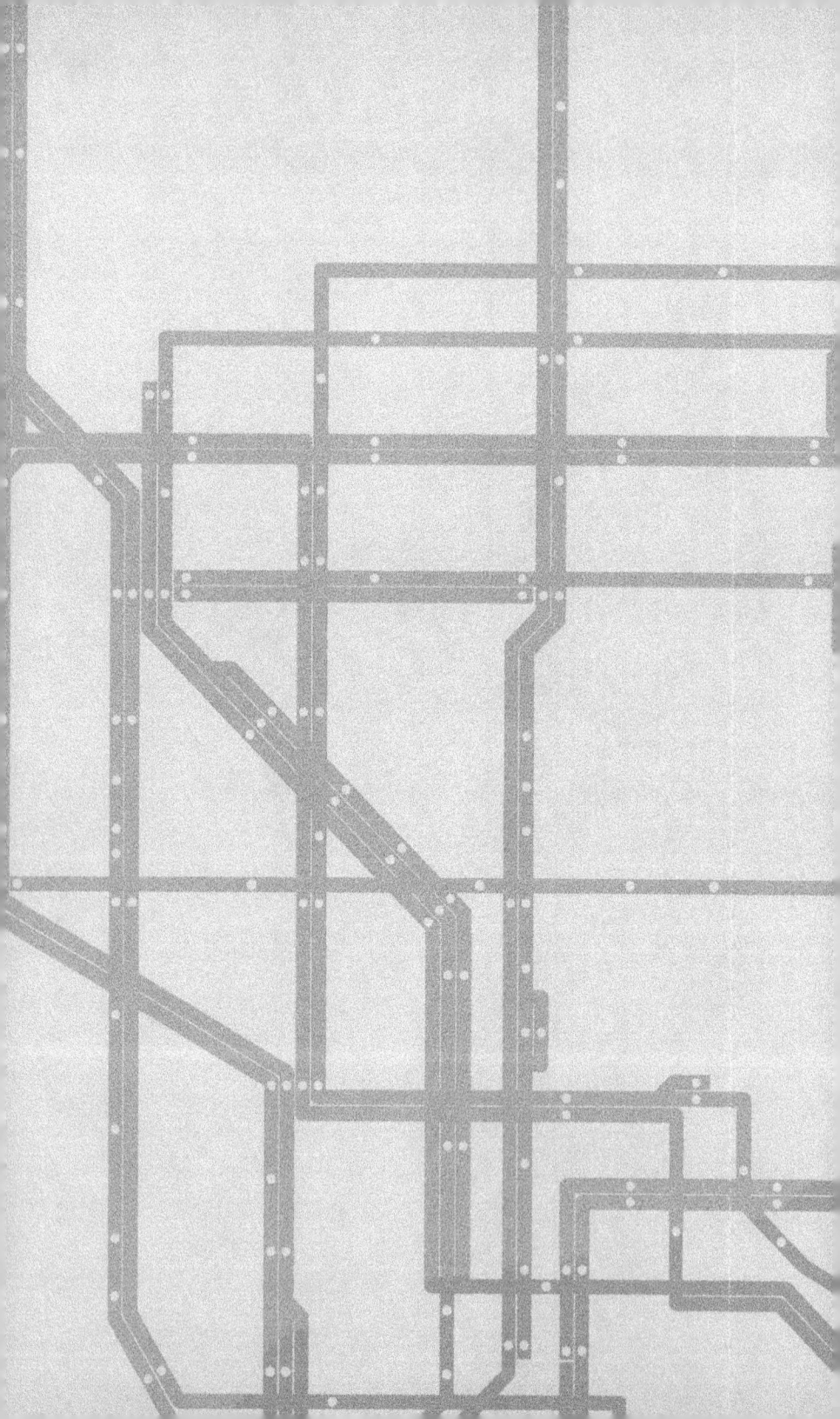

CHAPTER 1

WHAT IS THE GOSPEL?

Taco Bout the Good News

TWO WEEKS AND A TAMBOURINE

I first met C. Baxter Kruger in Ridgeland, Mississippi, just north of Jackson. He spoke at my parent's house church. I was twenty-something, married a handful of years, with a new little girl and singing lead in my band, Fringe—when I wasn't two weeks and a tambourine ahead.

"Two weeks and a tambourine ahead." That's what the good-natured pastor said after I led worship in a pre- 'Love Wins' Rob Bell[3]-enamored, 150-member Jackson, Mississippi, Baptist-adjacent church.

New to the South by way of New York, I was unused to dismissals being so polite. I almost missed it. But I'd grown up in the Church and, thus, was already well-versed in the

---
3 Rob Bell, *Love Wins: A Book About Heaven, Hell, and the Fate of Every Person Who Ever Lived* (San Francisco, CA: HarperOne, 2011).

loneliness of *"Christian"* rejection. I'd already been bloodied by the *"Buckle."*

Most North Americans reference the South as the *Bible Belt*. And most Southerners claim their city as the *Buckle*. But having lived in States—both North and South—plus a couple of Canadian Provinces, I've learned that the Buckle isn't confined to a region; it's the result of the Western Evangelical religious obsession with separation.

For me, those five years in Jackson were Buckle years.

In Mississippi, Christian Evangelicalism is the dominating religion—an identity intricately woven into the fabric of social hierarchy. You go to church on Sunday in the same way you celebrate America with BBQ and fireworks on the 4th of July. There's a church building on every street corner and two more in between; church membership is cataloged, and pastors collect them like baseball cards.

I love the Church—the Ecclesia. She raised me. I grew up in Her pews, theatre seats, and fold-up chairs. My deepest friendships have been formed in Her care. I've experienced Her compassion, kindness, generosity, wisdom, and grace. And, above all, I've encountered the love of Father, Son, and Holy Spirit through Her goodness.

I've also experienced hypocrisies, abuses, betrayals, and rejections in the church—the religious institution. I've listened to many a Western *"gospel"* message. You know them—the desperate *preach* where Jesus saves us from the wrath of His angry, sin-counting, hell-obsessed, back-turning Father.

> **THAT WELL-MEANING PASTOR WAS JUST ONE MORE GATEKEEPER IN A RELIGION OF GATEKEEPERS.**

So many have toiled under the onerous Western Evangelical message of separation—the religious obsession with retribution— the dualistic hierarchical preoccupation with good and evil, where the last often remain last, and the first often have pulpits from which they determine who's *"in"* and who's *"out."*

Jackson, Mississippi, is a fantastic town with beautiful people, but for me, it was the *Buckle*. It was where the separation message manifested in the most suffocating way. Between my personal wrestle with the lie that *the* good Father turned His back and living in the gargantuan shadow of monuments built to propagate and defend it, the rejection of that pastor's *two weeks and a tambourine* dismissal echoed in every fiber of my Christian being. It put words to my lifelong experience with the brutality of the institution's *polite* dismissal.

That well-meaning pastor was just one more gatekeeper in a religion of orphan gatekeepers.

And I imagine my experience resonates. Both the positive and the negative. The Church that loves. And the church that hates. The Church that restores and condemns, includes and excludes, blesses, and curses. Every day, I meet brothers and sisters who were raised in the religion of separation. And the trauma experienced in that disparity has everyone convinced their *"town"* is the *Buckle*.

The first time I met Baxter, I lived like an orphan—dismissed, insecure, lonely, and suspicious. To me, Baxter seemed *two weeks and a tambourine ahead*.

God has a wonderful sense of humor.

Baxter is not from Jackson. He lives in Brandon, Mississippi, just outside. And he'll correct you if you suggest otherwise. To him, the delineation matters in the same way I feel when a waitress offers Pepsi after I asked for Coke.

I'm sure what Baxter shared at my parents' house church was revelatory; he was already miles down the road of this Trinitarian good news, but I wasn't ready. And maybe he wasn't, either. After all, he's also experienced the Buckle's infatuation with separation and the rejection of anyone who dares believe that a good Father never looked away; that Love never leaves or forsakes—not once, not ever.

But I'm getting ahead of myself.

Regardless, that meeting introduced me to a fella I would later come to know as a friend.

After I launched the podcast, people kept saying, "You gotta have Baxter on!"

My first thought was, *You mean that smart fella from the Buckle town that rejected me?*

But those wounds have long since healed. They've become scars I occasionally show as testimonies of my Father's restoring nature.

As I continue to explore union, as I continue to find language for the Greater Love that laid His life down for us, His friends, the delusion of separation loosens its grip. I've tasted and seen that the Lord is good and only good, as Jesus reveals. I've discovered there is no shadow of turning in the Trinity (see James 1:17), and thus, I continue to grow confident in love.

Within the first minute of the podcast conversation, I was grinning. Baxter's warm southern charm didn't trigger—just the opposite—he sounded like home.

From the first word, we talked about the gospel—the good news that is actually only and always good! Not as a theological abstraction—I've never been able to keep up with academic confabulations—but as a living, breathing participation with LIFE.

Don't misunderstand; Baxter has academic chops; he can parse with the best of them. But you'd never feel less than or unseen while he did so. Just the opposite. His knowledge sits at the feet of LOVE, not the other way round. That's because Baxter is convinced God is love, and His love is always good, even better than we can imagine.

Baxter spoke about the gospel of Jesus—an other-centered, self-giving Greater Love. A friendship that shapes and transforms.

In every word, I felt the *good news* explode within my heart!

Baxter was one of our first podcast guests, and our conversation was foundational and, thus, the perfect place to begin this book.

WHAT IS THE GOSPEL?

Baxter is a kind fella, a Southern gentleman, and brilliant. It wasn't long before we discussed a shared hero in Scripture: the disciple, John, *"The one Jesus loved"* (see John 13:23).

We began by diving into the book of John, a text that has been a wellspring for me. Baxter shared how John's narrative isn't merely a collection of theological insights; it's a living testament to the ongoing dialogue between God and humanity. This dialogue reveals the very heart of our Christian faith, where everything ultimately points to intimacy and union with Father, Son, and Holy Spirit.

"Jesus came into our darkness not merely to rescue us but to illuminate it from within."

There's a reason they call it the good news, I thought.

You'll read that phrase often as it's a discovery I continually make—Jesus is simply astonishing, and the good news is always better than the last time I checked!

Baxter continued. "Jesus entered our darkness not to condemn us but to bring light and clarity. He didn't stand on the sidelines, judging our delusions and pain. Instead, He stepped into our mess, illuminating the shadows with His presence."

THE GOSPEL IS NOT GOOD ADVICE BUT GOOD NEWS ABOUT WHAT HAS ALREADY BEEN ACCOMPLISHED.

For years, Baxter has put language around the Trinitarian faith. And this early conversation was a foundational invitation for the podcast in the days and years ahead.

"Jesus stepped into our delusion, our pain, and our brokenness not as an outsider but as one of us, revealing the Father's heart in the midst of our deepest struggles." Baxter continued, "This is not a distant theological concept but a lived reality, a beacon of hope in the darkest nights of the soul."[45]

These words reminded me of another new friend and podcast guest, Francois du Toit, who said, "The gospel is not good advice but good news about what has already been accomplished."[6]

As Baxter shared, I was reminded of the countless times I've seen this truth play out in my own life and in the lives of those around me. And, of course, as a relational theologian—more on that later—I remembered Eva.

TO SEE HOW HE SEES

When my daughter Eva was an infant and even into her toddler days, she had an all-consuming attachment to her momma. Karen rarely went anywhere without her, including laundry rooms, bedrooms, and bathrooms.

---

4 Jason Clark and Derek Turner, hosts, *Rethinking God with Tacos*, podcast, adapted excerpts from "C. Baxter Kruger / Jesus Meets Us Inside Our Delusion," May 20, 2022, https://www.youtube.com/watch?v=HKfRdC9GayA.
5 Jason Clark and Thomas Floyd, hosts, *Rethinking God with Tacos*, podcast, adapted excerpts from "C. Baxter Kruger / Christ In You!," November 22, 2023, https://www.youtube.com/watch?v=JtDMHH7n2hs.
6 Jason Clark, host, *Rethinking God with Tacos*, podcast, adapted excerpts from "Francois du Toit / Jesus Is What God Believes About You." Sep 18, 2024 https://www.youtube.com/watch?v=4Sa9hs7o90E&t=2s

When Karen needed to leave the house without Eva, we had to be very strategic regarding her exit. Otherwise, we could have a potential near-nuclear crisis.

And then there were the occasions when Karen, without thinking, would get the mail! She would simply walk out the front door—without Eva!

I know!

The mailbox was only twenty-five feet from the house, and it would take no more than a minute before she returned. But if Eva happened to see Karen leave....

The sounds she made would break your heart.

And I would come running. I would scoop her up, hold her close, and whisper, "It's ok, honey; Daddy's got you. Momma is coming right back."

Even though I like to tell my kids that I just may be the world's greatest father, none of them would describe me as long-suffering. But even at my most impatient, I was never annoyed or angered by Eva's tears. I never belittled her inability to comprehend the situation.

As her loving dad, I recognized my little girl didn't understand that her momma was just outside the door. I was able to see from her perspective and value it. I positioned myself in her pain, confusion, disappointment, and lack of understanding.

"Daddy's got you; it's gonna be alright."

While I soothed her heart, I carried her to the front door. Why? So I could give her access to my perspective. Then, I lifted her so she could see out the craftsman door window—from my perspective. I pointed to Karen. "Look, there she is! She hasn't left you! Can you see Mommy?"

As a good dad, I fully immersed myself in her story while also inviting her into the whole story.

My point? God is infinitely better at fathering than I am.

In our brokenness or immaturity, we may perceive God and our lives through the lens of our heartbreak, disappointment, vanity, ego, ideology, self-reliance—the list is long. But all along the way, He is the loving Father running to us, scooping us up, positioning Himself in our pain, confusion, disappointment, and lack of understanding—immersing Himself in our story.

He is compassionate, kind, and loving. He is the Truth that sets us free. And all along the way, He is inviting us to transition from our perspective to His, from our story to the whole story — the one He's been telling since before the foundations of the earth.

This is the good news—God, in Christ, stepped into our experience. As my friend and often co-host, Derek Turner, says, "He became one of us to rescue all of us."[7]

REDISCOVERING THE GOSPEL

The conversation with Baxter traveled into union, inclusion, the incarnation, a Christological hermeneutic, and more—and we'll explore these topics with many other podcast friends in future chapters, but not before giving Baxter the final word—at least, in this chapter—on what the gospel *is*:

---

[7] Jason Clark, excerpts from *God Is (Not) In Control: The Whole Story Is Better Than You Think* (Independently published, A Family Story, 2017).

"Jesus has never shied away from our mess. Instead, He meets us right in the middle of our confusion and hurt, and He shines a light that dispels every shadow. At the cross, He stepped into the depths of our delusion, confusion, and pain and set us free. He is the light that reveals not just who He is but who we are in Him."

> **THE GOSPEL IS NOT WHAT JESUS DOES OR WHAT HE'S DONE; IT'S WHO HE IS AND WHERE HE IS.**

The gospel is the good news of what became of the Son of God and what became of the human race in Him. He died, we died; He rose, we rose; He ascended, we ascended. So, the gospel, in a nutshell, is Jesus."

It's just that simple and quite astounding. I thought.

Baxter continued. "The gospel is not what Jesus does or what He's done; it's who He is and where He is. Jesus is here with us as the Father's eternal Son, as the One anointed in the Holy Spirit, and as the Creator and Sustainer of all things."

That last thought nearly takes my breath away—every time I hear Baxter say it, it's better than the last time! The wisdom doesn't end there—in fact, Baxter is a wellspring. These observations, among many, really stood out to me:

- » "The gospel isn't that we invite Jesus into our lives—it's that He's already received us into His."
- » "The gospel is Jesus Himself with us and in us, sharing His mind, His heart, His joy, and His fellowship. It's always about Jesus and sharing in His life."
- » "Don't get complicated with the gospel; it's Jesus with us. And who is Jesus? The one who knows Holy Spirit and the Father."
- » And we are invited into this 'knowing.' We are awakening to this friendship, this union, this intimacy with the Father, Son, and Holy Spirit.

"In the end, it's all about relationship," Baxter said. "It's about knowing and being known by the One who loves us with everlasting love. And it's about living out that love in our everyday interactions, shining His light in a world that desperately needs to see it. This is our message, the truth we are invited to live by, and the hope we might share with all who will listen."

In Baxter's words, "This journey is one of discovery, transformation, and deep, abiding joy. It's about being present to the divine in every moment and responding with love."

As the conversation closed, I felt a deep sense of gratitude for those, like Baxter, who have dedicated their lives to the tambourine as they travel "two weeks" ahead in search of a God who looks like Jesus.

As my friend Dubb Alexander says, "God is good. He has always been good. He has always only ever been good.

He has always only ever been good in exactly the way Jesus revealed."

As my friend Bill Vanderbush says, "If I look at God and I don't see Jesus, I'm looking at something that's not God."

And as Bob Dylan wrote, "Hey, Mr. Tambourine Man, play a song for me. In the jingle jangle mornin,' I'll come followin' you."[8]

And that's what we're doing.

Jesus is the jingle jangle revelation of another way of thinking and perceiving. He is our native tongue. He made it possible for us to be re-born so we might re-discover His measureless love over and again. When He walked the earth, He redeemed our narrative so we could live in the transforming kindness and confidence of His affection. Jesus is the Good News, the Gospel, and He continues to transform my understanding by grounding me in the relational nature of the Trinity.

Baxter doesn't recall our first meeting, but he recently told me he loves connecting with anyone who rethinks God through a Christological lens, especially with tacos. Since we launched the podcast, I've been privileged to *conversate* and *revelate* with people like Baxter—those who've lived two weeks and a tambourine ahead in the heart of their Buckle. Those who are daily discovering and rediscovering Jesus and, through Him, a Father in whom there is no shadow of turning, and the indwelling kindness of Holy Spirit.

---

[8] Bob Dylan, vocalist, "Mr. Tambourine Man" by Bob Dylan, released March 22, 1965, track 8 on *Bringing It All Back Home,* Columbia Records.

I can't wait to introduce more tambourine men and women to you. I'm thrilled to share their jingle jangle in the coming chapters as we dive further into the always-good love of God!⁹¹⁰

---

9 Jason Clark and Derek Turner, hosts, *Rethinking God with Tacos,* podcast, adapted excerpts from "C. Baxter Kruger / Jesus Meets Us Inside Our Delusion."
10 Jason Clark and Thomas Floyd, hosts, *Rethinking God with Tacos,* podcast, adapted excerpts from "C. Baxter Kruger /Christ In Us!"

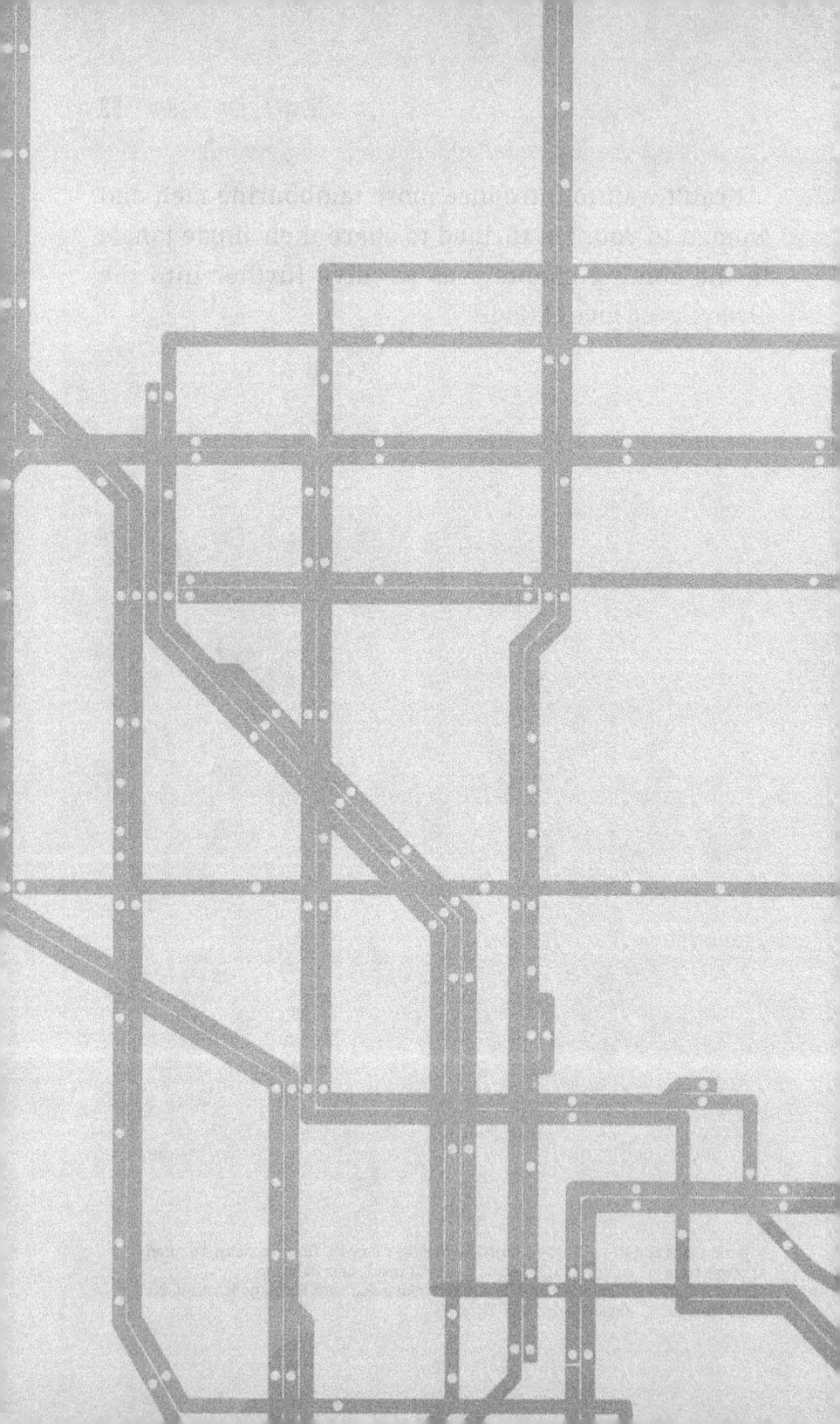

CHAPTER 2

THE CROSS

Where Love Set the Table

A GOD WHO DOESN'T OSCILLATE

That fan was the center of our universe, our delight and torment—our reward and punishment. For the brief seconds the air brushed across my clammy, tortured skin, I knew to my core that God was good, and I was loved. "Oh God," I sighed blissfully.

Then the damned thing moved on, and I began to doubt. "Oh God," I cried out again, this time with notes of desperation.

I was eight days into a thirteen-day whirlwind Philippines mission trip with a handful of saints. Now, five of us—the boys—were lying on the second floor of a two-story tin shack on the side of a volcano. Yeah, we were on an active burner—in case the natural heat wasn't enough.

And it was hot!

The Philippines is the hottest, most humid place I have ever been. New Orleans in July doesn't hold a candle to its suffocating heat. It was unworldly, unrelenting, and exhausting.

Oh God, there's a universe of meanings in those words.

"Oh God," I've said when the world was right and when it was wrong, but for the first thirty years of my life, I said it as if God were an oscillating fan.

Don't misunderstand. For my first thirty years, I knew God loved me like I knew the sun would rise, and I knew God was good. But sadly, that burning *"knowing"* within my heart was often contradicted by what I was taught about God on Sunday mornings, Wednesday nights, and any other time well-meaning substitutionary atonement preachers held court.

From most pulpits, during most of my life, God's goodness was presented like a fan that oscillated. God was always good, even when He wasn't.

You know, God was good but also sent bears to murder children (see 2 Kings 2:24), turned women into salt while raining hellfire down on entire cities (see Genesis 19:23-26), ordered angels to kill babies (see Exodus 12:23), and, of course, there's the book of Job, where God seems to have made a death deal with the devil.

For most of my life, God's goodness was dualistic—it was both a reward and a punishment. As a result, for those first thirty years or so, I wrestled with many a disorienting message from preachers who could biblically manipulate the goodness of God to present as an oscillating fan. And if I couldn't jive with their punishing separation interpretation, it was likely because I just didn't have enough faith.

In retrospect, the problem wasn't with the measure of my faith. The problem arose because of a very large flaw in my God lens.

It's called penal substitutionary atonement. And there isn't a Christian in the Western hemisphere that hasn't felt the horrific crushing weight of this abandonment theory.[11]

DEREK TURNER: BEYOND PUNISHMENT
"The cross is not about punishment or wrath but about love," Derek said.

Derek is a close friend and, for a couple of years, my co-host on the podcast. I love Derek. He is a pastor to his bones, loves well, and can unravel theological knots while staying rooted in compassion and kindness.

Derek has an unwavering commitment to Truth that sets people free. I count it a privilege to learn from and walk alongside him.

Occasionally, we would have a conversation that didn't include a guest but instead allowed us to revelate around the love of God. One of my favorite discussions was early on as we tried to one-up each other with the beautiful discovery that the cross wasn't at all the transactional, sin-focused horror story we'd been raised on.

Yeah, we talked about penal substitutionary atonement.

---
11 Jason Clark, excerpts from *Leaving and Finding Jesus* (Independently published, A Family Story, 2022).

THE CROSS IS NOT ABOUT SATISFYING GOD'S WRATH BUT REVEALING HIS UNWAVERING LOVE.

You know it. This atonement theory suggests that sin separates humanity from God. In this view, humanity turns its back on God through rebellion, and God, in His holiness, turns His back on humanity because He cannot look upon sin. The cross, then, becomes a transaction in which Jesus takes the punishment for our sin, which satisfies God's wrath, enabling Him to forgive humanity *if* we repent. This view emphasizes separation, retribution, and conditional reconciliation. And it's what most of us are familiar with.

The restorative gospel many are awakening to? This Trinitarian good news of union? It tells a different story—the original. When humanity sins and turns its back on God, God does not turn away. Instead, He moves toward us, relentlessly pursuing reconciliation. In Jesus, God steps into humanity's brokenness, bearing the weight of sin and dismantling the lie of separation. The cross is not about satisfying God's wrath but revealing His unwavering love. It reveals that God never leaves, even in our darkest moments.

If you're a visual learner, I'd recommend watching Brad Jersak's "The Gospel in Chairs." He juxtaposes the punitive distance of penal substitution to the healing nearness of union.[12] It's a game changer. But back to my conversation with Derek.

This gospel reframes the good news as one of union, not separation. It invites us to live in the truth that we belong to a Father who is always for us, whose kindness and love transform and restore all things.

"The cross wasn't about God needing a transaction (to be close to us)," Derek said, leaning in. "It was about Jesus stepping into our story, into our brokenness, and showing us that we were never separate."

Then Derek shared the phrase I've already noted. A phrase he's repeated faithfully on every podcast we've done together. And when he isn't on the podcast, like the one with John Crowder, I do my best to quote him—"God became one of us to rescue all of us."[13]

That thought was expanded in my conversation with Crowder, during which the dismantling of penal substitution and the rediscovery of a gospel-centered on union vibrated in every cell of my being!

JOHN CROWDER: THE PROBLEM WITH PENAL SUBSTITUTION AND A GOSPEL RESTORED

John Crowder has become a friend. He is the quintessential Tambourine Man and has been playing some beautifully disruptive rhythms for a long time. I am thankful for him and

---

12 Brad Jersak, "Brad Jersak – The Gospel in Chairs – Session 1," Filmed June 29, 2017 at Forgotten Gospel Conference, 29:47, *YouTube*, https://www.youtube.com/watch?v=N7FKhHScgUQ&t=3s.
13 Jason Clark and Derek Turner, hosts, *Rethinking God with Tacos*, podcast, adapted excerpts from "The Cross," January 6, 2021, https://www.youtube.com/watch?v=OmuvBv_sQSM.

his bold pursuit of the good news. John is thought-provoking, funny, and irreverent in all the best ways. And he's masterful when addressing fear-based theology.

JESUS DIDN'T SAVE US FROM AN ANGRY GOD. JESUS IS GOD SAVING US.

Every word from John invites us to a Christ-centered message of love, inclusion, and cosmic reconciliation, and very few on the planet can dismantle penal substitution better than John. But our conversation wasn't just a deconstruction; it was about rediscovering and rebuilding on Jesus, the Cornerstone.

"Thank God . . . Baxter Kruger nailed his colors to the mast on this . . . decades and decades ago." John wasted no time: "Jesus didn't save us from an angry God. Jesus is God saving us."

For years, penal substitutionary atonement has painted a picture of a divided Trinity: a wrathful Father appeased by the suffering of His Son. But as John pointed out, this atonement theory doesn't align with the God revealed in Jesus. "God's love didn't start at the cross—it was revealed there." John continued, "Jesus isn't saving us from God," he explained. "Jesus is God, saving us from sin, death, and the delusion of separation. . . . Jesus wasn't healing God's view of us; He was healing us."

The implications of this shift are profound, reframing the cross not as a courtroom drama but as a cosmic act of reconciliation.

HOW CAN WE TRUST A GOD WHO NEEDS TO PUNISH HIS OWN SON TO LOVE US?

I chimed in with my critique of penal substitution, emphasizing the relational damage it can cause. "When the only way we can get people into a relationship with God is to scare them, it's no longer good news." I continued, "How can we trust a God who needs to punish His own Son before he can love us?"

But that's what we were raised with—a separation-focused, fear-based theology that has shaped the Western church's message for generations.

This fear-based framework also distorts our understanding of judgment. "Does this mean God has no wrath?" John asked, anticipating the pushback. "Absolutely not. But there's a difference between the wrath of a father and the wrath of an executioner. Even God's wrath is a facet of His love. It's against the disease of sin that destroys His children, not against His children themselves." This redefinition of wrath—not as punitive but as purifying—invites us to see God's justice through the lens of love as restorative. But more on that later.

As the conversation unfolded, the early church's understanding of the atonement took center stage. "The first 500 years of Christianity were dominated by theologians who understood salvation as a cosmic victory," John explained. "Gregory of Nyssa, Origen, Athanasius—these guys weren't preaching a God who needed blood to appease His wrath. They were preaching a God who, through Christ, reconciled all of creation."

This recovery of the early church's theology is a transformative shift in how we understand God's character. "If God is love," John said, "then He can't act outside of that love. As George MacDonald wrote, 'Love loves unto purity.' And so, the fire of God is not something to be feared but embraced. It's the very fire that heals."

The West was raised on penal substitution, or separation, and thus the cross was a transaction, an exchange to satisfy a wrathful God. But the cross wasn't about appeasing God's anger—it was about healing humanity.

"The biggest problem here in the Western church is this separation thinking," John said. "It's the idea that there's distance between us and God, that Jesus has to bridge this gap because the Father can't even look at us. But that's a lie."

John didn't mince words as he critiqued the idea that Jesus died as a substitute to endure God's punishment for our sins. "This idea that the Father's turning on the Son, that Jesus is the whipping boy for the Father's wrath . . . it's preached as the gospel, but it's not. It's a demonic fairytale," he said bluntly. And I can't tell you how much I love John's bluntness. It's the truth that sets us free.

John highlighted the worst thing about penal substitution—that it misrepresents the Trinity by creating an illusion of division. "What happened on the cross wasn't the Trinity imploding on itself," John explained. "Jesus wasn't paying off some dark side of God. He wasn't fixing God's view of humanity. He was healing humanity itself."

"Come on," I said.

And he did. "Jesus was healing the human race. He was curing our human condition," he said, describing the cross as an act of reconciliation. "He stepped into the depths of our decay, sucked it into Himself, and pulled us out the other side as a new creation."

It's a perspective that challenges everything about how we view sin, judgment, and God's role in our redemption. "We've turned the cross into a courtroom drama where God is the judge, Jesus is the defense attorney, and we're on trial," John said. "But the truth is, the cross is a hospital, not a courtroom. It's where Jesus heals us, not where God condemns us."

This reframing exposes the transactional language that often infiltrates Western Christianity. "Religion builds an industry on the concept of separation," John observed. "It keeps people striving, desperate, and insecure, always trying to 'get closer to God.' But union means there is no distance to close. Jesus already brought us into the fullness of relationship with the Father."

John's thoughts reminded me of my friend and podcast guest, Carlos Padilla's statement, "Jesus didn't come to start a new religion. He came to end religion."[14] Man, that's good!

My heart burned; this is the gospel I have been growing sure of for years, and John has a way of describing it so we might be set free.

If Jesus is perfect theology, I thought, *then union is perfect theology.* Penal substitutionary atonement is built on separation, but the gospel is union. It's about a God who has always been with us, always been within us, always loved us, and always worked to heal us. And we are awakening to this reality—this finished work.

John's critique invites us to rediscover the beauty, depth, and power of the cross. It's not a transaction to appease a distant God. It's the ultimate act of love from a God who has stepped into our delusion of separation and revealed a Love that never leaves.

C. BAXTER KRUGER: A TRINITARIAN LOVE STORY

I know Baxter is getting serious billing early in this book, but for me, he is one of the foundational voices declaring this Greater Love, Trinitarian good news.

So, grab your chair and hang on; this is about to get even better!

In my second podcast conversation with Baxter, we dove into the cross—not just as a historical moment but as a

---

14 Jason Clark and Derek Turner, hosts, *Rethinking God with Tacos*, podcast, adapted excerpts from "Carlos Padilla / Walking in God's Power," May 5, 2021, https://www.youtube.com/watch?v=WSnC9SiBiIs&list=PLgimV9UoSbAIbXX447Gu_5-kGpLAO_eJO&index=146.

cosmic event that redefines everything we think we know about God and ourselves. "The cross is not a transaction to fix a legal problem," Baxter began, his voice steady yet passionate. It's a divine descent into our delusion, a rescue mission to meet us where we are."

He continued. "The Father, Son, and Spirit aren't spectators of human suffering; they're participants. Where was God when Christ was being crucified? God was in Christ. The Father wasn't distant, watching from the sidelines. The Father was in Jesus, holding Him and holding us."

Baxter's insistence that the cross reveals union rather than separation flips many of our Western Evangelical assumptions. "You actually believe Jesus had to pay the Father off?" an Orthodox bishop rhetorically asked him many years ago. "That has never crossed the mind of the early church. The cross isn't about appeasing wrath; it's about stepping into our darkness and bringing us home."

This shift in understanding the cross transforms how we see God. "When we damn Him, crucify Him, hoist Him up on the cross, what does the Father say? He says, 'I am holding my Son and my wayward children in everlasting mercy.' That's who God is. The cross is the ultimate revelation of the Father's heart."

Imagining the question Baxter's statement would raise with podcast listeners, I asked, "What about the wrath of God—something that has shaped so much of modern theology?" Baxter paused thoughtfully before replying, "Wrath isn't God's anger at Jesus. Wrath is God's opposition to our destruction. It's His 'no' to our delusion and death and

His 'yes' to our redemption. The cross is where that 'no' and 'yes' meet."

Baxter's vision of the cross includes a profound understanding of Christ's solidarity with humanity. "Jesus doesn't come to stand outside of us and point the way," he said. "He comes to become one with us, to step inside our brokenness and carry us out of it. He unites Himself with His bride in her delusion to deliver her."

The cross, in Baxter's words, is also deeply Trinitarian. "The Father, Son, and Spirit are indivisible," he explained. "When Jesus says, 'The Father is in me, and I am in the Father,' He's showing us that even on the cross, there is no separation. The whole Trinity is in this together, redeeming humanity from the inside out."

> **THE CROSS IS NOT A PLACE OF PUNISHMENT BUT THE ULTIMATE ACT OF LOVE, REDEMPTION, AND UNION.**

The cross isn't the end of the story; it's the beginning. "When we murdered Jesus, the Father transfigured that act into a new covenant—a union with us in our delusion. The light shines in the darkness, and the darkness doesn't understand it, but it can't overcome it either."

As our conversation ended, I asked Baxter how this vision of the cross shapes his life. He smiled and said, "You can't unsee it. Once you know the cross isn't about separation but union, you realize God has always been with us, even in our worst moments. The cross is God saying, 'I won't leave you. I am here. And I am making all things new.'"[15][16]

"I won't leave you." Those words burn with the gospel truth.

What if the cross is not a story where the Father looks away, but instead is a revelation that there is no shadow of turning in the Trinity?

NOR HAS HE HIDDEN HIS FACE

"A time is coming and in fact has come when you will be scattered, each to your own home. You will leave me all alone. Yet I am not alone, for my Father is with me" (John 16:32, NIV). Jesus spoke those words to His disciples before going to the cross.

That statement seems straightforward. The Father wasn't going anywhere—but if that's true, what do we do with Jesus's anguished cry on the cross: *"My God, my God, why have You forsaken Me?"* (Matthew 27:46, NKJV).

If I said, *"Our Father [who] art in heaven,"* most of you would continue with the next verse, *"Hallowed be thy name"* (Matthew 6:9, KJV).

---

[15] Jason Clark and Derek Turner, hosts, *Rethinking God with Tacos*, podcast, adapted excerpts from "C. Baxter Kruger / Jesus Meets Us Inside Our Delusion."
[16] Jason Clark and Thomas Floyd, hosts, *Rethinking God with Tacos*, podcast, adapted excerpts from "C. Baxter Kruger / Christ In Us!"

If I sang, "Baby, I'm just gonna shake, shake, shake, shake, shake," my wife and kids would sing, "Shake it off, shake it off."[17]

When Jesus, battered and broken, nailed to a cross and feeling the desperation of our loneliness and the ache of abandonment, cried out, *"My God, my God, why have You forsaken Me?"* everyone who knows Scripture looked up Psalm 22:1.

That's because Jesus quoted the first verse of the poet king, David.

In Jesus's day, it was culturally understood that when a teacher quoted the first verse of a Psalm, he intended to draw the listener's attention to the Psalm in its entirety. And every Jewish person could quote the following verse of Psalm 22 by memory, and the one after that, and the one after that....

As Davidic Psalms go, Psalm 22 is pretty standard. David wrestled through life's mountaintops and valleys with the raw authenticity that makes him an Old Testament favorite—except on this day, Psalm 22 became powerfully prophetic. On this day, David's words came to horrific life before their very eyes.

"My God my God, why have You forsaken Me," is followed a few verses later by (NIV):

"All who see me mock me, they hurl insults...." (v. 7)
"I am poured out like water, and all my bones are out of joint...." (v. 14)

---

[17] Taylor Swift, vocalist, "Shake It Off," by Taylor Swift, Shellback, and Martin Max, August 18, 2014, track 6 on *1989*, Big Machine.

"My mouth is dried up like a potsherd, and my tongue sticks to the roof of my mouth...." (v. 15)
"Dogs surround me, a pack of villains encircles me; they pierce my hands and my feet...." (v. 16)
"All my bones are on display; people stare and gloat over me...." (v. 17)
"They divide my clothes among them and cast lots for my garment...." (v. 18)

Then, in verse 24, the psalm prophetically reveals the nature of God and the relational dynamics taking place between Jesus and His Father on the cross. *"He has not despised nor abhorred the affliction of the afflicted;* **Nor has He hidden His face from Him***; But when He cried to Him for help, He heard"* (Psalm 22:24, NKJV, emphasis added).

JESUS STEPPED INSIDE ADAM'S DELUSION AND EXPERIENCED OUR SENSE OF ABANDONMENT.

Jesus, on a cross, in His darkest hour, experiencing the devastating betrayal behind the lie that has oppressed all humanity—the lie that God abandons, forsakes, and leaves—quotes a scripture that reveals the power of the gospel unto salvation: GOD DOES NOT LEAVE. GOD HAS NEVER LEFT.

The Father did not leave, never has. As the old hymn writer wrote: "There is no shadow of turning with Thee." At that moment, God was in Christ, on a cross, reconciling all humanity to Himself! (see 2 Corinthians 5:19)

Jesus, fully God and fully man, cried out, *"My God, my God, why have you forsaken Me?"* And it was our cry—yours and mine—a cry to know a Love that would never leave or forsake us; a cry birthed from the delusion of separation that tracks all the way back to Adam. Jesus stepped inside Adam's delusion and experienced our sense of abandonment. And in that moment, He cried out in a desperation that every one of us has felt, *"My God, my God, why would you leave?"*

And at that moment, the Father was with His Son; He hadn't left, abandoned, turned His back, or scorned Him. He was there. He knew His Son couldn't sense it, couldn't feel His always-good love, but He was there, loving His boy, proud of His Son, sharing His agony, and enduring the cross for the joy on the other side. He was there forgiving, and reconciling, and not counting our cruel and punishing beliefs and delusions about Him against us.

Jesus's next words were powerful: *"It is finished"* (John 19:30, NIV).

And the curtain of the temple, the veil that represented humanity's cruel and punishing thoughts about a God who abandons—a God who separates Himself from us—was torn in two (see Matthew 27:51).

Jesus then called out in a loud voice, *"'Father, into Your hands I commit My spirit.' When He had said this, He breathed His last"* (Luke 23:46, NIV).

Jesus knew He wasn't alone, and He called God, 'Dad.'[18]

A good Father does not leave, and Jesus knew this. His faith was firmly placed in the Truth that "neither death nor life, neither angels nor demons, neither the present nor the future, nor any powers, neither height nor depth, nor anything else in all creation, will be able to separate us from the love of God that is in Christ Jesus our Lord" (Romans 8:38-39, NIV).

By the way, that's where we place our faith—in the sure foundation of a Greater Love that never leaves.

Jesus revealed that regardless of our perspective, experience, ideology, or theology, our Father never leaves. Greater Love never abandons us. There is no separation in the nature of the Trinity, only in the mind and perception of humanity.[19]

> *"Once you were alienated from God and were enemies in your minds because of your evil behavior. But now he has reconciled you by Christ's physical body through death to present you holy in his sight, without blemish and free from accusation."*
> *—Colossians 1:21-23 (NIV)*

Dear friends, separation is not the gospel Jesus gave us. On the cross, a Triune God, in Christ, reconciled the

---
18 Jason Clark, adapted from *Leaving and Finding Jesus*.
19 Jason Clark, adapted from *Prone to Love* (Shippensburg, PA: Destiny Image Publishers, 2014).

world to Himself, *"not counting our sins against us"* (see 2 Corinthians 5:19).

On the cross, Jesus said, *"Father, forgive them; for they know not what they do"* (Luke 23:34, NKJV).

Then, before His last breath, He said, *"It is finished."*

Separation is not part of God's nature. There is no veil between heaven and earth—between God and humanity. That's why we call it the *good* news!

The cross is the ultimate act of love, redemption, and union.

So, let's dive into union.

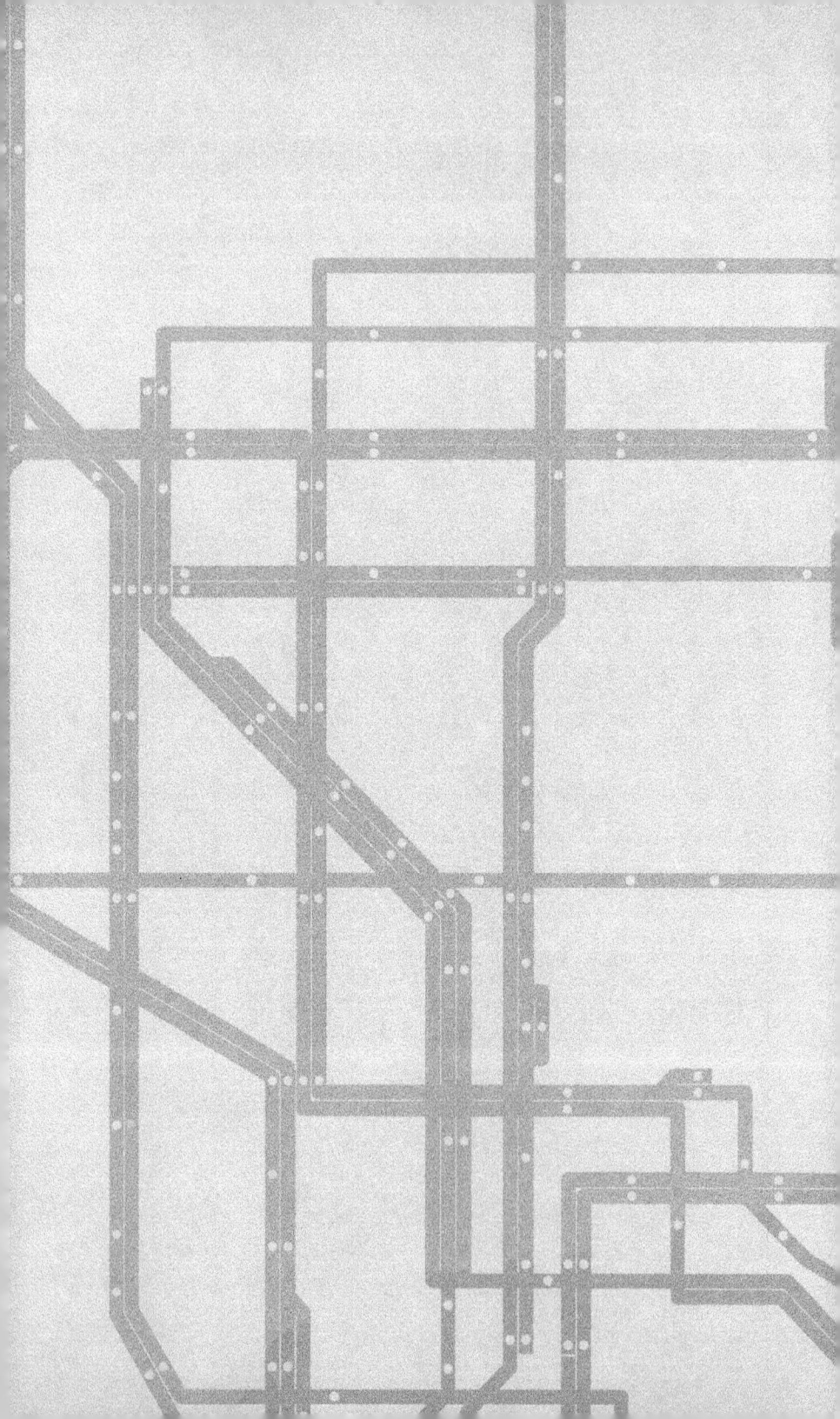

CHAPTER 3

UNION

One Shell, a Lot of Love

AN EXERCISE IN UNION

A few years ago, I attended a church service in which Bill Vanderbush spoke. Bill is a friend, a good man, and a fantastic communicator. He did an exercise I've since appropriated. I want to do it with you to set the table for this chapter's podcast conversations focused on union.

Ready?

Typically, I would ask you to close your eyes, but since you can't read with your eyes closed, let's skip that part. Take a deep breath and imagine a throne room. The throne could be ornate with jewels and gold engraved lion heads or a Carolina rocker. Use your imagination.

Got it?

Good.

Now imagine Jesus sitting on the throne. Take your time; we're in no rush.

Now place yourself in the room—anywhere you want; there is no wrong or right place.

This is the point at which I usually have folks open their eyes. Then, I ask questions starting with, "How many were able to picture the throne room?"

Nearly every hand goes up; I imagine yours would be among them.

Then, I ask, "How many were able to picture themselves in the room?" Again, nearly every hand goes up.

At this stage, I get more specific. "How many were near a door or a wall—somewhere away from the throne? Again, there's no wrong place." There are typically more hands.

Then I ask, "How many were at the feet of Jesus?" In my experience, most hands go up on that question.

Was that you?

"How many were sitting right *next* to Jesus?"

When Bill led this exercise and I sat in the audience, that fifth question brought Ephesians 2:6 to mind: *"And God raised us up with Christ and seated us with Him in the heavenly realms in Christ Jesus"* (NIV). I'd imagined myself sitting next to Jesus, so I raised my hand.

I thought Bill had finished asking questions. But the first set of questions had been the perfect setup for the last question that Bill, and now I, love to ask:

"How many were sitting on the throne?"

The finished work of the cross reveals there is no distance, no separation between us. Jesus went to a cross and took the lie of distance and separation to its conclusion.

JESUS IS PERFECT THEOLOGY. AND HIS INCARNATION REVEALED THAT PERFECT THEOLOGY IS ONLY PERFECT WHEN IT INCLUDES US.

The veil in the temple was torn, the delusion exposed; nothing can separate us from His love.

Jesus went to the cross and forever vanquished the lie of separation. "It is finished" (John 19:30), He declared.

Then He arose, and all creation rose with Him, ever awakening to our union—a burning discovery that we would be one just as the Father and Jesus are one (see John 17:21).

We have been invited to know the same intimacy, the same union. We have been invited to be with Jesus in the back corner of a throne room, at His feet, or sitting next to Him. But, oh Father, that we would awaken to a union in which we might sit on the throne in Christ.

Jesus is perfect theology, revealed as union. And His incarnation revealed that perfect theology is only perfect when it includes us.

As Baxter describes it, "Face to Face to Face." And we are included!

We have been invited to know the same union that the Father, Son, and Spirit share—perfect theology through friendship that reconciles the cosmos.[20]

BILL VANDERBUSH: THE GROUND BENEATH OUR FEET

Union. It's one of those words that can sound poetic, mystical, and sometimes abstract or untouchable. But when Bill talks about union, it's present, the very fabric of reality. And our conversation was focused on this reality!

"Union isn't something we strive for—it's the ground we already stand on. The problem isn't distance from God; it's the illusion of it," Bill said and continued. "The entirety of the concept of any heaven without Jesus encompassing it all is an afterlife perspective rooted in distance and separation." Bill noted that's the shift—realizing heaven isn't some far-off hope. It's Christ, right now, living in us and as us.

Bill's thoughts tear down the walls between sacred and secular, spiritual and physical. He calls out the separation paradigm that says righteousness is something we work toward: "We've made salvation a commodity—something you have to earn or possess. But Jesus is salvation."

Jesus didn't come to hand out golden tickets to heaven; He came to reveal the union that already exists. "I am in the Father, you are in Me, and I am in you," Jesus says in John 14:20, and Bill wouldn't let us forget it. "The gospel is scandalous grace—the kind that draws prodigals home without a lecture."

---

20 Jason Clark adapted excerpts from *Leaving and Finding Jesus*.

That's a holy selah—the kind of pause that invites us to rethink any faith that is defined by striving or earning.

Union is the invitation to live fully, freely, and intimately connected to the God who refuses to let us go. As Bill said, "Union with Christ is the lens through which we discover who we really are."[21][22]

And there's no one better to break that thought down than my tambourine friend, Francois.

FRANCOIS DU TOIT: THE DOOR WAS NEVER CLOSED

Every time I connect with Francois du Toit, it feels like he's pulling back a curtain to reveal what has always been true—revelation! It's like he's handing me a set of glasses that finally bring everything into focus. He's a walking encounter with the Love of God, and in every word is an invitation to experience our oneness with Father, Son, and Holy Spirit.

This is why, when you have him on your podcast, you hit record right away!

Francois doesn't do separation theology. There's no religion in him. He speaks like someone who's lived in the reality he's describing. "There is no separation, no distance," he said, his voice steady but full of fire. "We are in Christ, and Christ is in us. That's the gospel. It's not good advice; it's good news about what's already been accomplished."

---

21 Jason Clark and Thomas Floyd, hosts, *Rethinking God with Tacos,* podcast, adapted excerpts from "Bill Vanderbush / Reckless Grace," May 6, 2020, https://www.youtube.com/watch?v=pypRrodVBYI&list=PLgimV9UoSbAIbXX447Gu_5-kGpLAO_eJO&index=168.
22 Jason Clark host, *Rethinking God with Tacos,* podcast, adapted excerpts from "John Crowder and Bill Vanderbush / The Creator, Sustainer, and Reconciler of All Things," February 12, 2025 https://www.youtube.com/watch?v=xDn5nCexvW0&t=1s

That alone could've been enough to chew on for the rest of the conversation, but Francois kept going. "Religion thrives on two lies: distance and delay," he said, leaning in. "But God has canceled that. He's canceled every definition of separation." And I could feel it—like something heavy we don't even know we carry being lifted.

Francois doesn't speak in abstractions. He makes it real. "Faith," he said, "is not something we do. Faith is the fruit of our union." I laughed when he said that. Mostly because of how good it is. Also, I had been describing faith the same way for years.

We Western Evangelicals have been raised on the lie that the Father looked away, on the delusion of separation. And we've spent a lifetime trying to manufacture faith like it's some fragile thing that might slip through our fingers if we don't hold on tight enough. But Francois flipped that on its head. "Faith isn't something you chase—it's something that grows naturally when you wake up to the fact that you're already in Him."

Then he said something I'd been discovering in more profound ways. "We come from innocence." That's worth taking a minute to sit with. For most of us, our understanding of humanity starts with guilt. From the belief that we're fundamentally flawed and must work our way back to God. But Francois speaks the truth—union begins with innocence. We're not trying to earn our way into right standing; we're simply awakening to the truth of who we've always been in Christ.

As we paused our conversation "until next time," he left us with this: "The in-Himness of humanity has been largely underestimated. There's no 'us and them' in God. There's only union."

Most of us have spent much of our lives knock, knock, knocking on heaven's door when, as Francois noted with his jingle jangle smile, "The door was never closed to begin with."[23]

And that's a perfect introduction to the conversation my dad and I had with Paul Young.

PAUL YOUNG: YOU ALREADY BELONG

Paul is a living, breathing encounter with God's love. Talking with him feels like drinking coffee with a friend who's discovered the secrets to abundant life and isn't in the business of keeping them to himself. He's relational through and through.

"Union isn't something you achieve; it's something you wake up to," he said.

Let that sink in.

Most of us have spent our Christian years trying to pray harder, believe deeper, feel more connected—always chasing some elusive sense of oneness with God. But Paul's words land like cool water on a parched soul, or carnitas tacos for the famished heart.

---

[23] Jason Clark and Thomas Floyd, hosts, *Rethinking God with Tacos,* podcast, adapted excerpts from "Francois du Toit / Jesus Is What God Believes About You," April 24, 2020, https://www.youtube.com/watch?v=wjpqznUJRYE&list=PLgimV9UoSbAIbXX447Gu_5-kGpLAO_eJO&index=124.

> # JESUS DIDN'T COME TO CONVINCE THE FATHER ABOUT YOU. HE CAME TO CONVINCE YOU ABOUT THE FATHER.

Union with God isn't a distant goalpost but the very air we breathe. "You already belong," Paul said, a grin on his face. "You've always belonged. The cross didn't purchase your inclusion—it revealed it."

Yeah, it's worth pausing again.

"Jesus didn't come to convince the Father about you," Paul continued, "He came to convince you about the Father."

Paul's words speak to the good news our hearts have always known to be true, even when our minds have argued for the knowledge of good and evil.

And yet, if we surrender to love....

"The gospel isn't that we invite Jesus into our lives," Paul said, "It's that Jesus has already included us in His." Paul wasn't offering bumper sticker theology; he described the kind of love that meets us in the middle of our mess and refuses to leave.

Conversations with Paul tend to lead to more profound realizations that union isn't something to chase—it's a revelation.

Que Brent Lokker.

BRENT LOKKER: LIVING FROM UNION

Brent is a dear friend who embodies the kind of love that makes you feel seen, safe, and free to explore the depths of God's goodness. Our conversation centered on seeing what was always there—revelation. There's a moment in every journey where what we think we know falls away, and something deeper takes its place. That's revelation—not new information, but an unveiling of what has always been true. And at the heart of this awakening is union. Not something to earn, but the reality of our being.

For so long, much of Christianity has been filtered through the lens of the knowledge of good and evil—measuring, sorting, questioning. Am I in or out? Am I doing enough? What am I missing? But revelation isn't about acquiring more knowledge; it's about experiencing Christ within.

Brent pointed to Nicodemus, sneaking through the night to find Jesus, because something in his carefully built world wasn't measuring up. "He saw LIFE in Christ and wondered, 'What is it about you that my current life is not giving me access to?'" That's the ache so many of us know—the restless longing that won't let us settle for a faith of transactions and checklists. It's the whisper of something deeper, something we were made for: not a system, but a union. A life already ours, waiting to be seen—revelation.

Jesus doesn't invite us into another system of effort; He invites us to truly see Him. Brent put it this way: "Once you see (Him), you can't unsee (Him)." This echoes my friend Mike Zenker, who once said, "You can't hurry revelation."

And once you discover, you can't un-discover—which isn't even a word.

My point? Revelation is irreversible. It's about stepping into the reality of our union, awakening to His Greater Love-truth that sets us free.

And this changes everything. Brent shared how this revelation of union made anxiety fall away. "*I'm* not doing this interview. *We* are. As in, Jesus and me. It's a different feel." That's the shift—from trying to reach a distant God to simply being in the flow of love, in the rhythms of grace.

And when we see ourselves in union, we begin to see others that way, too. "The harvest is ripe. Look around at the people in front of you. They are already filled with (His) glory," Brent said, framing Jesus's words to His disciples through the revelation of union (see John 4:35).[24]

Nothing has changed. And yet, everything has; that's revelation.

Brent's reflections reveal a love that includes us without condition or effort. And that sets the table for the conversation with Rod Williams.

ROD WILLIAMS: UNION WITH DISTINCTION

Everyone knows Rod Williams. No matter what circle you find yourself in, Papa Smurf has already been there for years. I don't know the origin of his nickname, but I'm guessing it has to do with his full and impressive white beard. And also, maybe because when you connect

---

[24] Jason Clark, host, *Rethinking God with Tacos*, podcast, adapted excerpts from "Brent Lokker / Union" May 23, 2024, https://www.youtube.com/watch?v=CSZTqcTUGXo.

with him, you are immersed in a wisdom that expands head and heart.

Rod spoke about union with distinction. Within the Trinity, there is perfect union, but also distinction—Father, Son, and Holy Spirit are one, yet each is distinct in personhood. "We've been taught to think of union as erasing individuality," he said. "But true union celebrates our distinctiveness. Just like the Father, Son, and Holy Spirit are one but distinct, we are invited into that dance of love without losing what makes us unique."

That perichoretic image of the Trinity as a dance—mutual, joyful, endlessly creative—it is paradigm-shifting. It reminds us that this journey is about living fully as the persons God created us to be, embraced in the love of our Triune God.

But more on that later....

> **IF THERE IS NO SEPARATION BETWEEN US AND GOD, THEN THERE CAN BE NO SEPARATION BETWEEN US AND EACH OTHER.**

Rod also spoke about the delusion of separation we create in our minds. "The gap is between our ears," he said with a laugh. "God's not distant, but we've been conditioned to believe He is. The gospel doesn't demand faith—it supplies it. When you realize there's no separation, you stop striving and rest in the truth that you're already included.

Union with God isn't something to be earned. It's the natural state of our being. Jesus didn't come to make it possible for us to be united with God; He came to show us that we always were. This realization, Rod explained, moves us from a mindset of fear, punishment, and striving to one of peace, joy, and intimacy.

This is where the message of union becomes so practical. If there is no separation between us and God, then there can be no separation between us and each other. As Francois says, "There is no distance between us and God, and there is no distance between us and each other."[25]

THE HEART OF ONENESS

There's something beautiful about this journey of rediscovery—this rethinking done in the context of Greater Love. It's not a pursuit of knowledge; it's about knowing. It's about experiencing revelation, about waking up to what has always been true—that we are loved, that we belong, and that there is no separation between us and God. It's about learning to live from oneness, to rest in the love that has always been ours.

---

[25] Jason Clark and Derek Turner, hosts, *Rethinking God with Tacos*, podcast, adapted excerpts from "Rod Williams / Union with Distinction," January 31, 2022, https://www.youtube.com/watch?v=vAh-yILeO3w&list=PLgimV9UoSbAIbXX447Gu_5-kGpLAO_eJO&index=119.

My friend Dr. Matt Pandel,[26], who has been a podcast guest, says it this way. "We originate from the destination. We flow out of the Most Holy Place—not toward it." This is our original union!

Union is the good news that has the power to transform—to change everything. It's the message that has been burning in my heart before I had language to describe it, before the foundations of the world. It's bigger than deconstruction; it's the cornerstone upon which the cosmos rests. And it's a message I want to keep sharing, the throughline of every podcast conversation represented in this book. All creation is crying out for a deeper knowing that there is no separation, that we are all included, and that we are all deeply, endlessly loved.

---

26 Jason Clark and Derek Turner, hosts, *Rethinking God with Tacos,* podcast, adapted excerpts from "Dr. Matt Pandel / Living in the In-Between," July 12, 2023, https://www.youtube.com/watch?v=4y38BOWZ_uI&list=PLgimV9UoSbAIbXX447Gu_5-kGpLAO_eJO&index=89.

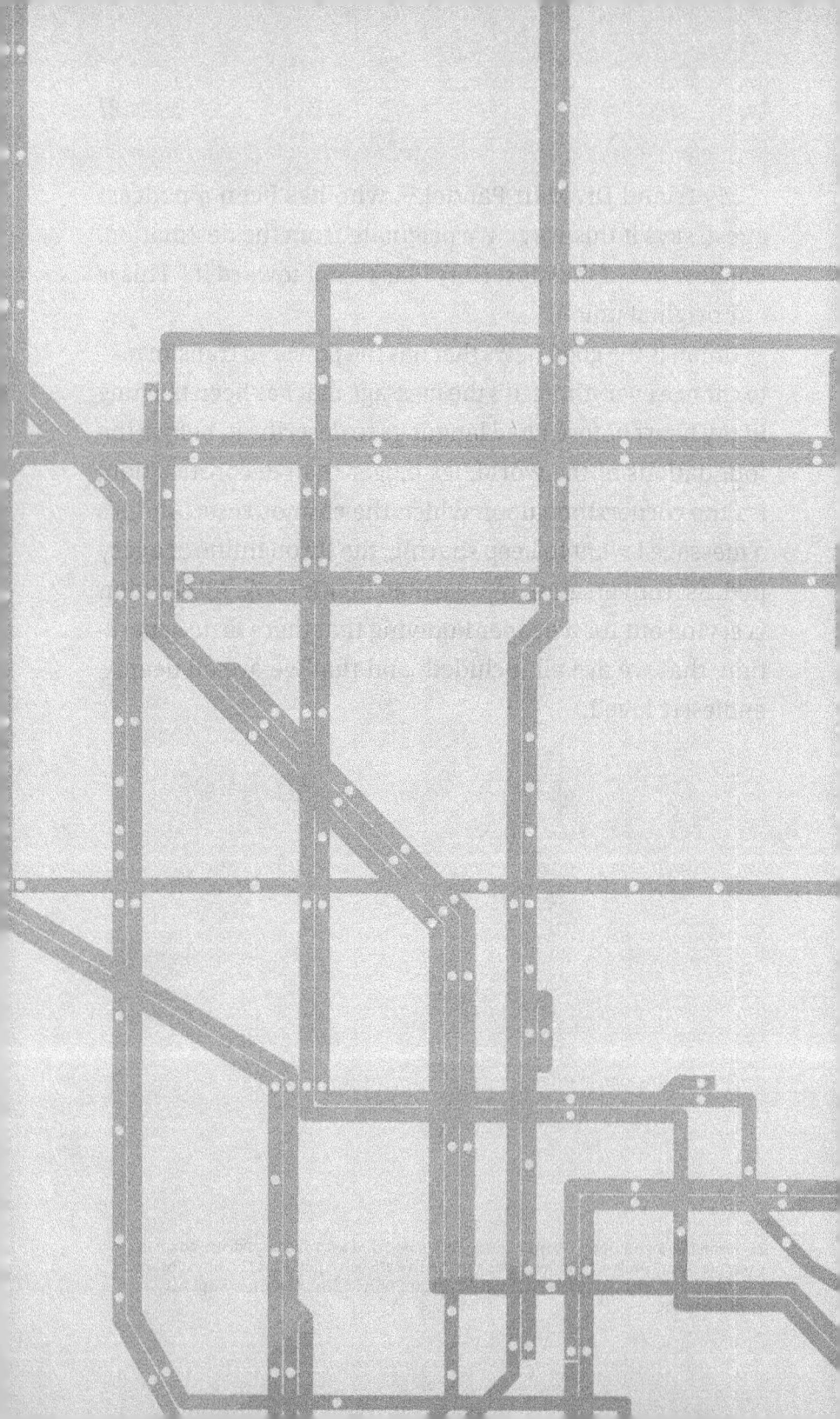

CHAPTER 4

A CHRISTOLOGICAL HERMENEUTIC

Seeing Christ in Every Bite

THE WHOLE STORY

"The Bible is not the object of our faith. Jesus is. The value of the Bible is that the Word of God always directs us to Jesus."
—Randall Worley, *Rethinking God with Tacos* podcast, "Questioning My Answers"[27]

Years ago, I stopped reading the whole Bible. You read correctly. For about two years, I only read the gospels. Well, that's not fully true; occasionally, I would brave my way into Psalms and Proverbs, but otherwise, I strictly and stubbornly stayed away from every book of the Bible except Matthew, Mark, Luke, and John.

---

27 Jason Clark and Derek Turn, hosts, *Rethinking God with Tacos,* podcast, adapted excerpts from "Randall Worley / Questioning My Answers," September 9, 2020, https://www.youtube.com/watch?v=Rxmy2tleGRs&list=PLgimV9UoSbAIbXX447Gu_5-kGpLAO_eJO&index=152.

You see, I had rediscovered Jesus in those pages, and I wasn't going to take my eyes off *Him*.

I love the Bible, the *whole* Bible. I believe the *whole* Bible is God-inspired. He can be found on all its pages. God has used the *whole* Bible to empower and instruct my faith from the beginning.

I remember my first picture Bible; I was five and so proud to have my very own. My dad read the *whole* book to me over the following months.

I still have my One Year Bible; I read the *whole* of it when I was thirteen.

When I was eighteen, I went to Bible College, where I studied the *whole* Bible.

I love the *whole* Bible and continue to grow in my love and knowledge of it. But when I intentionally stopped reading the *whole* Bible for those two years, I did so for a reason. I had some unlearning to do.

Understand—during those two years, I was not denying the *whole* Bible; I was resetting my lens. I had caught a glimpse of something hidden in plain sight. Jesus is perfect theology, and I could not look away.

> **JESUS IS PERFECT THEOLOGY—THE CLEAREST AND TRUEST WAY TO KNOW WHAT GOD IS LIKE.**

Over those two years, the eyes of my heart adjusted, seeing in a way they never had before. Greater Love was awakening within me, and I couldn't afford to look away from the gospels—the four books that are the clearest representation of Jesus—not even for a moment. I wouldn't risk it lest my eyes revert to their old way of seeing, and I lose sight of the glorious revelation—union!

In Jesus, I discovered my core conviction, my *whole* theology: God is love, His love is always good, and I exist to awaken and grow ever sure.

It's that simple.

In those two years, I discovered that Jesus is the perfect revelation of what love looks like, acts like, sounds, dreams, and teaches like.

Jesus is perfect theology—the clearest and truest way to know what God is like. He is the beginning, the end, and everything in between. He is everything before and everything after, measureless in love, infinitely good.

For most of my life, I'd endeavored to develop *whole* thoughts about who God was by reading my *whole* Bible. By that, I mean that for too long, I had allowed Job's description of God to carry as much weight as Jesus's.

That's just dumb.

I am not suggesting that God can't be discovered in the book of Job, but where Job's life is full of questions, Jesus is the answer.

And Jesus is the *whole* answer. Jesus is the *whole* truth. Jesus is the *whole,* perfect revelation of God. Jesus is what the *whole* Bible is about. Jesus is what everything before points to and what everything after is built upon. Jesus is the *whole story*—His, yours, and mine.

During those two years in the gospels, I began seeing in a way I had never seen before. My old eyes, old thought patterns, and old understanding of God were being renewed. I began seeing life in a new way. I discovered a better language, my native tongue. I discovered a truer paradigm, the Kingdom of Heaven—Family. The mysteries were being revealed; the hidden things were being made plain.

God is love; His love is always good!

And my good and loving God looks like Jesus. And I fixed my eyes on Him and only Him as the *Author and Perfecter of my faith,* as the *whole story.*

The revelation of Jesus as the *whole story* began shifting my perspective, my foundational approach to our relationship—to every relationship, actually. It changed my perspective on every circumstance; it also changed how I would eventually read the *whole* Bible.

I am again reading the Book cover to cover. But I approach it differently. I look for Jesus, perfect Love, on every page. And I am daily becoming better at finding Him.

Which reminds me of a quote from Chris Green, who has been on the podcast a few times. "The Gospels say that all of the Scriptures—and by which they mean what we call the Old Testament—all of the Scriptures speak of Jesus. I think that's true."

Jesus is my lens, my Christological hermeneutic. His narrative is my true narrative. His perfect love is my conviction. His goodness is my faith. Every question I have, every relationship or circumstance, every scripture, including the tension Job seems to represent, is measured against the immeasurable revelation of Jesus.

> **IN ALL WAYS, JESUS IS MY HERMENEUTIC—THE METHOD BY WHICH I INTERPRET AND UNDERSTAND.**

Jesus is the *whole gospel*, the *whole story*—the perfect, unrestricted, all-consuming, life-transforming, ever-expanding revelation of sovereign love.[28]

Those two years spent solely in the gospels taught me that if my understanding of God doesn't look like Jesus, I need to rethink.

But it took me many more years to find those words. And for most of that time, I thought I was pretty much alone in my Jesus hermeneutic.

Then I launched a podcast. Turns out I wasn't.

BRIAN ZAHND: READING THE BIBLE THROUGH A JESUS LENS

In Brian's first appearance on the podcast, I grinned ear to ear the whole time. Brian approaches Scripture with a

---
28 Jason Clark adapted excerpts from *God Is (Not) in Control: The Whole Story Is Better Than You Think*

Christocentric hermeneutic—a Jesus lens that frames the Bible as a signpost pointing to the Word made flesh. Brian is a prophetic pastor-poet who can speak to Bob Dylan's jingle jangle in ways the rest of us envy. I hold deep respect and affection for how he gently yet boldly reimagines the gospel through the lens of Jesus.

I'd read his book, *Sinners in the Hands of a Loving God*.[29] I was a little salty when I first heard his title, as I'd been drafting my own *Saints in the Hands of a Loving God*. Turns out, Jeff Turner's brilliant *Saints in the Arms of a Happy God*[30] and Brian's masterpiece beat me to the punch.

Clearly, the *good news* of a nonviolent, restorative, and infinitely kind God was in the ether. It seems even as we Westerners stumble over our idolatrous certainty around literalism and inerrancy, Jesus just keeps revealing *Himself* as the Word of God.

And Brian has been championing this liberating Truth. And like all good communicators, he did this with a story about speaking to teens at a church camp in Colorado.

During one youth camp, Brian opened with Exodus 21:20-21—the passage about the rights of a slave owner to beat their slaves. After reading it aloud, he asked, "How many of you disagree with this?"

One by one, every hand went up.

Brian leaned in, "So, you disagree with the Bible?" He paused, then eased the tension, "You should."

---

29 Brian Zahnd, *Sinners in the Hands of a Loving God: The Scandalous Truth of the Very Good News* (Colorado Springs, CO: WaterBrook, 2017).
30 Jeff Turner, *Saints in the Arms of a Happy God* (Jeff Turner, 2014).

He continued, "Do you think you have a superior moral vision concerning the subject of slavery than the Bible does?"

He paused again to let the uncomfortable question sink in. Then he eased the tension by answering for the kids and for everyone who has listened to the podcast since.

"You do, and you should."

Brian wasn't dismissing Scripture; he was inviting us to wrestle with it honestly. He explained that our discomfort highlights the need to read everything through Jesus. "Jesus presides over our interpretation of Scripture," he said.

This approach emphasized our Protestant context, where there is a tendency to view the Bible as an inerrant, infallible document. Zahnd continued. "While the Bible is inspired, it is not the final revelation of God—that role belongs to Jesus. . . . the Bible itself cannot be the foundation that we build upon. The apostles are very clear—the foundation is Jesus, and Jesus changes everything."

As I listened to Brian, I noted how his interaction with the youth didn't stop at intellectual engagement; it was deeply pastoral. He wanted them—and us—to see that grappling with difficult texts is part of a faithful, mature Christian life. "Jesus presides over our interpretation of Scripture," he explained. "If a particular interpretation of a verse doesn't look like Jesus, if you can't see Jesus fulfilling it, then we set it aside (until we get revelation). If a passage of Scripture appears to contradict the radical love and inclusive message of Jesus, it requires careful re-examination," he said.[31]

---

[31] Jason Clark, host, *Rethinking God with Tacos*, podcast, adapted excerpts from "Brian Zahnd / Jesus Is the Interpretation," June 8, 2020, https://www.youtube.com/watch?v=w5u-IKzAPYQ&list=PLgimV9UoSbAIbXX447Gu_5-kGpLAO_eJO&index=164.

Brian described my two-year journey, during which I set aside certain scriptures that appeared to contradict Jesus's radical love, only to later discover a Christological interpretation. I've since met so many who, like me, have determined that if a passage doesn't align with Jesus, it needs Christocentric rethinking.

And Brad may be chief among them.

BRAD JERSAK: A MORE CHRISTLIKE WORD

Brad Jersak is a widely recognized author, teacher, and theologian who carries profound wisdom grounded in love. Another Tambourine Man who has gone two weeks ahead, I'm grateful for the way he invites us into a fuller, more beautiful vision of God.

I hadn't read Brad's *A More Christlike Word, Reading Scripture the Emmaus Way*[32] when he first came on the podcast. So, I was thrilled as he took this Christocentric hermeneutic to transformative depths—"the Bible serves as a witness, not the destination."

As a young theologian, Brad wrestled particularly with the Old Testament text, which seemed to depict God as harsh or violent in apparent contradiction to the God of love revealed in Jesus:

> This shifted for me when I joined the Mennonites.... my mentor there was Reverend Peter Bartel, who showed me how the Anabaptist tradition or the Mennonite tradition taught us to read Scripture.

---

32 Bradley Jersak, *A More Christlike Word: Reading Scripture the Emmaus Way* (New Kensington, PA: Whitaker House, 2021).

> What they would say is, "Don't think of the whole Bible as an equal revelation. Don't even think of it as flat, where all the books are on the same plane—as if genealogies or census lists have the same authority as the words of Jesus.
>
> Instead, you bend your Bible upwards where the gospels are. That's the pinnacle or peak of revelation because Christ alone is perfect theology."
>
> It was Peter who encouraged me to ask the question, "How does this passage point to Jesus?" He helped me see that everything in the Bible—whether it's law, prophets, psalms, or letters—is either prefiguring Jesus or reflecting on Him. That changed everything for me.

I love how Brad wrestled with the seeming disparity between the God depicted in the Old Testament and the love and mercy of the God revealed through Christ in the New. I know that wrestling. And I love how God, through Peter's insight, helped shape Brad's hermeneutic: "What if the point of those stories isn't about revealing who God is, but about revealing how humanity misunderstood Him?"

That question is worth some serious reflection and reminded me of a quote by theologian, writer, podcaster, and another *Tacos Podcast* guest, Pete Enns. "God let His kids tell the story."[33]

---

[33] Jason Clark & Brooke Waters, hosts, *Rethinking God with Tacos*, podcast excerpt from "Pete Enns / Finding A Bigger God" October 16, 2024, https://www.youtube.com/watch?v=lbo_mrGDCR0&list=PLgimV9UoSbAIbXX447Gu_5-kGpLAO_eJO&index=22&t=3113s

But what I most loved about the conversation with Brad was how he spoke to my sense of loneliness when I first stubbornly yet tentatively leaned into my Jesus hermeneutic—those two years when I only read the gospels. I'd thought I was alone, only to meet folks like Brian and Brad and Kruger and Crowder and...

> But it wasn't just contemporary voices. Brad continued. "What I learned from the early church fathers, especially through the mentorship of Archbishop Lazar Puhalo, is that they approached Scripture with a threefold lens: literal, moral, and spiritual. But their literal sense was very different from our modernist, literalistic way of reading. They didn't see the text as a rigid set of facts to be dissected but as a living story meant to convey deeper truths."

Brad noted that many of our church fathers emphasized Jesus as the pinnacle of revelation. "If something in Scripture contradicts what Jesus revealed about God, then we have to understand it as a human projection, not divine reality."

Brad continued. "When the church fathers read the Old Testament, for example, they didn't abandon it, as Marcion did, nor did they literalize it in the way we often do today. Instead, they engaged it deeply, asking, 'How does this prefigure Christ and His gospel?' How do the Law, the Prophets, and the Psalms point to Christ? They believed every figure—whether it was Abel, Isaac, Joseph, or Moses—foreshadowed Jesus in some way."

If you're unfamiliar with Marcion, so was I at the time. Briefly, the early church did not consider Marcion (c. 85–160 AD) an "early church father" but rather a heretic. He also wrestled with the disparity between the God presented in the Old Testament as opposed to the God Jesus revealed in the New. His solution? Throw out the Old Testament. He rejected it entirely and proposed that the God of the Hebrew Scriptures (whom he saw as wrathful and legalistic) differed from the loving and merciful God whom Jesus revealed in the New Testament.

I have been accused of being one of Marcion's followers a time or two, so it was helpful to learn about him. But like Brad, I am no Marcionite. I, too, find my footing with the early church fathers. And I, too, love the whole Book!

"For them, Scripture wasn't a flat text to be dissected and debated. It was a unified testimony that led to Christ. They understood that the Bible isn't the Word of God; it bears witness to the Word of God, and that Word is Jesus. Everything bends toward Him, either pointing forward to His coming or reflecting back on His life, death, and resurrection."

"Are you telling me our early church fathers would approve of my two-year Christological resetting of my lens?" I asked Brad and received a resounding "Yes."

I was not alone. Our early church fathers' approach to interpreting Scripture was Jesus—a walking, talking *Word who became flesh*—revelation of other-focused, self-giving love.

And still today, we have fathers and mothers endeavoring to provide this same hermeneutic.[34]

Voices like Brian Simmons continue in this narrative, seeking to unveil the love of God through the lens of Jesus.

THE BIBLE MINUS LOVE EQUALS FALSE TEACHING.

BRIAN SIMMONS: INTERPRETING SCRIPTURE — THE LOVE THAT UNVEILS GOD

Sitting down with Brian, the translator of The Passion Translation, is like opening a window to a world where Scripture comes alive, where words breathe and beckon us into deeper intimacy with God. His approach to interpreting Scripture isn't merely academic—it's relational. It's about seeing the heart of God through the lens of Jesus, who revealed, in every word and action, that God is love.

Derek was my co-host for the conversation, and we were both wrecked by Brian's rich confidence in God's affection!

"The Bible minus love equals false teaching," Brian said early in our conversation, a statement so succinct yet so weighty it felt like it hung in the air, demanding we sit with it. For Brian, Scripture isn't a rulebook, it's a love letter, an

---

[34] Jason Clark, host, *Rethinking God with Tacos*, podcast, adapted excerpts from "Brad Jersak / High Christology," April 2, 2020, https://www.youtube.com/watch?v=_iWAYL4XgVo&list=PLgimV9UoSbAIbXX447Gu_5-kGpLAO_eJO&index=175.

invitation to encounter the living God who is deeply in love with His creation.

Brian's journey into Bible translation began during his missionary years with the Payakuna people in Central America, but it wasn't until an encounter with God's divine love in 2008 that his calling crystallized. "I had a holy, heavenly visitation," he shared, "A supernatural encounter, and for some reason, this tends to really irk my critics, but you know, it's okay if Jesus comes to Muslims around the world . . . but God forbid He would come to a Christian pastor like me. But He did."

As a relational theologian—more on that soon—I love Brian's recognition and normalization of a relational God who speaks to us!

That sacred and transformative moment became the catalyst for what would become The Passion Translation. "(God) promised that He would help me with the translation. . . . He has kept that promise," Brian stated, describing how the Holy Spirit would breathe on the manuscripts, revealing insights and layers of meaning that he might not have seen otherwise.

That encounter didn't just set him on a path; it shaped how he approached every verse and every phrase. For Brian, translating Scripture is about unveiling the God revealed in Jesus. He approaches every verse through the lens of divine love.

Brian began his work on the Passion Translation with the Song of Songs. And it speaks volumes about his approach. "The Song of Songs is the heart of God placed in the heart of the Scriptures to get into the heart of every one of us," he said. "It is not a book of erotica. It is not X-rated. . . . It is a beautiful symphony of love." For Brian, this ancient song of longing and intimacy mirrors the divine romance between Christ and His bride. Song of Songs is not about rigid doctrines or debates; it's about, as Brian put it, "a glance of love (that) ravishes the heart of Jesus."

> **IF YOU READ SCRIPTURE WITHOUT LOVE, YOU'LL MISS THE HEART OF GOD.**

Brian challenged the hyper-literalization of Scripture, a trend he sees as a roadblock to experiencing God's love. "To hyper-literalize what obviously is metaphoric misses the depth and beauty embedded in the Scriptures," he explained, advocating for deeper engagement—one that invites us into the relational and allegorical layers within Scripture. "When you open the Bible with a love lens, you'll read it the way God has written it—to feed and correct us ... to transform us."

Derek asked how viewing Scripture through the lens of love changes the way he approaches difficult or divisive passages. His response was profoundly relational. "Love is always the basis," he said. If you read Scripture without love, you'll miss the heart of God." He described how historical and cultural contexts can help us understand passages that are often used to exclude or wound. But his ultimate guide is Jesus.

A Christological Hermeneutic

In his words was an invitation. What if we approached Scripture as a means of discovering a God who so loved the world that He became one of us?

"To rescue all of us," Derek finished, and I smiled.

Connecting with Brian, I couldn't help but feel inspired. His hermeneutic sees every word through the eyes of Jesus, allowing us to discover, over and again, that God is love.

In Brian's hands, Scripture becomes what it was always meant to be: a window into the heart of a God who longs to be known, not through fear or rules, but through relationship.

This lens of love leads to one of Brian's most compelling insights: union with Christ. "When (Jesus) said it's finished, it wasn't just about the work of the cross. It was about the perfected union that He has given us," Brian shared with a quiet intensity. "We don't add anything to it; we can't subtract anything from it. It's a completed work." This union, this oneness with Christ, is central to Brian's translation and teaching.[35]

And this is a beautiful way to transition to one of my favorite people.

We've had two guests on the podcast who have written Bible translations, Brian and Francois du Toit.

The incredible thing about those conversations is how both men were open to questions about the translation process—both are brilliant with jot and tittle—but the only thing they truly wanted to talk about was how profoundly loved we are.

And union!

---

35 Jason Clark and Derek Turner, hosts, *Rethinking God with Tacos,* podcast, adapted excerpts from "Brian Simmons / The Passion Translation & the Fiery Love of God," May 19, 2021, https://www.youtube.com/watch?v=4ho1ax0mCCg&list=PLgimV9UoSbAIbXX447Gu_5-kGpLAO_eJO&index=125.

FRANCOIS DU TOIT: LIVING FROM HIS DIVINE EMBRACE

In the shadow of the majestic Swartberg Mountains, nestled far from the bustling world, Francois du Toit and his wife, Lydia, have carved out a sanctuary. It is there, amidst the serene beauty of South Africa, that they have dedicated their lives to translating and sharing the transformative message of the Mirror Bible.

Connecting with Francois and Lydia, even through the ethereal threads of a virtual call, felt like being enveloped in the warmth of an old friend's embrace.

From the moment we began, Francois's vibrant spirit and profound humility shone. His laughter was infectious, his words a blend of deep wisdom and childlike wonder. He greeted us with the exuberance of a grandfather, making the physical distance melt away.

Our conversation traversed many paths, but at its heart was the theme of rediscovering the gospel as union. "Man began in God. You are the greatest idea that God has ever had. . . . You can't choose Union. You don't choose to be one with God. You can only awaken to the truth of your union with the Father, Son, and Spirit." Francois said. And this awakening is discovered in Jesus."

Francois's journey into this revelation began before his translation work. He recounted his early days, a time marked by a legalistic approach to faith, where the Bible was a book of rules rather than a love letter from God. But as he delved deeper into the Scriptures, he began to see them through a different lens. "I realized that the Scriptures are about unveiling the heart of the Father," he said. "They are about revealing our true identity in Christ."

Central to Francois's work is the Mirror Bible, a translation that aims to reflect the true essence of the original texts. He explained how this project was born from a desire to help people see themselves as God sees them. "The Mirror Bible is about living from the place of embrace," he said. "It's about understanding that we are already included in the divine fellowship."

THE SCRIPTURES ARE SOCIAL, AND SALVATION IS SOCIAL.

Throughout our conversation, Francois returned to the theme of living from embrace. He painted a vivid picture of what this looks like in daily life. "Imagine waking up every morning with the assurance that you are already embraced by God," he said. "There's no striving, no performing. Just living in the reality of His love."

He challenges us to see the gospel as an all-encompassing embrace. "The gospel is not good advice; it's good news. It's the declaration of what has already been accomplished." Francois said with a passionate glint in his eye. This foundational belief drives his translation work in the Mirror Bible, which aims to reflect the essence of the original texts in a way that speaks directly to the heart.

Francois is not interested in theological debates. "It's not about arm-wrestling someone with theological information. It's about unveiling the Christ in them," he emphasized. His focus or methodology is always on the relational aspect of Scripture; on how it reveals our inclusion in the divine fellowship.

> **THE BIBLE IS NOT A BOOK WRITTEN FOR INDIVIDUALS; IT'S WRITTEN FOR HUMANITY. IT BELONGS TO US AS A REVELATION OF GOD.**

"We are never out of His thoughts. You cannot be abandoned. It's impossible for the Father to abandon the human race," Francois concluded. This approach to Scripture is profoundly personal, offering a life-changing revelation of God's unfailing love and our eternal inclusion in His family.

And it's about family—community. And no one speaks to this better than Father Kenneth Tanner[36][37]

---

[36] Jason Clark, host, *Rethinking God with Tacos*, podcast, adapted excerpts from "Francois du Toit / Awakening to the I Am-Ness of God," September 18, 2024, https://www.youtube.com/watch?v=4Sa9hs7o90E&list=PLgimV9UoSbAIbXX447Gu_5-kGpLAO_eJO&index=12.

[37] Jason Clark host, *Rethinking God with Tacos*, podcast, adapted excerpts from "Francois du Toit / Jesus Is What God Believes About You." https://www.youtube.com/watch?v=wjpqznUJRYE

FATHER KENNETH TANNER: SEEING JESUS IN THE MOSAIC

I love Father Kenneth. He is a compassionate man who loves and thinks in the deep end of life. Talking with him about Scripture was like walking into a treasure trove of wisdom. His approach to reading the Bible is profoundly Christ-centered and deeply communal, a perspective that feels both ancient and timely. From the start, Kenneth emphasized, "The Bible is not a book written for individuals; it's written for humanity. It belongs to us as a revelation of God." That shift from "me and the Bible" to "us and the Bible" reframes everything.

> **WHEN WE REARRANGE THE SCRIPTURES THE RIGHT WAY, WE SEE THE IMAGE OF JESUS.**

For Kenneth, Scripture comes alive when it's read through the lens of Christ—together. He shared how his understanding of the Bible expanded: "I never really started seeing everything about Jesus until I started praying with Orthodox Christians, reading Scripture with them, entering their worship, and living in that space." This wasn't just about intellectual discovery but about experiential connection, a sacred dialogue that helped him see Jesus more fully.

> **WHEN JESUS IS THE HERMENEUTIC, WHEN YOU'RE LOOKING FOR THE PRESENCE OF JESUS ON EVERY PAGE, THERE'S SO MUCH FREEDOM.**

Kenneth leaned on 2nd century Greek Bishop Irenaeus's metaphor of an ancient mosaic to explain this. "When we rearrange the Scriptures the right way, we see the image of Jesus," he said, pointing out how reading with the whole Church—across traditions and centuries—helps us avoid misinterpretations. He noted that without this communal engagement, it's easy to get the "hypothesis wrong" and distort the picture.

He also emphasized the freedom that comes from this approach. "When Jesus is the hermeneutic, when you're looking for the presence of Jesus on every page, there's so much freedom," he said, contrasting it with the rigid literalism many of us grew up with. This freedom is essential as it allows us to wrestle with the text, even the seemingly hard parts, without losing sight of God's goodness.

Ultimately, Kenneth reminded us that "the Scriptures are social, and salvation is social." Reading the Bible together, with Jesus at the center, draws us not only closer to Him but also to one another. It's an invitation to see the big picture of Christ in community, across time and tradition—a way to let Scripture shape us as one body.[38]

This communal Christological hermeneutic is a beautiful invitation to reset our lens and discover God in Christ, together.

MY HERMENEUTIC

> *"Jesus is the dictionary in which we look up the meaning of words."*[39]
> —Eugene Peterson, Author of *The Message Bible*

When I write, I hope to present ideas in a conversational tone as though we're connecting over a good cup of coffee with a little Baileys, a generous amount of cream, and my wife, Karen's, berry rhubarb pie, which was an early possibility—Rethinking God with Berry Rhubarb Pie.

The fact is, I like to make suggestions through storytelling and what-if questions, but I've been told that on occasion, maybe—you know, every once in a while—I could just state my conclusions plainly.

When it comes to hermeneutics, the method by which we interpret Scripture, this is me making it plain.

Jesus, Greater Love, is my hermeneutic—a Christological hermeneutic.

I approach Scripture in search of Jesus, the *"Word Who Became Flesh."*

---

38 Jason Clark and Thomas Floyd, hosts, *Rethinking God with Tacos,* podcast, adapted excerpts from "A Body of Which I Am a Member," July 29, 2020, https://www.youtube.com/watch?v=DQ5o9_Yuwpg&list=PLgimV9UoSbAIbXX447Gu_5-kGpLAO_eJO&index=158.
39 Eugene H. Peterson, *Christ Plays in Ten Thousand Places: A Conversation in Spiritual Theology* (Grand Rapids, MI: Eerdmans, 2008), 103.

Jesus is the whole revelation of what God is like, and the cross is the clearest way to know Him and how He feels about us.

WHAT IF ANY BELIEF ABOUT THE NATURE OF GOD THAT CONTRADICTS CRUCIFORM LOVE, EVEN IF IT'S BIBLICAL, IS UNTRUE?

God has always been like Jesus, whether we knew it or not. That's true today and was true for our Old and New Testament brothers and sisters.

The Apostle Paul put it this way, *"For I resolved to know nothing while I was with you except Jesus Christ and him crucified"* (1 Corinthians 2:2, NIV). I share that same resolve in all things, including my approach to Scripture.

Now, here are some *what-ifs.*

What if any belief about the nature of God that contradicts cruciform Greater Love, even if it's biblical, is untrue?

What if Scripture is an inspired collection of books that reveals how poorly humanity has thought about God in light of how good the God Jesus revealed truly is?

What if the whole point of the Book is to empower deeper revelation of reconciling love, a greater discovery of the Truth that sets us free, and an awakening to our union in Christ?

What if we were meant to search Scripture so we might recognize the *"Word Who Became Flesh"* in every person standing before us?

What if we can know our hermeneutic is true based on whether we love God, our neighbor, and ourselves more? I'm thankful to my friend Randall Worley for that thought.[40]

For me, interpreting Scripture is not rocket science; it's relational theology 101. But what did you expect? I'm a relational theologian, which I write about in depth in the next chapter. But first, one more what-if:

What if even our approach to Scripture is about a Love who laid His life down for His friends?

Plain and simple: Jesus is my hermeneutic.

When I read Scripture, I'm not just looking for facts or rules. I'm searching for the Word made flesh. As Brad Jersak noted, "Every page, every story, every letter bends toward Him.[41]

Jesus is perfect theology. And when I lose sight of that, I know it's time to return to the gospels and fix my eyes on the Author and Perfecter of my faith.

Because, in the end, it's all about love. And His name is Jesus.[42]

---

[40] Jason Clark, *Rethinking God with Tacos*, adapted excerpts from "Randall Worley / Questioning My Answers."
[41] Jason Clark, host, *Rethinking God with Tacos*, podcast, adapted excerpts from "Brad Jersak / High Christology." March 31, 2020. https://www.youtube.com/watch?v=_iWAYL4XgVo
[42] Jason Clark, adapted excerpts from *Leaving and Finding Jesus*.

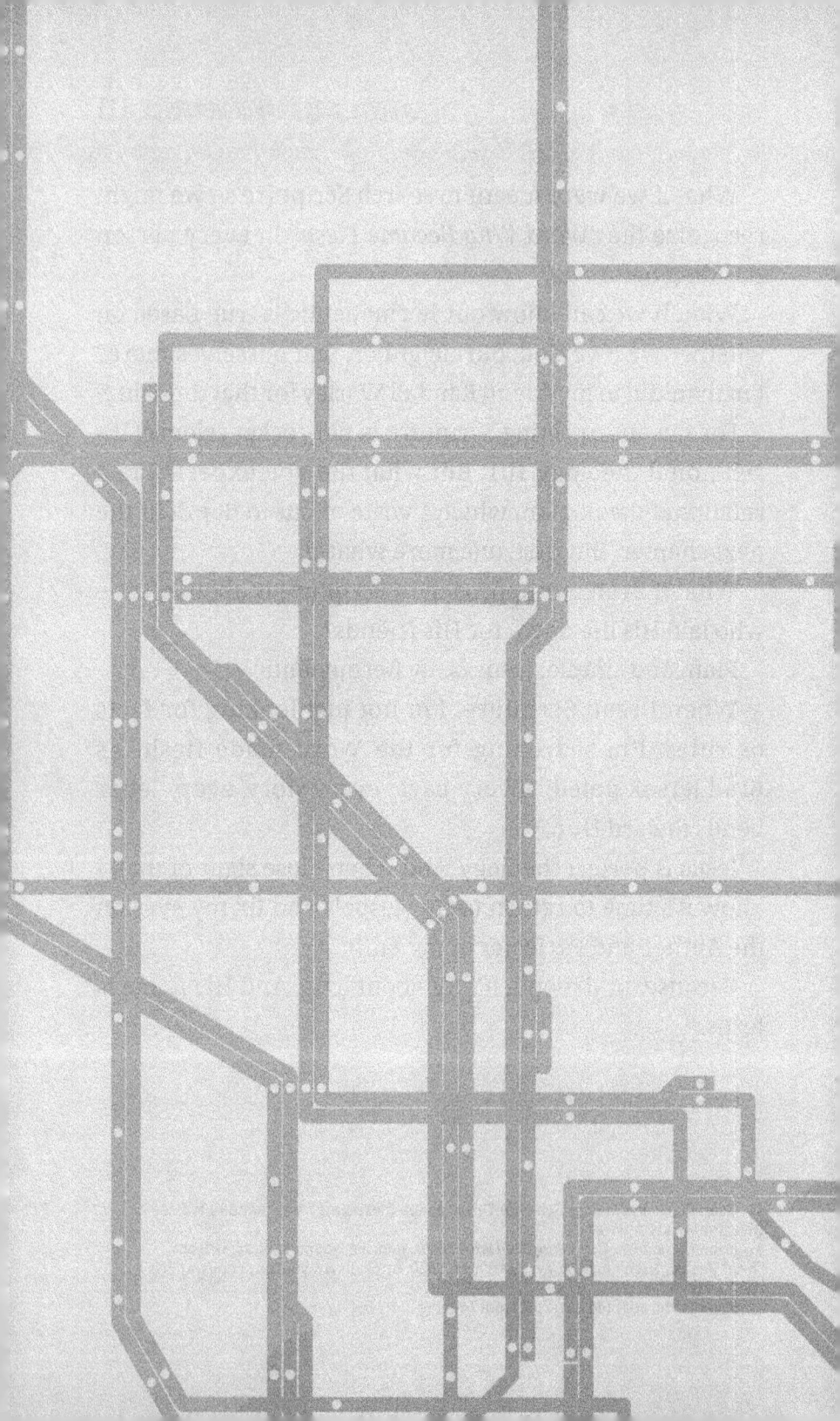

CHAPTER 5

RELATIONAL THEOLOGY

Tortillas Together

A RELATIONAL THEOLOGIAN

If you've been in the church for half a minute, you've bumped into terms like "systematic theology" or "biblical exegesis"—phrases that feel like they belong in a sterile lab rather than the unpredictable, messy, and beautifully relational reality of human existence.

I'm not prolific with language that doesn't apply to my relational way of being. I'm not wired for academic approaches to knowledge. I appreciate those who parse through jot and title, but I'm all about experiential knowing.

I'm a right-brained fella making my way in a left-brained world where Western Enlightenment is the consensus paradigm by which to navigate theology. Thus, I have often felt disqualified from discussing deep-end thoughts about God. I am not alone.

This is why my heart exploded when I first heard speaker, writer, and podcast guest Graham Cooke refer to himself as a relational theologian. It was well over a decade ago, and he didn't expound, but that term arrested me with the truth of the gospel. I embraced it and have spent every day since exploring and expanding upon it.

> **TO ME, IF YOU AREN'T A RELATIONAL THEOLOGIAN, YOU'RE DOING IT WRONG.**

Jesus was a relational theologian—a walking, talking expression of relational theology. He was a son, a friend, and a brother. He revealed God as a Father, and everything He did was a revelation of love. God is love—not theoretical—but a love that is given and received.

To me, if you aren't a relational theologian, you're doing it wrong.

Some of my academic friends have pushed back, referring to me as a "practical theologian" — I'm good with that. But I prefer the term "relational," as its impact is evidenced in practical transformation. In other words, let's keep the horse in front of the cart.

At its core, being a relational theologian isn't about nailing down every doctrine with precision. It's about asking how God's love breathes and moves through the cracks and corners of real life—how love transforms, reconciles, and restores.

This isn't theology that collects dust on a shelf—it's theology with dirt under its nails and a pulse that syncs with the heartbeat of humanity. LOVE isn't an abstract puzzle to solve or knowledge to acquire; He's the fires within us, wrapped in the fabric of our lives—Jesus's Greater Love burning at the center and the edges, in the beginning, and the end, the before and after, and everything in between.

For the relational theologian, Jesus isn't just the centerpiece of faith; He's the interpretive key to everything. If a passage in Scripture feels harsh, cruel, or out of sync with the radical, cross-shaped Greater Love Jesus embodied, relational theologians don't sweep it under the rug. They lean in, ask questions, and let trust lead the dance.

Relational theologians don't dismiss the Old Testament or cherry-pick verses; they search for Greater Love, the Word who became flesh, within its pages. It's about reading everything through the lens of Christ crucified, risen, and ascended. Jesus isn't a plot twist; He's the whole story, the boundary lines, and the quiet whisper that rewrites everything.

Relational theology isn't a monologue. It's an ongoing conversation. It lives in the overlap between ancient voices, modern mystics, and the neighbor you run into at the coffee shop.

Yeah, lots of coffee.

And berry rhubarb pie.

And tacos, of course.

And relational theology works in the context of consent.

BRAD JERSAK: EXPLORING RELATIONAL THEOLOGY

Brad Jersak often reflects on God's "consenting love"—a love that never kicks down the door but patiently waits for our "yes." This resonates deeply with relational theologians. God isn't in the business of forcing His way in. He always waits for the invite.

Jersak, who has a PhD, by the way, and can play in all the academic spaces, considers himself right-brained as well. I was grateful that he understood and valued my right-brained limitations while adding brilliant left-brain cultural and historical foundations for our relational approach to all things.

During our conversation, he shared, "Jesus didn't come to give us a new religion; He came to reveal the relational heart of God—a Father who loves us unconditionally." That's the essence of relational theology: it's not about rules, rituals, or getting doctrine "right." It's about connection and the journey.

Brad described how this relational perspective reshaped his understanding of God. "If we start with the idea that God is love, then everything else—justice, holiness, even judgment—has to flow out of that love," he said. This is profoundly practical. It reframes how we see ourselves, our neighbors, and the God who refuses to be distant from us.

Brad also pointed out that this relational approach is embodied in Jesus. "When you look at Christ, you're seeing the perfect revelation of God's nature. Every act ... was an expression of self-giving, other-centered love."

That's what relational theology looks like to me: a God who meets us in our mess, steps into our pain, and transforms us—not through punishment or fear, but through a love that never lets go. A love that is trustworthy, patient, and makes room for our "yes." That's the heartbeat of the gospel.

Let's be honest, though. Relational theology can get messy. It doesn't tie our understanding up with a neat little bow. There are always more questions than answers. But for those who are growing in relational trust, paradoxes aren't problems to solve but mysteries to hold. Tension exists, but it's wrapped in trust. And that's the beauty of it. Faith, through this lens, isn't about clutching for certainty, but about growing in humility, love, and the willingness to walk forward with open hands—together.

To me, relational theology is gathering around a fire, where life's highs and hardships are shared. I'm grateful for systematic thoughts; I'm just noting that transformation happens in community, first with the Trinity and then with one another.

And that's been my hope for every *Tacos Podcast* conversation —that right and left-brain would merge around a metaphorical fire, maybe with some tacos, and lean into better thoughts about God than the last best thoughts we've had.

I love my conversations with the Krugers, Jersaks, and Chris Greens of the world—fellas whose hearts beat faster at the thought of a relational God. And I'm thankful for the study they have done in the pursuit of love.

And I'm thankful for you, the relational theologians who, regardless of how your brain works, have made Greater Love the high watermark of your faith.

Five chapters in, the fire has moved from pine kindling to oak and is putting off some good heat. So, pull your camp chair closer and help yourself to the chips and salsa, cause there are so many more relational theologian friends I want to introduce you to.[43]

THOMAS JAY OORD: OPEN AND RELATIONAL THEOLOGY

When I first sat down with Thomas Jay Oord to discuss his book *Open and Relational Theology*,[44] I knew we were stepping into deep waters. Tom is a brilliant relational theologian who has letters in front of his name. And like so many of my academically gifted friends, he's relational first. For years, we have wrestled with an image of God that felt distant and unmoved by the daily grit of human life. And I'm thankful for men like Tom, who are painting a picture of a God who feels, loves, leans in, and listens.

Tom's theology rests on a simple idea: God is relational. And he believes it.

"Our actions," he said, "actually affect God." That's a profound statement if you spend a minute with it. We've grown up with a fixed, cosmic version of God—unshaken,

---
[43] Jason Clark, host, *Rethinking God with Tacos*, podcast, adapted excerpts from "Brad Jersak/He Searched Until He Found Them," October 18, 2023, https://www.youtube.com/watch?v=AtjZj1a94Dw.
[44] Thomas Jay Oord, *Open and Relational Theology: An Introduction to Life-Changing Ideas* (New York, NY: SacraSage Press, 2021).

unaffected, watching from a distance. But Tom cracks open that image. In his view, the future isn't locked in place. It's open, dynamic, and shaped moment by moment by both God and humanity.

> ## IT'S THE KIND OF LOVE STILL MOVING IN OUR LIVES TODAY—NOT BY FORCE, BUT BY INVITATION.

"If the future is open, does that mean God doesn't know what's coming next?" I asked. Tom grinned, clearly ready. "Exactly. God knows every possibility, but the future unfolds in real-time. It hasn't happened yet, so even God is leaning forward with us."

Christ isn't distant or untouchable. He is right here in the thick of it—weeping, laughing, and breaking bread with us.

This relational perspective points to love not just as something God does, but as who He is. This is the kind of love that led Jesus to forgive His executioners from the cross. And it's the kind of love still moving in our lives today—not by force, but by invitation.

For someone steeped in the language of God's omniscience, this is a radical shift. But I think Tom is onto something. You see, open theology is a very relational way by which to know and trust God.

It highlights the nature of love in the context of consent. And let's face it; love isn't love outside of consent. . . .[45]

Enter Jonathan Foster.

JONATHAN FOSTER: THE THEOLOGY OF CONSENT

Jonathan is amazing. He has traversed the heights and depths of life with God and discovered a trust that is grounded in love.

In the heart of our conversation is a beautiful way of seeing God—a vision Jonathan calls the "Theology of Consent." It's an idea both disarming and profound: that love, at its core, requires consent. Not just our consent but God's as well. Jonathan suggests that the very structure of the cosmos is built on this relational, non-coercive love.

As he shared his thoughts, I was struck by how much this reframes the way many of us have been taught to think about God. God doesn't operate through control or force, but through a deep, vulnerable relationship with creation. "Jesus didn't die to appease God's anger," Jonathan explained. "He consented to love. And in that love, God invites us all into the best possible future."

Jonathan's vision is beautifully disarming in its simplicity yet carries a profound transformative truth: love, by its very essence, cannot exist without consent. This consent isn't one-sided; it flows in both directions, shaping how we experience God and how God interacts with us. Jonathan proposed that this mutual, non-coercive relationship

---

45 Jason Clark and Derek Turner, hosts, *Rethinking God with Tacos*, podcast, adapted excerpts from "Thomas Jay Oord / Open & Relational Theology," March 30, 2022, https://www.youtube.com/watch?v=_Prsa-0algE.

stitches together the fabric of creation itself—a dance where God leads, but only as far as we allow and follow.

> **GOD IS A RELATIONAL THEOLOGIAN, AND HE DESIRES TO KNOW US AND TO BE KNOWN.**

"God's love is never manipulative. Love coerced isn't love at all." Jonathan continued. "Consent is God's way of honoring the dignity of our humanity, allowing us to freely choose love in return."

Those words underscore the radical vulnerability inherent in divine love—a love that refuses to violate our will, even when it aches for connection.

Here's another way to say it: God is a relational theologian, and He desires to know us and to be known.[46]

RYAN PENA: THE GOD WHO REWRITES OUR STORIES

Jonathan's *Theology of Consent* tangibly plays out in real life. The conversation Derek and I had with Ryan Pena speaks powerfully to this.

Ryan is one of those people you meet and instantly feel at home with—like you've found a long-lost brother.

---

46 Jason Clark and Derek Turner, hosts, *Rethinking God with Tacos*, podcast, adapted excerpts from "Theology of Consent," April 5, 2023, https://www.youtube.com/watch?v=FvIARg_sAzI&list=PLgimV9UoSbAIbXX447Gu_5-kGpLAO_eJO&index=92.

From the moment we connected, his passion for Jesus, his humility, and his deeply relational approach to theology inspired me. Ryan carries the kind of wisdom that only comes from wrestling with big questions and finding Jesus in the process.

"There are pages in your heart I didn't author," he felt the Lord whisper to him during a quiet moment of prayer. The words landed with both the weight of conviction and the lightness of hope.

Ryan described how this wasn't a reprimand, but an invitation. God wasn't standing over him with red ink, marking errors. Instead, He was seated beside him like a gentle editor, a friend ready to help rewrite the story, restoring what was distorted and erasing lies that had been drawn over time.

This wasn't just about small tweaks in theology—it was about identity. "Some pages God rewrote, while others," Ryan said, "He tore out completely." This divine act of authorship wasn't invasive but consent-driven. "He asked for permission to reshape the way I saw Him—and the way I saw myself." Talk about rethinking!

The shift was profound. Ryan had grown up with an image of God as a distant master to serve, but through this relational experience, he realized, "God isn't looking for servants; He's looking for sons and daughters." I couldn't help but add my "yes and" to the conversation. "He is looking for friends!" I said. Ryan nodded with enthusiasm. The move from performance to intimacy, orphan to son or daughter, servant to friend, unravels the religion of striving. This Christian life isn't a transaction; it's a relationship!

"God's love isn't interested in coercion or control," Ryan said. "It's about freedom—freedom to let Him author the pages that lead to healing, restoration, and wholeness."

> **HE WAITS FOR OUR "YES"—THE SACRED CONSENT THAT WELCOMES HIS GRACE DEEPER INTO OUR LIVES.**

Ryan's journey fits like a missing puzzle piece into the larger picture of relational theology. It reveals that transformation isn't about God forcefully rewriting our stories but about our Heavenly Father's patient and loving collaboration with us. This divine authorship respects the integrity of our personal journeys, gently inviting us to reimagine life through the lens of His love and our friendship. The God Ryan encountered stepped into the narrative not to override but to tenderly offer new perspectives, redeeming the broken chapters without discarding the essence of who we are.

God's relational authorship means He meets us in the middle of the mess, amid our humanity, offering to pen words of healing and hope where fear once lived. He highlights the beauty already present, drawing out the gold buried beneath years of striving and misunderstanding.

Ryan spoke about how our Father values our voice in the story. He waits for our "yes"—the sacred consent that welcomes His grace deeper into our lives. In this way, divine transformation becomes a shared creation, a story co-authored in love and trust.[47]

THE FREEDOM TO CHOOSE

I asked Jesus into my heart when I was five. It was the first time I tried to give Him control. He awakened my heart powerfully. I knew His friendship and authority, but He didn't take control. He did something infinitely better; He introduced His Spirit within me.

Over the years, as I grew in the revelation of Greater Love, as I awakened to our union, He became my Lord, my Comforter, my Provider, my Father, my Friend; and all along the way, in every discovery of His perfect love, I would try to give Him control.

I had been told that's what He wanted.

But God is love, and He would not take control; not only that, He didn't seem to want it.

His passion has always been that I would grow intimate with Him as Father, Son, and Holy Spirit and discover the freedom, power, and authority of self-control —that I would know His indwelling friendship.

---

[47] Jason Clark and Derek Turner, hosts, *Rethinking God with Tacos*, podcast, adapted excerpts from "Ryan Pena / God is Good; Jesus Is the Model," November 29, 2023, https://www.youtube.com/watch?v=4Al46u1Y6GQ.

The fact is, God has never been, nor will He ever be, interested in controlling us. Love cannot operate freely in that context. You see, control is the antithesis of relational trust.

No, God is a relational theologian, and His passion is that we would receive the gift He paid such a high price to give. The freedom of self-control is discovered as we surrender to love and awaken to union, a relational indwelling.

We are invited to live intimately one in the Father, Son, and Holy Spirit—fully experiencing the freedom of self-control. We are invited to live a Spirit-filled, Spirit-breathed life in the mutual consent of in-dwelling love.

We are invited to surrender to self-giving, other-centered love, to lay our lives down so we might know what it is to live in the wonder of His eternal life.

We are invited to live in the relational narrative that will transform us, our families, and every area of influence.

We are invited to revelation and intimacy as a way of our being.

When we live as relational theologians, we are the freest people on the planet, empowered to be loved and to love in the same transformative ways Jesus loved.[48]

REWRITING OUR STORIES: THE JOURNEY OF RELATIONAL THEOLOGY

In the end, relational theology calls us to a table, not just as students, but as sons and daughters rediscovering the heart of the Father, as brothers and sisters journeying with Jesus, as friends of the Holy Spirit. This is the relational

---
48 Jason Clark, edited excerpts from *God Is (Not) In Control.*

truth in which we live theologically authentic. It is where we discover that:

Love is our doctrine.

Kindness, our dogma.

The goodness of God, our creed.

We aren't passive spectators but active participants in a divine conversation, one that invites us to see the Trinity in the stories we live and share.

> **GOD IS NOT DISTANT, DETACHED, OR DOMINEERING. HE IS RELATIONAL, PRESENT, AND PATIENT.**

Relational theology invites us to trade control for connection, knowledge for knowing, and rules for trust. It reminds us that God's love is a living, breathing reality that transforms us from the inside out. This is the Greater Love that waits for our consent, meets us in our pain or missing of the mark, and partners with us to rewrite the pages of our lives with hope and healing.

I've had the joy of connecting with Jersak, Oord, Foster, Pena, and so many more Tambourine Men and Women, echoing a truth that resonates deeply: God is not distant, detached, or domineering. He is relational, present, and patient. His love honors our freedom even as it invites us to deeper co-surrender. This is the kind of theology that transforms our lived realities, bringing reconciliation, restoration, and abundant life!

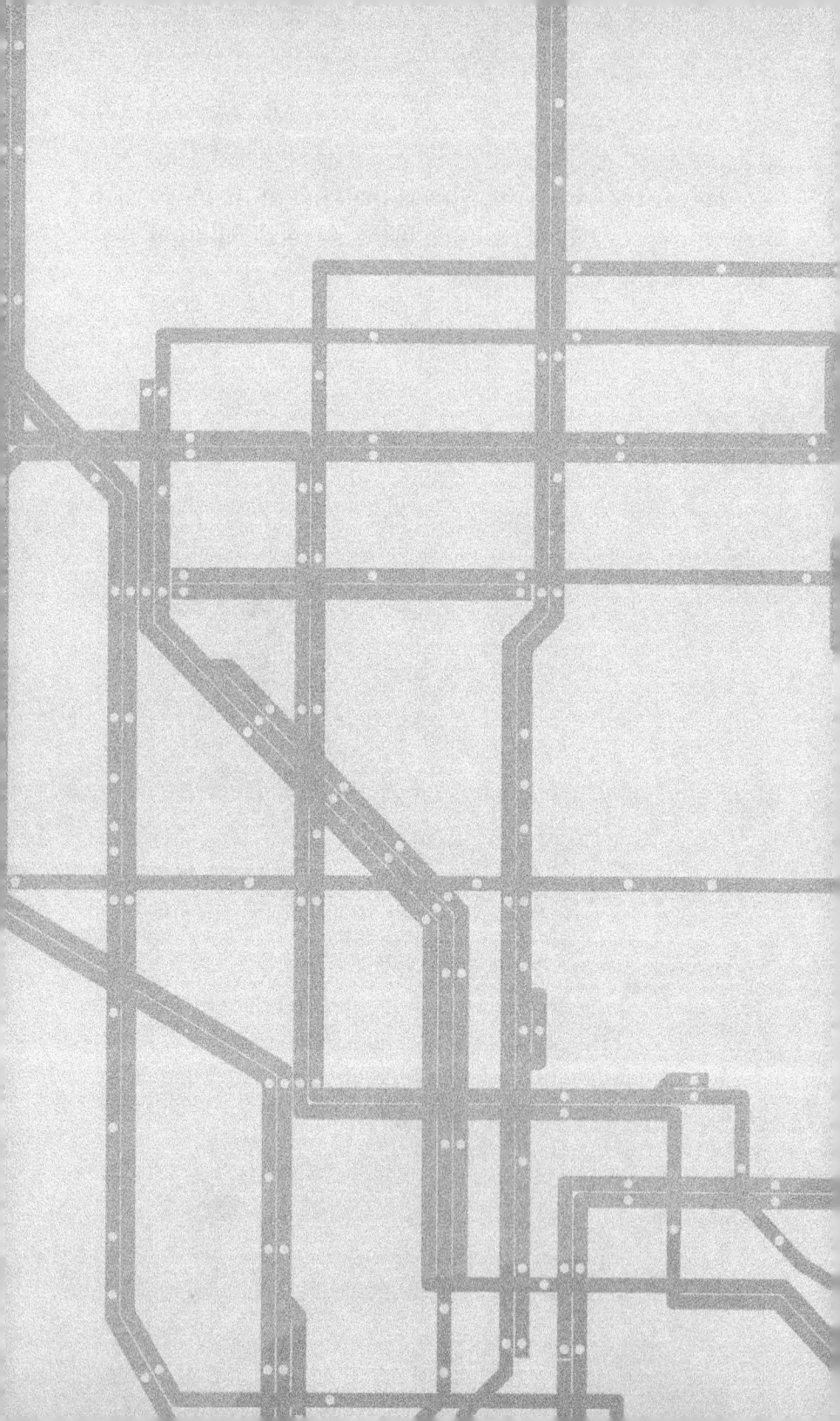

CHAPTER 6

ON DECONSTRUCTION

Taco Salad

ON DECONSTRUCTING

I remember the first time I heard the term *"deconstruction."* It was many years ago.

While I grasped the metaphor, the word didn't resonate. I'd certainly done some spiritual deconstructing in my life, but I am inclined to use a descriptor more in line with *"reconstruction."*

This is partly because I'm a *"glass half full"* guy—at least, I want to be. Nevertheless, my faith journey has been less about the spiritual structures I tore down and more about the spiritual structures with which I replaced them. Thus, my faith journey would be better described with transformative words like rethinking, reimagining, repenting, or reconstruction.

My faith journey? It's been about relationship, mercy and grace, forgiveness, reconciliation, and restoration—reconstruction. It's more of a remodel than a tear down—but yeah, every remodel needs some deconstruction, and that's the word that seems to connect with so many of us church kids these days.

It's a violent word and limited for sure, but I get it. You see, most of us church kids were raised, in some form or another, under the abusive penal substitutionary lie of separation.

We grew up in the limited violent dualism of retribution. We grew up in the religion of hierarchy of distance and delay, in the knowledge of good and evil where the last often remain last, and the first often have pulpits from which they determine who's *"in"* and who's *"out."*

We grew up under the political banner of what and whom the Church was against, even when it was at the expense of what and whom we were for, even when it compromised character, integrity, kindness, compassion, mercy, and grace.

THE ONLY THING THAT'S CHANGED IS AT WHOM THE ROCKS GET THROWN.

We grew up with Church leaders often conflating Jesus with a punishing, systematic theology and then making excuses for every cruel thing said or done in its defense.

This onerous separation theology gave birth to a revolution, and when people revolt, they often start by tearing things down.

When we react to something, we create an equal and opposite reaction. Just so, part of the deconstruction movement is an equal and opposite reaction: still participation in cruel punishment, still striving down the all-too-familiar road of separation and lack. The only thing that's changed is at whom the rocks get thrown.

For some, maybe those most abused by the church's infatuation with separation—and we are many—deconstruction has become an outright demolition with no plan for the future. For these folks, there is no *baby in the bathwater*, and their journey vacillates between days of cathartic meltdowns and days of nihilistic numbness.

For others, deconstruction is a holistic response. We are intent on discovering an authentic connection with God and humanity. We are leaning into a kindness that empowers repentance, and we are being transformed. We are madly in love with Jesus, but we are rethinking the cruel and punishing certainties about the God we were often raised with.

My friend and podcast guest, Schlyce Jimenez, says it this way: "Jesus told me one time . . . you never rebelled from Me. You rebelled from a version of Me that was never Me."[49] I think that statement deeply resonates with many of us, especially those who listen to or watch the *Tacos* Podcast. Our deconstruction has been an excavation—digging down

---
[49] Jason Clark and Derek Turner, hosts, *Rethinking God with Tacos,* podcast, adapted excerpts from "Schlyce Jimenez / The Path," May 4, 2023, https://www.youtube.com/watch?v=ReYgW1P5gcE.

to find the Cornerstone, the Greater Love that we can trust and thus build upon.[50]

BRIAN ZAHND: BEFORE YOU LEAVE, GO DEEPER

Brian Zahnd has walked this road. In another of our conversations in which Derek co-hosted, Brian admitted he's a bit weary of the word "deconstruction." "But I respect it," he said. "Because it names something real. Something unavoidable for most of us."

Zahnd pointed out that the term "deconstruction" has roots in Jacques Derrida's work—originally a literary theory aimed at exposing hidden power structures in texts. But when applied to faith, the word takes on a different weight. "It sounds too much like destruction," Zahnd said. "And that's not what I'm advocating. I prefer words like rediscovery or reorientation. Before you leave, go deeper."

Deconstruction isn't about destruction—it's about peeling back layers to rediscover the richness that lies beneath. Brian continued, "Sometimes I think what people are done with is a shallow Americanized Christianity. Well, yeah, that's my story too."

Brian recounted when he began questioning the faith he had known for years. He was a successful pastor, "by every measure that American Christians like to use to determine success. But I began to feel thin. It felt too consumerist, too American." And so, he set out to find something deeper, richer.

---

50 Jason Clark, edited excerpts from *Leaving and Finding Jesus*.

"I just backed up as far as I could," he said. "I started reading the Church Fathers for the first time. I began to take them in order—Polycarp, Justin Martyr, Irenaeus, Athanasius—and it began to change me."

Brian wasn't abandoning faith but returning to its roots. "I felt like what I knew deserved a better Christianity than the one I had experienced."

What I loved about Brian's thoughts was they were restorative. "It's not about tearing everything down with no plan for rebuilding," he said. "If we're not careful, it can become an end in itself, and that's where people get stuck."

His advice to those questioning their faith was simple but profound: "Go deeper. Maybe explore outside of what you feel is no longer sustainable. Look at some of the other expressions of faith. Try to find the best of orthodoxy, Catholicism, Anglicanism, and mainline Protestant thought. There are gems there."

> **I'M CONVINCED WHAT ENDURES IS JESUS'S OTHER-CENTERED, SELF-GIVING LOVE.**

And, of course, He followed this with his Jesus hermeneutic. "Jesus is what God has to say," he declared. "If it doesn't look like Jesus, then we need to question how we're interpreting." He wasn't just talking about Scripture; he was referencing how we navigate our faith and the church.

"There's never been a golden age of the church. The church has always been more or less a train wreck. But even the angriest atheists rarely mount a sustained attack on Jesus. There's something about him that endures."

I'm convinced what *endures* is Jesus's other-centered, self-giving love. I've learned I can put my faith there, even as I navigate the unsettling uncertainties of deconstruction. Jesus is our Cornerstone.

"Jesus will save our faith. He'll save us," Brian said. "Even when everything seems to be on fire, faith is still possible. Faith doesn't have to perish in the ashes of theological deconstruction."

Maybe faith isn't about our certainty but about trust in the midst of the mystery.[51]

BRIAN MCLAREN: FROM CERTAINTY TO MYSTERY

Brian was such an encouraging fella to talk with. Gentle, kind, and steady. He has been a pioneer in the deconstruction movement, not by choice but because he has been rejected by some who can't yet imagine a God as good as the one Brian is convinced of. Brian has learned to live in the response of love, or as Thomas Oord says, "the logic of love," even when we can't understand.

---

51 Jason Clark and Derek Turner, hosts, *Rethinking God with Tacos*, podcast, adapted excerpts from "Brian Zahnd / When Everything's on Fire," November 12, 2022, https://www.youtube.com/watch?v=d_j0sESZ4Vg.

"Certainty has nothing to do with reality," McLaren said. "People are certain about all kinds of falsehoods. Faith isn't about certainty—it's about trust."

Brian's deconstruction journey began, in part, with questions about the Bible's portrayal of God. McLaren, like Zahnd, found solace in reading the Bible literarily rather than literally. And Brian was convinced God was good.

He recounted a profound realization from the heart of God: "You've never had a thought of me that is too good." That moment became a cornerstone in his evolving faith. "It gave me permission to say, 'human language is never going to contain God.' The best language can do is point." The difference, he explained, lies between pointing and grasping. "If you think you have God in your hand, you're not pointing. And you can pretty much be sure God is not in your hand."

This shift—from grasping for certainty to embracing the mystery of God—has shaped Brian's interactions with critics and skeptics alike. "I've written myself out of a couple of different churches," he shared with a wry smile. "It's better to be rejected for who you actually are than to be accepted for a false image of yourself." This vulnerability—the willingness to traverse rejection—is a hallmark of those undergoing deconstruction. If you listen closely, you'll hear the transformative jingle jangle of Brian's faith.

For Brian, deconstruction isn't just about dismantling harmful beliefs but about creating space for something new. "Deconstruction is not destruction," he said. "It's lovingly telling the story of something." This framing invites a posture of curiosity and compassion, both for oneself and for the structures being questioned. It allows for a kind of holy demolition—a tearing down with the intent to rebuild.

Another way to say it, "If you're not safe to question, you're not safe to grow." That's from my friend and podcast guest, Mike Zenker.[52]

Still, the path of deconstruction can be lonely. "If people go to a lot of their churches and say what they actually think and believe, they'll just be asked to leave," Brian acknowledged. "In a sense, they have good reason to leave because they're not wanted as they are." For those navigating this isolation, he offered practical advice: "Find at least a couple of friends with whom you can be honest. And honestly, podcasts like yours are helping people find each other."

I want to pause a moment and acknowledge Brian's words. My favorite thing about the podcast is all the ways I and others have connected because of it. On this awakening journey into the ever-expanding love of God, we aren't alone! I can't tell you how encouraged I was by Brian's words—and still am to this day. They warm my heart. But back to the conversation.

Brian spoke about the stages of faith that many encounter during deconstruction. He described four key phases—simplicity, complexity, perplexity, and harmony. "We all start in simplicity," he said. "That's the stage of dualism—right and wrong, good and bad.

---

[52] Jason Clark and Derek Turner, *Rethinking God with Tacos*, podcast, "Mike Zenker / Understanding Forgiveness," August 23, 2023, https://www.youtube.com/watch?v=qVDIS-DzkTo&list=PLgimV9UoSbAIbXX447Gu_5-kGpLAO_eJO&index=83.

But eventually, life pushes us into complexity, where we realize the world isn't as simple as we thought."

DECONSTRUCTION BECOMES A CYCLE OF GROWTH—A SHEDDING OF OLD SKINS TO MAKE ROOM FOR NEW LIFE.

For some, this leads to perplexity, a stage marked by deep questioning and skepticism. "Perplexity is the stage of deconstruction," Brian noted. "It's where you say, a lot of what I was taught is actually harmful, and I have to scrutinize it." But there is hope beyond perplexity.

"Harmony," Brian explained, "is where we realize that love is the ultimate guide. It's not about having all the answers, but about walking in the light of that love, even when the path ahead is unclear." In this way, deconstruction becomes a cycle of growth—a shedding of old skins to make room for new life.

As our interview wrapped up, I was thankful for Brian's unwavering belief in the goodness of God, even amidst the questions and uncertainties. "Jesus never had a thought about God that was too good," he reminded. And in that statement lies the essence of deconstruction—a stripping away of the lesser, distorted images of God to reveal the boundless love at the heart of the gospel—Jesus.

And of course, that's the whole point of the podcast—can we have a better today, than the last best thought we had about Him?

In a world that often values conformity, Brian's journey is a testament to the beauty of questioning, the courage of transformation, and the grace that meets us in the in-between.

Which is the perfect place to have my friend Randall Worley enter the conversation.[53]

RANDALL WORLEY: QUESTIONING MY ANSWERS

I followed Randall Worley for fifteen years before meeting him. He was a voice of wisdom and encouragement, and in the last several years, I also have the great joy of calling him a friend.

Derek co-hosted this conversation and also calls Randall a friend, so our conversation pretty much started in the deep end.

TRUE FAITH ISN'T THREATENED BY MYSTERY—IT THRIVES IN IT.

---

53 Jason Clark and Derek Turner, hosts, *Rethinking God with Tacos,* podcast, adapted excerpts from "Brian McLaren / Faith After Doubt," June 9, 2021, https://www.youtube.com/watch?v=LBO7pIcYgAk.

Randall's book, *Questioning My Answers*,⁵⁴ was the centerpiece of our discussion. It is so good and releases grace and wisdom for those who are trading their theological certainties for love. Randall's approach to those who are deconstructing is gentle and weathered. There is no bitterness, no desire to burn everything to the ground. Instead, Randal exudes a quiet, confident joy in embracing the mystery of faith.

"The opposite of faith isn't doubt," he told us, "it's certainty." That one thought can unravel so much and reminded me of my friend Rob Smits' words: "The gospel I was raised in tied faith to certainty—you weren't allowed to change. But the real gospel is ever-expanding."⁵⁵

Randall reminded us that true faith isn't threatened by mystery—it thrives in it. Mystery, he explained, isn't a problem to solve but a space to inhabit. In the absence of mystery, faith shrinks into rigid dogma, and dogma leaves little room for awe. "When we reduce God to something we can fully grasp, we've made an idol out of our understanding," he said.

Deconstruction, as Randall described it, is not about destruction for destruction's sake. It's about love. For this simple relational theologian, there was one sentence Randall said that encapsulated the journey of deconstruction.

"If what you're discovering causes you to love God more, love yourself more, and love people more, it's the truth," he

---

54 Randall Worley, *Questioning Our Answers: A Manifesto for Spiritual Searchers* (Randall Worley, 2018).
55 Jason Clark, host, *Rethinking God with Tacos,* podcast, adapted excerpts from "Robin Smit / Behold The Lamb," April 8, 2025, https://www.youtube.com/watch?v=l8O1V2ycxBQ&list=PLgimV9UoSbAIbXX447Gu_5-kGpLAO_eJO&index=3&t=2726s.

said with the kind of conviction that only comes from experience. "Even if it offends people." Those words have stayed with me. Why? Because relational theology is that simple.

If your deconstruction leads to Greater Love, it's the truth—period. And that can be trusted in a way that settles hearts.

Many people fear deconstruction because it feels like a slippery slope, mostly because they have been told this. But like a father, Randall settles our hearts with the truth that sets us free. "God is not insecure," he reassured us. "He's not defensive when we raise hard questions."

Essentially, what Randall went on to say is that the heart of deconstruction is the pursuit of a deeper, more authentic relationship with God. It's not about tearing down belief systems to live in nihilism, but about removing the barriers that prevent us from experiencing God fully.

Randall discussed the beginner's mind. "Jesus told the disciples, 'Unless you become like a child, you can't access the kingdom'" (see Matthew 18:3). Randall explained that this childlike posture is not about ignorance or naivety but about curiosity and openness.

> **FAITH, AT ITS CORE, IS NOT ABOUT HAVING ALL THE ANSWERS BUT ABOUT BEING WILLING TO ASK THE RIGHT QUESTIONS.**

"When a child is born, their brain is shaped like a question mark," he said with a smile. "But over time, we drive that curiosity out of them. We give them answers instead of teaching them to ask better questions."

Throughout our conversation, Randall returned to the theme of mystery. "If we remove mystery from our relationship with God, we're doomed to monotony," he warned. "Mystery is what keeps the relationship alive. Without it, faith becomes a list of doctrines rather than a living, breathing experience."

"God conceals things for us, not from us," he said, referencing Proverbs. "It's the glory of God to conceal a matter and the glory of kings to search it out" (Proverbs 25:2, BSB).

Deconstruction is not an end but a beginning. It's an invitation to step further into love, into the boundless mystery of God, and realize that faith, at its core, is not about having all the answers but about being willing to ask questions that lead to the discovery of union!

MATTHEW HESTER: REBUILDING

Matthew Hester is my friend and has been both a guest and co-host. He always adds depth and wonder to our conversations. There are so many Tacos guests I could have highlighted for this chapter—Brad Jersak, Pete Enns, Jeff Turner, and more—but I love Matthews's grace and insight into this faith journey. He has written a book titled The Rorschach God. It invites folks to explore and rethink their thoughts about God, it's a Christological de- and reconstruction. I can't recommend it enough.

This conversation occurred on Randall Worley's rented condo balcony overlooking a South Carolina beach. If you listen closely, you can hear the waves.

"Deconstruction," Matthew began, "is a word charged with emotion. For many, it symbolizes the tearing down of harmful beliefs, especially those that portray God as punitive or distant." He paused, reflecting. "But what often gets overlooked is the process that must follow: reconstruction. It's not enough to dismantle old structures; we have to rebuild, and we must do so on the cornerstone of Jesus's love."

Hester's words were a call to hope—that even in the tearing down, something beautiful can rise.

"Look at the Emmaus Road," I suggested, which I often reference. It's one of my favorite stories about how Jesus helps us both de- and reconstruct. I continued, "Jesus doesn't reveal Himself until He's walked with them and listened to their pain and confusion. He walks with them hidden, as a Stranger, to reintroduce Himself. He is unfamiliar to them, even though they had followed Him for three years.

The Emmaus Road Jesus, as a Stranger, deconstructs their misconceptions not through argument but through presence as the Word in the flesh spoke to their burning hearts. It's only after they see Him in the breaking of the bread that they realize the truth: He was with them all along. And He was better than they could have ever imagined."

Matthew nodded. "That's the essence of relational theology. It's about recognizing that God isn't waiting for us to get it right before He engages with us. He's in the mess, on the journey with us, guiding us out of our delusions and into the light of His love."

The conversation moved to the deeply personal. We shared stories—his, mine, and those of others we've encountered—of people hurt by the church, disillusioned by doctrines that seemed more about control than compassion. "But what keeps me hopeful," I said, "is the belief that love wins in the end. When we see God as He truly is, through the lens of Jesus, we find that He's not the God of our fears, but the God of our deepest hopes."

Matthew agreed. "That's why we must approach Scripture, and indeed all of theology, with a hermeneutic of love. If what we believe about God doesn't look like Jesus, we miss the point."

And isn't that the ultimate journey of de AND reconstruction? I thought.

In that moment, as the waves crashed below us, I was thankful for Matthew and all those who have released wisdom and grace to the church who is rethinking. They have given us a restorative perspective that reveals deconstruction isn't the end—it's the beginning of a journey towards a fuller, richer faith.[56]

---

56 Jason Clark and Derek Turner, hosts, *Rethinking God with Tacos,* podcast, adapted excerpts from "An Emmaus Road Deconstruction with Matthew Hester," November 22, 2022, https://www.youtube.com/watch?v=x1iIvygnY_w.

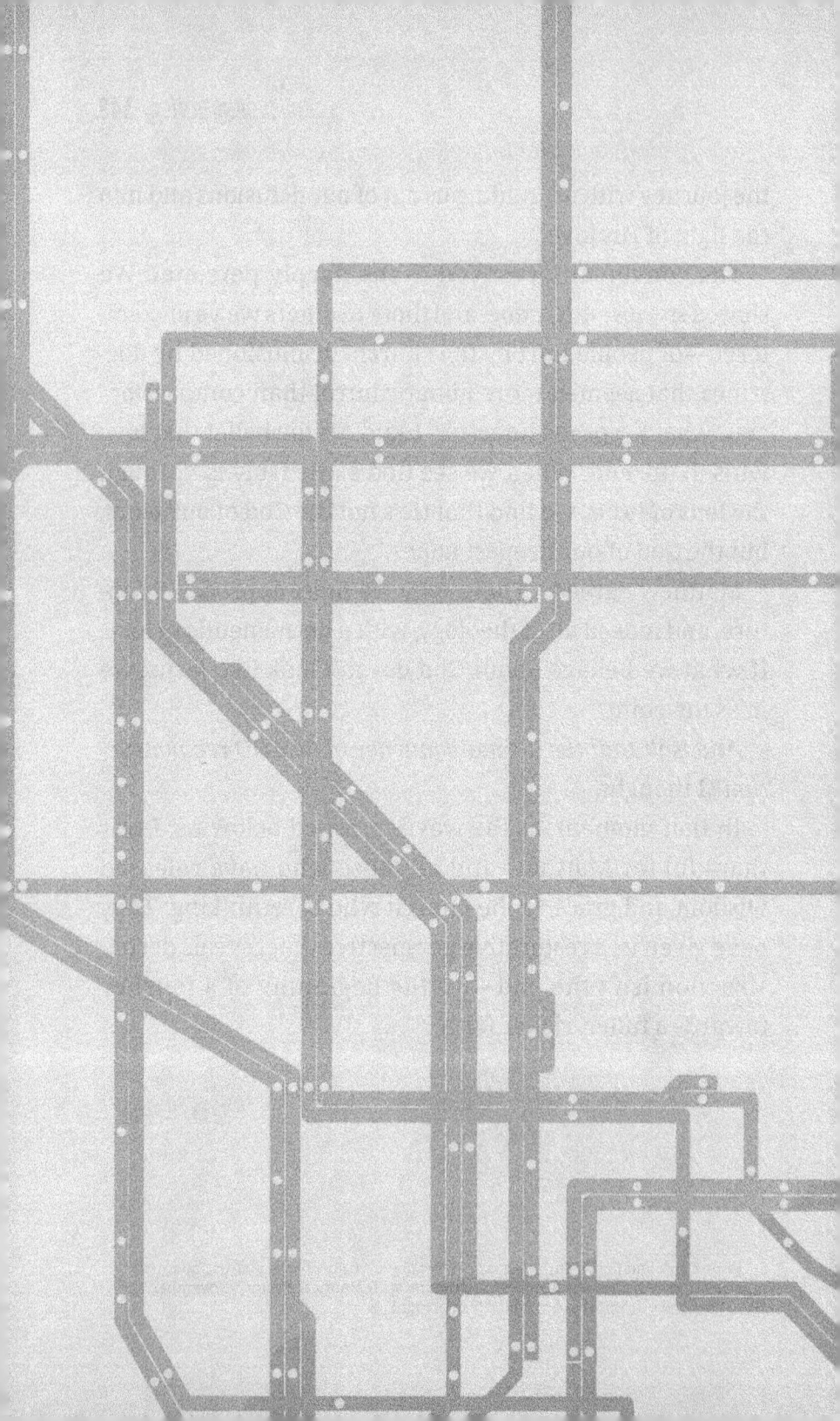

CHAPTER 7

TRINITARIAN FAITH

Guac, Queso, Salsa

C. BAXTER KRUGER: AWAKENING TO THE RELATIONAL HEART OF THE TRINITY

If you want to see Baxter light up, ask him about the Trinity. The moment the word is spoken, he steps into a reality he's been living for decades—where everything, from the smallest acts of kindness to the vast mystery of the cosmos, flows from the eternal love of the Father, Son, and Spirit.

The early Church Fathers used the word "perichoresis" to describe the mystery of the Trinity's relationship—a word formed from peri, meaning "around," and chōreō, meaning "to make room" or "to move." While not directly related to choreography in origin, the word beautifully evokes the image of an eternal, divine dance—Father, Son, and Spirit moving in perfect unity, love, and mutual indwelling.

Baxter refers to it as the circle dance, an eternal exchange of love between Father, Son, and Spirit. "Perichoresis—the divine dance of the Trinity—is at the heart of the gospel," he said. It's not mere doctrine. It is the relational fabric of reality.

"The Trinity is not a hierarchy, not a chain of command—it's a fellowship, a communion, an eternal relationship of love." And here's the kicker: *we are eternally awakening to this communion!*

> **JESUS DIDN'T COME TO CREATE UNION; HE CAME TO AWAKEN US TO THE UNION THAT ALREADY EXISTS."**

"The Trinity is mutual indwelling without the loss of personal distinction. It is the face-to-face-to-face perfect love Jesus displayed." Baxter continued, "And Jesus scoops us up in the incarnation and carries us into that measure of fellowship."

This is relational participation. We don't lose ourselves in God—we find ourselves fully alive in Him.

The heartbeat of this Trinitarian faith is the insistence that Jesus didn't come to *create* union; he came to *reveal* the union that has always been. "Before creation, before time itself, there was face-to-face oneness," Baxter said. "The Father, Son, and Spirit weren't lonely or lacking. They were overflowing with love, and creation is the fruit of that love."

Baxter drew on this to remind us that in Christ, we see not only God revealed but humanity restored in union with the Trinity.

The revelation of the Trinity confronts our inherited separation mindset. The idea that God is "up there" and we are "down here" has lodged itself so deeply into Western Christianity that it's hard to see past it. But Baxter is relentless in exposing that delusion. "The Trinity is not a distant committee in the sky," he declared. "They are family, and they've always called us home."

They have always been our home!

This Trinitarian faith is deeply rooted in the wisdom of the early church fathers. Baxter quoted Athanasius to emphasize God's relational nature: "The God of all is good and supremely noble by nature; therefore, He is the lover of the human race." The Trinity is fundamentally about love. Love that doesn't hold humanity at arm's length but draws us into divine life itself. Baxter continued. As Athanasius so beautifully put it, "God became man so that man might become God." In other words, He stepped fully into our humanity, not to condemn it, but to heal and restore it, and draw us into His divine life. He became what we are so that we could become what He is—by grace.

This is theosis—co-crucified, co-risen, transformed by grace, sharing in the divine life, participating in the very nature of the Trinity.

> **IN CHRIST, WE SEE NOT ONLY GOD REVEALED BUT HUMANITY RESTORED—RESTORED IN UNION WITH THE TRINITY.**

Then, as if my heart wasn't already overflowing, Baxter invited Scottish theologian T.F. Torrance into the conversation. "The Trinity is the ground and grammar of theology,"[57] Baxter noted weaving Torrance's insights into the relational fabric of the discussion before quoting T.F.: "The Triune God is a communion of love—Father, Son and Holy Spirit—who has opened Himself to us and drawn us within that communion." The Torrance brothers, T.F. and J.B., bridged the gap between ancient understandings of God's relational being and the modern distortions that make God seem distant. "To think of God apart from the Trinity," Baxter said, "is to lose sight of His very essence." And that essence is relational through and through.

By the end of our conversation, my head was spinning, but my heart was Emmaus-Road burning. "We're awakening to the reality that the Trinity's life has always been in us, and we get to live in response to that," Baxter concluded.[58]

This is the invitation—the lived reality of union! It's not about striving or earning, but about recognizing that every

---
57 T.F. Torrance, The Ground and Grammar of Theology (UNKNO, 2001).
58 Jason Clark and Thomas Floyd, *Rethinking God with Tacos,* adapted excerpts from "C. Baxter Kruger / Christ In You!"

moment, every relationship, and every breath is infused with divine love. In the Trinity, separation is revealed as the lie it's always been. We are, and always have been, held in the relational heart of Father, Son, and Holy Spirit.

DALE HOWIE: A JOURNEY INTO TRINITARIAN LOVE

Dale Howie is a mutual friend of Baxter and me, and we agree—Dale is all right! If you've spent any time in our online Tacos Zoom Communities, you know him. He hosts online gatherings where everyone is welcome. Spend a half-minute with Dale, and you'll feel seen, valued, and loved. Spend another half-minute with him, and you'll realize his theology is expressed through stories that invite us to ask deeper questions.

Dale's story is full of faith-shaking questions and faith-inducing answers. The loss of his stillborn son, Nathan, became a pivotal moment. Holding Nathan, he confessed, "I knew I didn't have any idea who God was." Before that moment, Dale had been certain regarding the nature of God, fundamentally so, if you know what I mean. But that raw vulnerability propelled him into a season of deep questioning. These questions reshaped his faith and revealed a God of love and relationship. That heartbreaking moment became a springboard for a deeper exploration of divine love, leading him to know Heavenly Father's embrace even in life's most painful experiences.

One of Dale's lifelines during that season was the writing of 19th-century Scottish writer, poet, and theologian George MacDonald. "MacDonald's sermons weren't about individual quotes," Dale shared. "It was the big picture, the vision he cast of a loving Father." MacDonald's poetic portrayal of God as an endlessly loving Father clarified Dale's theological journey and helped him see that the Trinity's essence is not independence but self-giving love. Inspired by MacDonald and mentored by Baxter, Dale began to encounter the Trinity not as a theological abstraction but as the essence of all reality—a living communion that invites humanity to participate.

> **THEY CREATED BECAUSE THEIR LOVE WAS TOO GOOD TO KEEP TO THEMSELVES.**

Dale stopped defining faith through systematic certainty. Instead, faith became the Trinitarian fruit of his communion with Father, Son, and Holy Spirit.

"Faith isn't a muscle you flex or a fuel tank you fill," he explained. "It's a position—a resting in the faith of the Son of God, who loves us and gave Himself for us." We are invited to discover a relational awakening to a shared divine life.

Thus, faith is the response of awakening to our shared love relationship in the Trinity.

"The Father, Son, and Spirit didn't create out of need," Dale said. "They created because their love was too good to keep to themselves." This radical vision of union with the divine turned Dale's focus from performance to participation—to being swept into the eternal love shared within the Trinity.

"The Trinity is not a diagram or a doctrine." Dale said, "It's an eternal invitation to participate in divine love." And this is a perfect way to invite Crowder back into the conversation.[59]

JOHN CROWDER: THE DANCE OF DIVINE LOVE

John speaks of the Trinity with a contagious passion. "The Trinity isn't about rules or doctrines," he said. "It's about love—pure, unbroken, eternal love."

John spoke of the Trinity as the ultimate picture of relationship—a divine dance of mutual love and self-giving. "When we see that God has never been alone, that there's always been plurality in the Godhead, we understand that He's always desired family." This idea transforms faith from a solitary pursuit to a communal celebration. In this eternal dance, we find not only our place but our identity, as God's invitation has always been to draw humanity into His relational life.

John's critique of Western Christianity's separation thinking challenges deeply held assumptions. "The biggest problem here is this idea that we're separate from Jesus," he said. "The Trinity demolishes that illusion."

---

[59] Jason Clark and Derek Turner, hosts, *Rethinking God with Tacos*, podcast, adapted excerpts from "Dale Howie / Unspoken Sermons on The Good News of Inclusion," June 22, 2021, https://www.youtube.com/watch?v=GxMi3at-NGw.

JESUS IS PERFECT THEOLOGY. AND IF JESUS IS PERFECT THEOLOGY, THEN UNION IS PERFECT THEOLOGY.

John addressed a common theological distortion: "We (the Western church) don't believe in the divinity of Jesus in practice; we make Him less than the Father, as if He's negotiating on our behalf. But in the Trinity, there's no hierarchy—only love and equality."

John's words reflect the Nicene Creed. I thought ".... God from God, Light from Light, true God from true God, begotten, *not made;* of the same essence as the Father...."

"This is clearly revealed in Jesus's words, 'Anyone who has seen me has seen the Father'" (John 14:9, NIV), I said, my hurt bursting. Jesus was a walking, talking revelation of the love and equality shared between Father, Son, and Holy Spirit. I continued. "Jesus is perfect theology. And if Jesus is perfect theology, then union is perfect theology." John nodded and brought it home. "We are already part of the divine dance—that is the heartbeat of the gospel."

"I think that's why we call it Good News," I said.

John agreed.

THE ETERNAL DANCE

The Trinity is the essence of existence. This relational God—Father, Son, and Spirit—invite us to live in the circle dance of love. The lie of separation crumbles in the light of this truth: we are already in union with the Trinity, woven into the fabric of divine love. This truth doesn't just transform how we see God; it reshapes how we see ourselves and the world. The invitation is clear: join in the eternal dance. Let love be your rhythm.

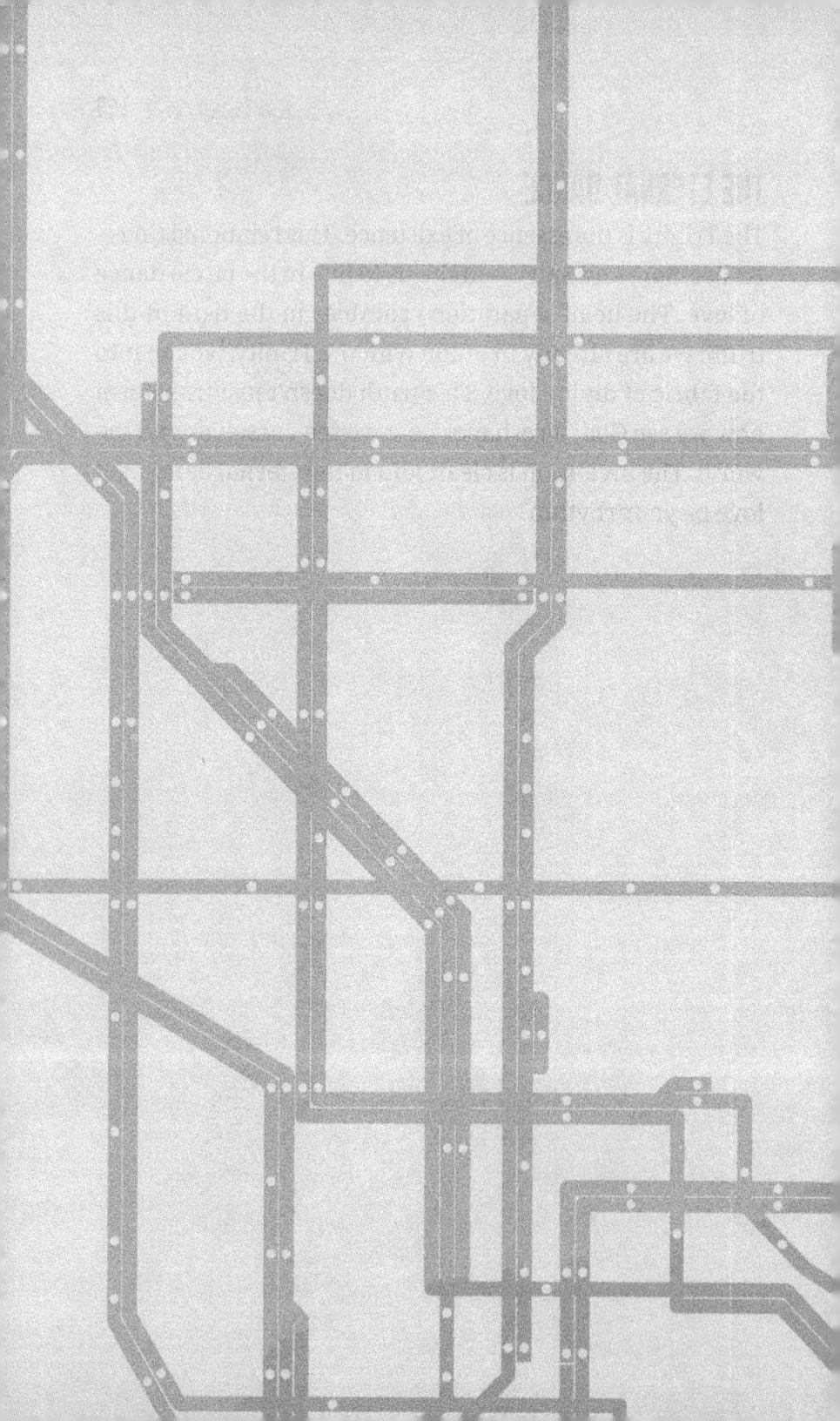

CHAPTER 8

THE INCARNATION

When the Word Ate Tacos

JOHN CROWDER: THE INCARNATION, A COSMIC EMBRACE OF HUMANITY

I kick this chapter off with John because he has a way of cutting to the quick. For instance.

"In his very being, Jesus has united humanity to divinity." Told ya.

The incarnation is where the Trinity's measureless love meets humanity in the flesh, binding creation to Himself in the person of Jesus Christ. "Jesus is our union with God," John continued, capturing the heartbeat of the incarnation: God with us, God as us, and God for us." John continued, "The infinite... comes down to humanity so that humanity may ascend to infinity."

This transforms how we relate to God and understand ourselves... if we lean in.

And I was leaning in.

"He (Jesus) is the union of creation to its creator," John said. This shifts the focus from human effort to divine initiative, reminding us that union is not achieved—it's discovered and explored.

John was mindful of how this truth could be misinterpreted. He critiqued movements that veer toward a vague "Christ consciousness." "They're on to a truth," he said, "but so often it gets off of the actual concrete person of Christ." I nodded.

The incarnation is Jesus.

Period.

"(Jesus) is the meeting place of God." John concluded.

Thus, the incarnation is a declaration of humanity's intrinsic worth. It's an affirmation of God's deep investment in creation, drawing all creation into Himself through Christ.[60]

And this is a good place to introduce my friend, Cherith.

CHERITH FEE NORDLING: THE RADICAL UNION OF DIVINITY AND HUMANITY

I love talking with Cherith. She is a brilliant relational theologian with letters in front of her name. She is kind, and I feel Holy Spirit's great affection through her words. As the daughter of Gordon Fee, her legacy is steeped in love for God and humanity, and her work invites us to live from our union with God, embrace our humanity, and discover the better gospel.

---

60 Jason Clark, host, *Rethinking God with Tacos,* podcast adapted excerpts from, "John Crowder / Trinitarian Theology." May 25, 2022, https://www.youtube.com/watch?v=DiNPFgZMxC0&t=3181s.

Cherith's passion for the incarnation invites us to rediscover what it means to be human. Her podcast reflections revealed the incarnation as an intimate, life-altering reality. Every word further anchored us in the everyday experience of being beloved.

JESUS DIDN'T STRIVE FOR THE FATHER'S APPROVAL; HE LIVED FROM IT.

"The incarnation isn't just about God temporarily wearing human skin to perform miracles and die for our sins. It's about the permanent union of divinity and humanity, a mystery that redefines what it means to be truly alive." Cherith's words were grounding and breathtaking. Jesus didn't come as a divine fixer-upper, swooping in to repair us and leave. No, His becoming human unveiled a truth far more profound: our humanity was never the problem. Instead, it was the place God chose to dwell.

"The incarnation reveals the worth of our humanity," Cherith noted, reflecting on how, for much of her life, she had seen the incarnation as a temporary solution: God putting on human flesh for a while, completing the mission, and returning to His divine form. "But that's not the story," she said. "Jesus didn't just become human to fix us; He became human to show us what it means to be fully alive, to unite us to God in a way that can never be undone." She continued with quiet conviction, "Jesus lived from a place of already being loved, and that's where we are invited to live, too."

This "permanently human gospel," as Cherith defined it, radically reshapes our understanding of God. It reveals a Creator who doesn't view our humanity as an obstacle to overcome but as a gift to embrace. In Jesus, God entered the fragility and beauty of human life, showing us that our bodies, emotions, and experiences—all of it—are the sacred space where divine love manifests.

"We're not called to escape our humanity," Cherith said, "but to live into it, in union with God." Jesus's life didn't avoid the messiness of pain, suffering, or limitation. Instead, He entered fully into those spaces, redeeming them from within. "Suffering isn't a sign of God's absence," Cherith explained. "It's the space where God's love often becomes most tangible."

Those words burn with the goodness of God and offer a profound invitation. If God, in Christ, has entered our suffering, then our pain isn't a sign of divine displeasure—it's a place where divine love can be encountered. The incarnation reveals that Jesus didn't bypass the hardship of being human but transformed it through His resurrection and ascension. His love doesn't skip over the broken places; it heals them, breathes life into them, and awakens us to union.

The incarnation invites us to embrace our humanity as the sacred ground where God meets us. Cherith's words remind us that our fragility and imperfections are not evidence of failure but of belovedness. The incarnation proclaims that we are already seen, known, and loved.

And in this truth, there is freedom to stop striving and rest in our worth as God's beloved. It's a freedom that whispers: You are enough. Right here, in your beautifully human life, God is with you.[61]

Which perfectly sets up my conversation with Felicia.

FELICIA MURRELL: LOVE, EMPATHY, AND THE INCARNATION

Felicia Murrell is a guide, a friend, and a fellow traveler on the journey toward deeper faith and inclusion. She encourages me to see the world through an empathetic lens and to trust in a love that is always bigger than fear.

When I started writing this book, I knew exactly which chapter would feature Felicia. Her thoughts on the incarnation are life-changing! She speaks about it as a love story woven into the fabric of creation. She writes the same way. Her reflections linger like poetry, each thought resonating with the truth that God's love is both invitation and revolution.

"What was the treasure of the incarnation through the eyes of Jesus?" she asked Holy Spirit one day in her prayer time. "And Spirit said back to me, 'Empathy.'"

This single word captures the incarnation's essence. It's God stepping into humanity not as an outsider but as one of us. Consider a God who embodies love in its most empathetic form. "The incarnation is God saying, 'You are worthy of being known, loved, and redeemed just as you are,'" She

---

61 Jason Clark and Derek Turner, hosts, *Rethinking God with Tacos,* podcast, adapted excerpts from "Cherith Fee Nordling / A Permanently Human Gospel," April 9, 2023, https://www.youtube.com/watch?v=bt3W9bmaTAU.

continued, "The incarnation is God stepping into the circle of humanity, saying, 'I see you, I feel you, I am with you.'"

I was reminded of what my friend and podcast guest, David Tensen, said. "That is Jesus—the most empathetic act—stepping into flesh and becoming humanity with us."

This incarnational empathy reshapes how we see ourselves and each other; it invites us to be fully loved and to become love.

This empathetic view of the incarnation also rejects the separation-based hierarchical dualism of "us versus them," I thought. And Felicia seemed to hear my thought. "What the incarnation teaches us is that there's no 'them.' We are all invited into the same love."

This empathetic love dismantles barriers, both internal and external. She continued. "Empathy helps us let go of our need to control or fix." This is a liberating way to approach relationships, especially with those who seem different from us. "Every person you encounter is someone God loves deeply," she said. "The incarnation isn't just about Jesus saving us; it's about showing us how to live in love."

This love, she emphasized, is never coercive. "God doesn't force us to change. Instead, love invites us to be transformed.... Empathy," she continued, "isn't just a reflection of God's love; it's an invitation to embody it.... The love of God transforms us—not by force but by entering our story and inviting us into His."[62]

And it is an invitation to co-creation.

---

[62] Jason Clark, host, *Rethinking God with Tacos*, podcast, adapted excerpts from "Felicia Murrell / Empathy; The Treasure of the Incarnation," January 17, 2023, https://www.youtube.com/watch?v=zCOqH3Enupo.

Which is the perfect setup for my friend, Andre Rabe.

ANDRE RABE: ALL CREATION IS INCARNATION

Andre Rabe is a storyteller, theologian, and philosopher. He is kind and generous. His insights are profound and personal, weaving together a faith story that invites participation and imagination. I'm thankful for his vision of union and co-creation with God.

Andre brings a cosmic perspective to the incarnation, one that, like Crowder, refuses to confine it to a single moment in history. "All creation is incarnation," he declared, inviting us to see the divine woven into the very fabric of existence. The incarnation isn't just about Jesus's birth; it's about the ongoing union of heaven and earth, a story that continues to unfold.

"The universe has a direction," he said. "It is moving toward greater meaning and beauty. It's an unfinished story, and we are invited to co-author it with God." I love how this perspective transforms the incarnation from a static event into a dynamic reality we're called to participate in.

Andre is a relational theologian!

> **THE ESSENCE OF YOUR LIFE ADDS VALUE TO GOD.**

Thus, union is the center of everything for Andre. "God doesn't stand behind us with a rod," he said. "God stands in front of us, opening up possibilities." This God of consent invites us into relationship, offering freedom and partnership rather than coercion. The incarnation, then, is a collaborative dance, an ongoing act of love that includes all creation.

Andre's insights challenge the dualism that separates the sacred from the secular. Jesus's life shows us that the sacred is not confined to certain spaces or moments but is present in every aspect of creation. In the incarnation, there is no "us and them."

To bring it home, Andre also spoke of the incarnation as a declaration of our worth. "The essence of your life adds value to God," he said. Maybe read that sentence again. It is a stunningly staggering thought—that our existence enriches God. It empowers us to see ourselves and others as participants in a divine love story that is still being written.

Andre's reflections also invite us to consider the ongoing nature of the incarnation. How do we, as individuals and communities, participate in this unfolding story? Are we open to the possibilities God places before us, or do we resist the movement of love in our lives? These questions call us to a deeper awareness of our role in the world and our relationship with the divine.[63]

Maybe we are created to create incarnationally?

Enter Curt Thompson.

---

[63] Jason Clark, host, *Rethinking God with Tacos*, podcast, adapted excerpts from "Andre Rabe / All Creation Is Incarnation," March 20, 2024, https://www.youtube.com/results?search_query=andre+rabe+all+creation+is+incarnation.

CURT THOMPSON, MD: IMAGINATION IS INCARNATION

Curt Thompson is a psychiatrist, speaker, and author whose work bridges neuroscience, faith, and the deep human desire to be known. His insights on imagination, vulnerability, and the incarnation are profound, practical, and lead to a richer experience of God's love. Curt walks with wisdom and humility and invites us into a journey of beauty and healing. My conversation with him felt sacred.

> **WE DON'T PRACTICE LOOKING FOR BEAUTY BECAUSE WE'RE TOO BUSY SCANNING FOR DANGER.**

I was stirred as he dove immediately into the incarnation as an invitation to participate in God's creative work. Curt's words were like windows into a larger story, reframing how we see beauty, imagination, and the embodied reality of God's love.

From the start, he emphasized that the incarnation isn't just about Jesus stepping into flesh; it's an ongoing invitation for us to step into God's story. "God's primary mission has not changed," he said. "Genesis chapter 3 doesn't mean we suddenly forget about Genesis 1 and 2."

How often do we live like the fall of Adam is the headline? I thought. Curt went on to remind us that we're living in a

Genesis 1 and 2 reality where God's creative, redemptive purposes are very much alive. "We are practicing for the age that's coming," he explained, "where beauty and goodness will fully emerge."

"Come on," I said. Curt was speaking to our imagination in an incarnational way, and I was picking up what he was laying down!

"We don't practice looking for beauty because we're too busy scanning for danger," he said, hitting on something so true. Our imaginations are often hijacked by fear or shame, focused more on protecting ourselves than creating beauty. Curt's perspective turned that narrative upside down. "Moving from imagination to incarnation means bringing what we envision with God into real time and space," he said. This, he explained, isn't abstract theology—it's deeply personal and transformative.

"Jesus's capacity to see beauty just around the corner in the man with the withered hand or the woman caught in adultery has everything to do with his connection to the Father," Curt shared. My heart was exploding. Jesus, one with the Father and Holy Spirit, revealed an incarnational imagination. And it was relational, practical, restorative, and miraculous.

"It is in those vulnerable spaces that the beauty of healing begins to emerge." This, he noted, is what makes the incarnation not just a theological idea but an embodied reality we're invited to live.

"You will see beauty as you create beauty, as you become beauty," Curt said, and those words have lingered long after the conversation ended. *What a stunning incarnational reality!* The invitation is to imagine what beauty could look like in our lives and step into it, co-creating with God as His hands and feet in this often-broken world.

Curt wrapped up our conversation with: "God is so confident in you. Even when you fail, He's no further away than before." That's the incarnation—not just God with us, but God in us, drawing us into the sacred work of healing and restoration— on earth as it is in heaven.[64]

THE INCARNATIONAL NATURE OF LOVE

The incarnation is the thread of divine love and union woven through the very fabric of existence. This is a love that steps into the mess, beauty, and ordinariness of our humanity, binding heaven and earth in Christ. It's a love that whispers, "You are enough. You are beloved. You are mine." And in this union, we find liberty—not to escape our humanity but to live fully into it, redeemed and embraced.

The incarnation tells us that love is embodied. It's the tangible, self-giving, fiery presence of a Love who refuses to let go of His creation. And it's this Love, this measureless, scandalous, incarnate Love, that draws us together and transforms us.

So, here's to the God who has not only come near but has united Himself to us forever. May we live as incarnational people, stepping into the circle of divine love and inviting others to do the same.

---

64 Jason Clark, host, *Rethinking God with Tacos,* podcast, adapted excerpts from "Curt Thompson MD / Imagination To Incarnation," February 14, 2024, https://www.youtube.com/watch?v=qAWUNQabe6E.

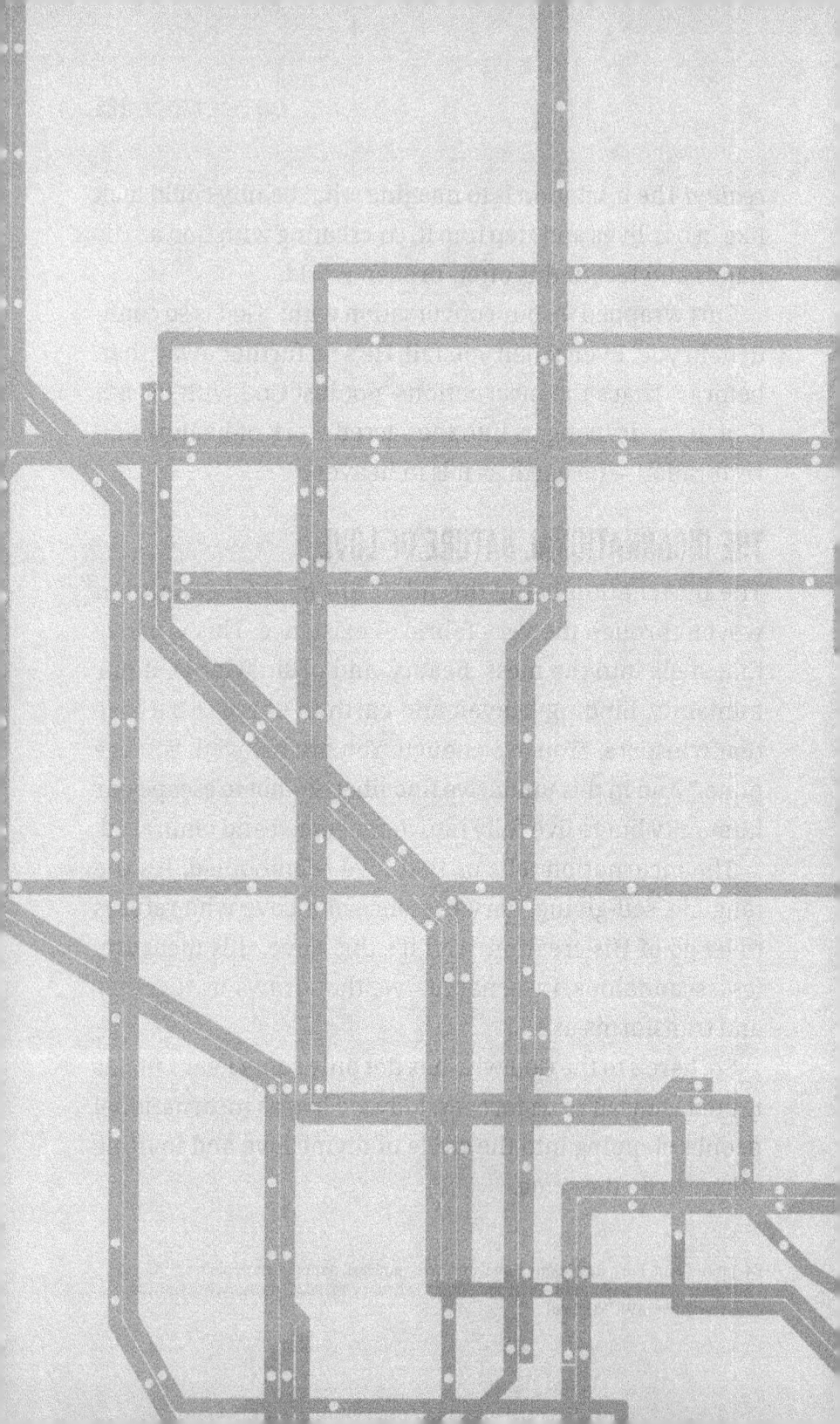

CHAPTER 9

IDENTITY

You Are What You Eat

A GOOD STORY

Jesus's story isn't just the greatest; it's the framework for understanding our own. His life answers the age-old question: Who are we? At its core, His story confronts the crisis that permeates our story—the crisis of identity.

This crisis has plagued humanity since Adam and Eve's fateful choice in the Garden of Eden. Their agreement with the serpent's lie of separation created a delusion regarding their identity that's echoed down the generations. That lie still whispers, "We're not enough." But in Christ, we are learning how to live confidently in our beloved identity.

Jesus perfectly faced the crisis of identity. He lived amid constant questions and accusations regarding

His identity, yet He remained sure. He was His Father's beloved Son—always.

Consider His birth: miraculous yet surrounded by scandal. To the outside world, His origin story appeared shameful, born of a virgin in circumstances that defied human understanding. From the start, His identity was questioned. Yet, even as a child, He was sure. The one story we have from His youth—found in Luke 2:49—reveals this confidence. At twelve, when His parents found Him in the temple after days of searching, He responded, "Didn't you know I had to be in my Father's house?" This wasn't precocious arrogance; it was the beloved identity declaration of someone who knew exactly who He was.

> **JESUS DIDN'T COME TO MAKE US ELIGIBLE FOR SONSHIP; HE CAME TO REVEAL THAT WE ALREADY BELONG.**

Throughout His life, Jesus faced relentless challenges to His identity. Religious leaders tried to discredit Him. Entire towns rejected Him. Government officials doubted Him. Even His disciples, those closest to Him, questioned Him. Yet, Jesus never wavered. He lived fully sure of His identity, modeling what it looks like to stand firm as a beloved child of His Father. When asked by the Jewish leaders,

"Are you the Son of God, then?" (Luke 22:70, ESV), Jesus, knowing the suffering ahead, answered simply and powerfully: "Yes, I am."

Imagine a life where external circumstances don't dictate your sense of self—this is the freedom Jesus modeled. His story invites us to step into that same assurance, knowing our identity is anchored in the unwavering love of our Father.[65]

LLOYD CLARK: LOVE TELLS A BETTER STORY

Lloyd is my dad. I am made in his image and likeness. And thankful for it. My dad is the kindest, wisest, bravest, and most generous man I know; he is the OG Tambourine Man. I hope to be like him someday. And of course, he's my best friend. When he joined the podcast, it was more than a conversation. It was a slow, sacred unfolding of how love dismantles the religion of separation and shame. We discussed beloved identity, my dad's journey into discovering union.

> **"RELIGION DOES EVERYTHING IT CAN TO GET TO THE FATHER. OUR FATHER DID EVERYTHING TO GET TO US."**

---

65 Jason Clark, *Prone to Love.*

"After almost sixty years of religion, I had no answers, just questions, shame, condemnation, and this deep sense of foreboding that I couldn't shake," Dad shared. "It took me sixty years to awaken to the truth of His love for me." My dad's voice was full of awe as he described the gospel as an invitation to rediscover who we really are. "Religion had told me all of my life who I wasn't. The gospel is about who I am! Beloved."

All religion, including the "Christian religion," starts with separation. "Religion does everything it can to get to the Father." My dad said, "Our Father did everything to get to us."[66] That sentence dismantles every ladder we've ever tried to climb in the name of worthiness. It calls us down from our striving. It invites us to surrender to our Father's eternal kindness.

"Years ago, I heard my Heavenly Father tell me, 'You have always been my dream come true, and it has nothing to do with your behavior or performance!'" My dad said, his eyes lighting up as if he was hearing it for the first time. Those words were an invitation to childlike faith, to discovering my dad was enough, just as he was.

"The gospel isn't complicated," Dad said. "If a kid can't get it, then it's not the gospel." It's not the first time I've heard him say that, but it makes my heart swell every time. It's relational theology 101. The gospel is simple: He loves us, His love is always good, nothing separates us from His love, and we are growing sure.

---

[66] Jason Clark and Derek Turner, hosts, *Rethinking God with Tacos*, podcast, adapted excerpts from "Lloyd Clark / I Am Enough," January 20, 2021, https://www.youtube.com/watch?v=u4sty2mJE5E&list=PLgimV9UoSbAIbXX447Gu_5-kGpLAO_eJO&index=154.

"I spent sixty years believing a distorted gospel, living under the foreboding cloud of separation and a distorted identity. God's good; I'm bad; try harder!" Dad said. "But Love tells a better story. Love rewrites our story." God is good, I am loved, and I am awakening to innocence. That is the childlike definition of 2 Corinthians 5:21.

I love the Mirror translation:

This is the divine exchange: He who knew no sin embraced our distortion; he appeared to be without form; this was the mystery of God's prophetic poetry. He was disguised in our distorted image and marred with our iniquities; he took our sorrows, our pain and our shame to his grave and birthed his righteousness in us. He took our sins and we became his innocence.

That's the heartbeat of beloved identity—the exchange of shame for innocence, separation for union, striving for rest. We are loved and we love.

JAMIE AND DONNA WINSHIP: DISCOVERING TRUE IDENTITY THROUGH LOVE

The moment I heard Jamie and Donna talk about identity, I was a fan. Our conversation is a favorite as we kept competing with thoughts about how good God is and how profoundly Jesus loves us. Jamie and Donna are wellsprings of wisdom and grace. They are practical theologians who are transformation-focused and provide a line-on-line strategy that helps us experience the love of our heavenly Father so we can live confidently in our identity in Christ.

Burdened with the lie of separation, many of us Western Christians have this tendency to live like orphans, like we're standing outside the Father's house, waiting for an invitation to come in. Or worse, waiting to earn our place at the table. But Jesus didn't come to make us *eligible* for sonship; He came to reveal that we *already belong*. That's why the language Jamie and Donna use isn't about "achieving" identity but about *receiving* it.

Donna puts it: "Your true identity overflows into every area of life almost effortlessly. When you live in the truth of who God made you to be, you no longer have to strive or convince anyone of your worth. You simply are, and that is enough."

> **THE INVITATION WAS NEVER TO FIX MYSELF—IT WAS TO TRUST THE ONE WHO ALREADY MADE ME WHOLE.**

That's it, right? We simply *are*. And discovering our *being* happens through a growing trust of the One who holds our *being*. And trust doesn't come from doctrine or effort—it comes from encounter. It comes from *knowing* Greater Love—from experiencing Jesus in the quiet, in the chaos, in the moments when we feel like we've lost ourselves completely, only to hear Him whisper, *You were never lost to Me.*

And this is where the false self begins to crumble. The false self is built on fear, on lack, on the lie of separation that tells us we have to *become* something to be loved. It keeps us trapped in cycles of striving and exhaustion. But Jamie describes the breaking of that illusion:

"If it's burdensome to you, you're not meant to carry it. The false self thrives on burdens, but Jesus said His yoke is easy and His burden is light. We must let go of what's false to embrace what's true."

Trust is always personal, relational, and about union, first with God, then with ourselves, and finally with one another.

Jamie and Donna kept returning to this truth—that identity is never discovered in isolation. Jamie said it plainly, "You cannot separate your identity from your relationship with God and with other people. It can only develop in relationship."

Jamie and Donna highlighted how relationship is what makes the Kingdom of God different from every other system of this world. It's not built on hierarchy or competition. It's a family. And in a family, no one has to prove their right to belong. No one has to earn a place at the table. We are already seated. We are already home.

Jamie is passionate about shifting from a scarcity mindset to one of abundance. The lie of scarcity is the foundation of the false self—it tells us there isn't enough to go around. Not enough love, not enough favor, not enough room. But Jamie challenged that thinking:

"People live in a scarcity model. They believe there's not enough time, not enough jobs, not enough love. And if they believe there's not enough, they eventually believe they are not enough."

"Come on," I said. My heart was on fire.

BELOVED IDENTITY ISN'T SOMETHING WE ACHIEVE; IT'S SOMETHING WE WAKE UP TO.

What if we trusted that our Father is good, that He is generous, that He isn't withholding anything from us? That there is no lack in Love, and we are enough? I thought.

Beloved identity isn't something we achieve; it's something we *wake up to*.[67]

And the moment we wake up, we realize—we were never outside the house, never separate from the family, never anything less than fully loved, fully known, fully belonging.

That, my friends, changes everything.

And is also a good way to introduce my friend, Justin Stumvoll.

---

[67] Jason Clark, host, *Rethinking God with Tacos,* podcast, adapted excerpts from "Jamie & Donna Winship / Our True Identity," February 16, 2022, https://www.youtube.com/watch?v=hv0TVQlhUS8&list=PLgimV9UoSbAIbXX447Gu_5-kGpLAO_eJO&index=123.

JUSTIN STUMVOLL: LOVE IS THE KEY

"You can't hate yourself into wholeness. You can only love yourself there—the way God does," Justin said. His words cut through the noise of religious striving and self-condemnation.

There's a moment in every life-changing conversation where something clicks—a truth so profound and simple it rearranges the way you see the world and yourself. That's how it felt talking to Justin about identity and God's love. It was the first time we met, but he felt like a brother who had discovered the same transformative love I knew and put similar language around the experience. Since that first podcast, Justin has become a dear friend and a voice of grace in my life—someone who doesn't just talk about the love of God but lives it in a way that reminds me who I truly am.

"Worthiness isn't something we earn." I responded to his statement, "It's who we are because of who our Father is."

> **TRUE FREEDOM ISN'T THE ABSENCE OF STRUGGLE; IT'S THE PRESENCE OF LOVE IN THE MIDST OF IT.**

Justin took the reins: "The voice of accusation convinces us that we're not loved, and we partner with it until it shapes how we see ourselves." That voice, Justin explained, is the root of so much of our mess. It whispers lies about our worth, wraps our failures around us like chains, and keeps us stuck in cycles of shame. Then he dropped the key to heart, mind, strength, and soul transformation: "The kindness of God doesn't just lead to repentance—it transforms us."

"Repentance," Justin continued, "isn't about groveling in guilt or trying to earn our way back to God. It's about turning toward love, letting kindness rewrite the lies we've believed. . . . God doesn't stand outside your mess waiting for you to clean up," he said. "He climbs into it, into the very places you think disqualify you, and He loves you there."

Justin continued, "When you realize God is kind and patient and doesn't need you to perform for Him, you stop performing for yourself." That's freedom. And it's evidenced through transformation.

"If you want to know who you are, you must know how loved you are. Everything about your identity flows from that." Justin said, and my "Come on" couldn't have been more sincere. Knowing God's love isn't just an emotional experience; it's the foundation of everything—our relationships, purpose, and ability to step into the messiness of life with courage.

"When you stop judging yourself and start seeing yourself the way God does, healing begins. It's not about pretending the mess isn't there; it's about letting love into it." That's where true transformation happens—not in denial but in letting love reparent and restore us.

"You're not defined by your failures or fears. You're defined by love—God's love,"[68] Justin concluded. That's the truth that anchors, empowers, and sets up our conversation with Kim.

KIM HONEYCUTT: KNOWN AND LOVED

If we don't know we're loved, how can we possibly know who we are?

That question lingered as Derek and I connected with Kim Honeycutt, a psychotherapist, TEDx speaker, and founder of ICU Talks. Kim is a friend who helps folks discover grace and freedom. She's walked the road of shame, rejection, and addiction and come out the other side—not because she finally got it together, but because she discovered she was loved and accepted.

We talk a lot about identity in church circles, but too often, it's framed as something we must secure through effort—becoming more Christlike by trying harder. As the previous conversations have already noted, identity isn't something we achieve; it's something we awaken to as we discover God's kindness. We've always been known, always been loved, always been included in the divine embrace— our journey is simply learning to live from that reality.

---

68 Jason Clark, host, *Rethinking God with Tacos,* podcast, adapted excerpts from "Justin Stumvoll / Love Is the Key," June 5, 2022, https://www.youtube.com/watch?v=DAcmyImw-KE&list=PLgimV9UoSbAIbXX447Gu_5-kGpLAO_eJO&index=115.

For Kim, that journey began in a house where love and fear had become indistinguishable.

"When your initial bond is pain, you believe pain is the bond," she told us. Her mother, struggling with mental illness, couldn't nurture or connect with her. "So, fear and love got coupled, nurturing and chaos got coupled." By the time she was eleven, she had already found her way to alcohol—her first form of escape.

"My parents had a party, and I learned that adults did dumb things like set their drink down and turn around. So, I stole their liquor, got really drunk, had my first blackout, and came to in the bathtub with a line of vomit from my bed to the bathroom." She came to as her mother was screaming at her, but something had shifted. "This time, I didn't care. She always screamed at me. She always told me something was wrong with me. But now I had found a numbing agent that helped me not to care that she didn't like me."

> **SHAME IS A GIFT—IT'S LIKE AN STD. SOMEONE ELSE HAS TO GIVE IT TO YOU.**

That numbing agent became her survival mechanism. "I became a daily drinker at that point, and I stayed that way—through being arrested, through treatment centers—until the age of twenty-four, when I came to at Mercy Detox. Something just shifted that day. I called out to God to help me, and He answered. I have not had a drink since, and that was twenty-five years ago."

"The thing about shame is that it never starts with us—it's inherited," Kim said. "It's not something we're born with, but something given by those who were meant to love us. Shame is the belief that I'm not good enough," Kim paused. Then added, "Shame is a gift—it's like an STD. Someone else has to give it to you."

That reminded me of what my brilliant friend and podcast guest, Cory Rice, once said, "Brokenness is what happened to you—it's not who you are."[69] How much of our self-perception has been shaped by voices that were never speaking the truth to begin with?

For Kim, that self-perception had to be unlearned, piece by piece. "One of the main things I did when I got sober was write on my mirror, You are wrong. Because so much of my (healing) journey was learning that what I was taught about who I am was wrong."

We do a thousand things in life and call it personality. We call it preference, habits, identity. But Kim pushed back.

"Personality is not who you are. It's who you aren't. It's what you present so people don't get any closer to you—so they won't hurt you."

---

[69] Jason Clark and Derek Turner, hosts, *Rethinking God with Tacos,* podcast, adapted excerpts from "Cory Rice / Saints Not Sinners," January 24, 2024, https://www.youtube.com/watch?v=hEwBS60kE5E.

The lies we inherit about ourselves keep us from living in the fullness of love. And for many of us, religion hasn't helped.

YOU DON'T GET A SAY IN HOW HE FEELS ABOUT YOU.

"When I was drinking and drugging, people kept telling me about this God who loved me so much He sent His Son for me. And they kept telling me I was worthy of that. And when you're drinking every day and can't even get yourself to eat food, you don't believe you're worthy of anything."

Then, she got sober. She finally accepted that maybe she was worth the blood of Jesus. But that's when the message changed.

"I went to church, and once I said I believed I was worthy of the Son who died for me, *that's* when they told me to stop thinking about myself, stop making it about me, and go be of service to God."

Isn't that how it goes? We preach grace until someone believes it, and then saddle them with religious duty. And that's not identity. That's striving, earning, the same road of separation so many of us have travelled.

Kim had to unlearn the lie that God's love must be maintained through effort. She had to wake up to the truth that she was already included, already known, already home, already one. "You don't get a say in how He feels about you," I said, and continued, "And how He feels about you is revealed through what Jesus did on the cross. And He hasn't changed His mind, and He never will. Jesus is what God has to say about you. You are worthy, loved, accepted, enough. You are the apple of His eye!"

Derek followed up, "When we know we are loved, we stop striving for belonging and start living from it. But knowing that love takes time. Transformation takes time."

Kim responded, "Jesus was crucified on Friday, buried everything for us on Saturday, and rose again on Sunday. That's transformation," Kim said. "If it took Jesus three days, what's it gonna take for us?"

Shame wants us to believe we're on the outside looking in, unworthy of the love that has always been ours. "Shame says you're not enough, but God says you are everything to Him."[70] Kim said as our conversation ended.

And that is grace—a grace that transforms how we believe and empowers us to live in our true identity. It's also the perfect way to introduce Katie.

---

70 Jason Clark and Derek Turner, hosts, *Rethinking God with Tacos,* podcast, adapted excerpts from "Kim Honeycutt / Shame and What to Do with It," February 7, 2021, https://www.youtube.com/watch?v=rhVayuwXXaQ&list=PLgimV9UoSbAIbXX447Gu_5-kGpLAO_eJO&index=151.

KATIE SKURJA: BREAKING FREE FROM SHAME AND EMBRACING TRUE IDENTITY

I sat digitally across from Katie Skurja, leaning in as she unraveled the power of grace like it was the very air we were meant to breathe. Katie described grace as the force that dismantles shame and reawakens us to the truth of who we've always been. "Grace is the empowering revelation of how God actually sees you," I said, barely containing my excitement to add to the conversation. Katie agreed, "It's not a distant hope or an abstract mercy—it's here, now, shaping us, pulling us back into union with the One who calls us His own."

Katie is a brilliant and compassionate guide into the heart of identity. Her insights on grace, union, and God's love are transformational.

Katie has spent years working with people buried under the weight of shame. She shared about a client who felt utterly consumed by it. "She (Katie's client) told me her shame was at *a ten thousand*," Katie recalls. "But shame is a liar, a force that glues itself to our souls and distorts our identity."

To break through it, Katie uses what she calls the "paradox prayer."

Instead of trying to fight shame head-on, she invites people to hold two truths in tension: "Even though I feel like a failure, I am loved and accepted by God." This prayer is not denial—it's defiance against the lie of shame.

> **WHEN WE AGREE WITH JUDGMENTS ABOUT OURSELVES THAT CONTRADICT GOD'S TRUTH, WE EMPOWER SHAME TO SHAPE OUR IDENTITY.**

Katie said, "In three rounds of the paradox prayer, her [client's] shame level dropped from ten thousand to ten. . . . It was like watching her step out of a storm into a place of peace."

"Shame is rooted in judgment," she explains. "When we agree with judgments about ourselves that contradict God's truth, we empower shame to shape our identity." And this is where grace intervenes as the greater force that restores what shame distorts. "Grace is the only force more powerful than shame," Katie said.

Shame isolates; grace restores. Shame condemns; grace redeems.

Grace is the gentle, unrelenting voice of God's love continually awakening us to the reality of our union.

Katie drove this point home with an urgency that made me sit up straight. "When we say, 'Even though I've failed, I am loved and accepted by God,' we're giving up our right to judge ourselves." She continued, "In the presence of God, there's only room for one Judge." Come on!

How much of our lives have been spent on trial before a jury that only existed in our minds?

Katie shifted the conversation toward how grace reframes our mistakes. "Even if I did a shitty thing, that's not who I am," Katie said. "Who I am is rooted in the unchanging truth of the Imago Dei—the image of God within me." That's the battle, isn't it? To stop defining ourselves by our worst moments. To believe that grace confronts our sin narrative by rewriting our entire story.

But grace doesn't stop at personal restoration. It transforms the way we see each other. I said as much: "When we see ourselves through the lens of grace, we can begin to see others the same way." Katie agreed and noted that grace isn't just an individual experience—it's relational. It's the glue that holds everything together. "We won't hurt others if we're rooted in the truth of God's grace toward us."

The conversation circled back to union—the heartbeat of grace. "When I believe God's view of me, everything changes," Katie said. "Grace doesn't just forgive; it transforms. Grace is not an event—it's an unfolding journey of remembering who we are and who we've always been. "Grace teaches us to live from our true identity, not in spite of it but because of it," Katie concluded. "And in that place, we find the freedom to be fully ourselves, fully loved, and fully alive."[71]

---

[71] Jason Clark and Thomas Floyd, hosts, *Rethinking God with Tacos*, podcast, adapted excerpts from "Katie Skurja / Discovering Our Humanity," August 26, 2020, https://www.youtube.com/watch?v=C9lMOj_96rw&list=PLgimV9UoSbAIbXX447Gu_5-kGpLAO_eJO&index=159.

True identity isn't striving to become something new but waking up to the reality that all things have been made new.

Let's keep waking up with my friend, Catherine Toon.

CATHERINE TOON: LOVEOLOGY, AWAKENING TO OUR TRUE IDENTITY

I want to give my friend Catherine the last word. She is a radiant voice of love, carrying the message of God's infinite affection with theological depth and personal warmth. Whenever I talk with her, it feels like family—like we grew up in the same house, speaking the same language of grace and union. And her thoughts about our identity are pretty dang good!

"Our sense of self starts and ends in the epicenter of love," Catherine said. I agreed. Everything about who we are flows from God's infinite affection. Catherine's language for this is beautiful, even disruptive—she calls it "Loveology." It's the study of God as love, a lens that changes everything. It's also an amazing song by Regina Spektor.

> **GOD IS SMARTER THAN OUR STUPID.**

Catherine's passion for this topic shines through every chapter of her book, *Marked by Love.* She says, "You are literally a poem to the world cut out of the same bolt of fabric as your Creator."[72] Pause and take that in. Our identity isn't just an afterthought or a mystery we're trying to unravel. It's intentional, woven into the very essence of who God is—LOVE. When we begin to see ourselves through that lens, we're stepping into the truth of our original design.

"The Word needs to become flesh in us," Catherine said. "This requires an experiential encounter with this God who utterly adores us." Catherine continued by encouraging us to encounter God personally—to sit in the truth of who we are as His beloved.

"Oh, an incurable humanist you are." Regina sings in her Loveology song,[73] and I hear it as Catherine talks. For many, the hurdle to experiencing love is the "yeah, but." Catherine knows this struggle: "The problem is we don't know how adored we are." We don't know how much of an incurable humanist God actually is!

Then Catherine said something I think should go on a t-shirt.

"God is smarter than our stupid."

I laughed and interrupted to add my 'Yes, And.'

"God is love. And He is really good at loving. And His love never ends, no matter how far we wander."

Catherine added, "Love marked me before I was marred by anything else."[74]

---

[72] Catherine Toon, *Marked by Love: Unveiling the Substance of Your True Identity* (Imprint Publishing, 2017).
[73] Regina Spektor, vocalist, "Loveology" by Regina Spektor, released June 7, 2022, track 9 on *Home, Before and After,* Sire Records.
[74] Jason Clark and Derek Turner, hosts, *Rethinking God with Tacos,* podcast, adapted excerpts from "Catherine Toon / Loveology," July 18, 2024, https://www.youtube.com/watch?v=1OFWYu5OrhI&list=PLgimV9UoSbAIbXX447Gu_5-kGpLAO_eJO&index=31.

So here's the takeaway: we are more loved, seen, and known than we can imagine. As Catherine put it, "God doesn't blush about His love for us."

At its heart, identity is not something we achieve but something we awaken to—rooted in the unwavering love of God. The religious voices of shame and striving may try to define us, but grace tells a greater story: We have always belonged. Our identity is secure in love. The invitation is clear: let go of the false self, embrace grace, and live fully as who we were always meant to be—beloved, known, and whole.

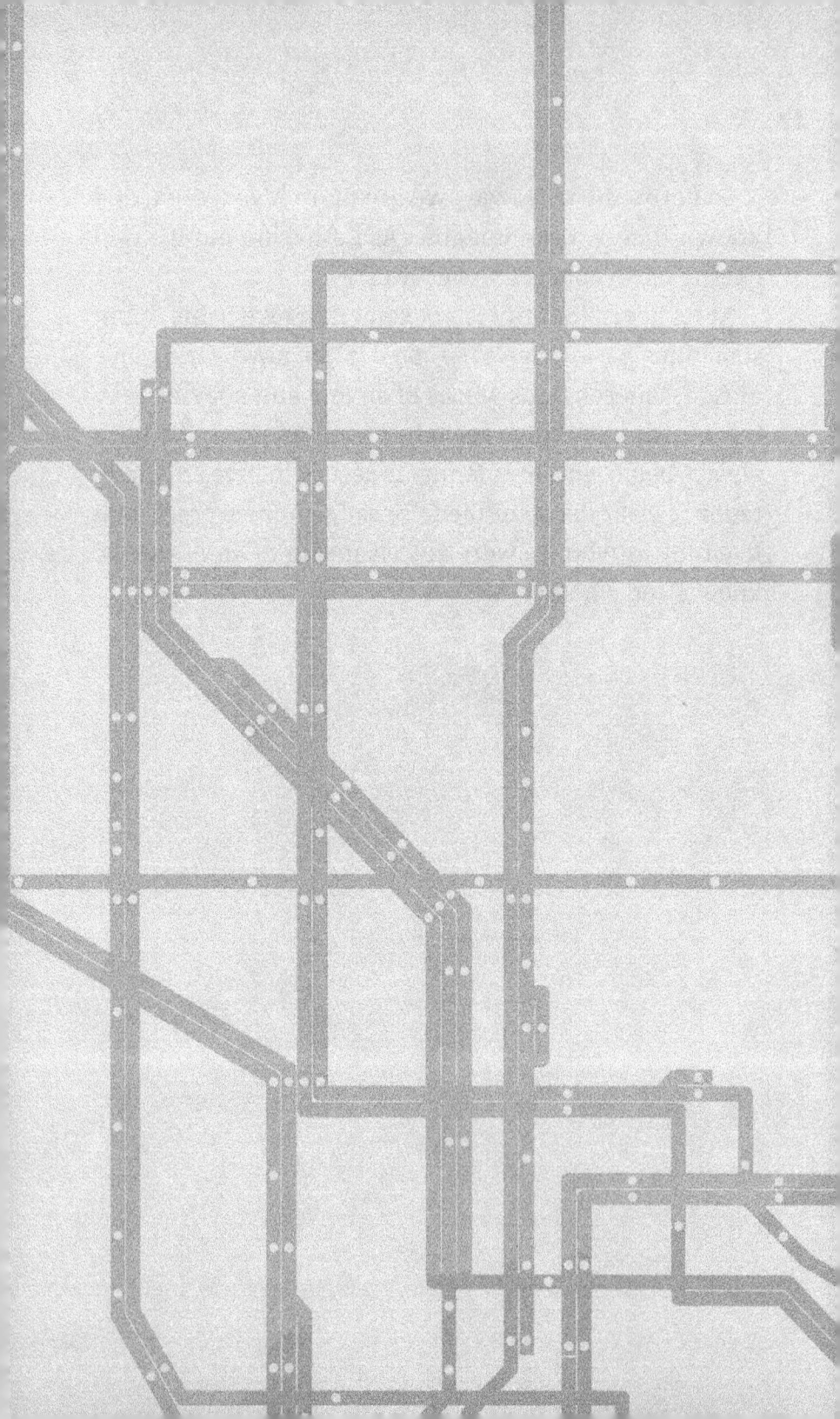

CHAPTER 10

A PATH TO WHOLENESS

The Whole Enchilada

DR. CAROLINE LEAF: WIRED FOR LOVE

Dr. Caroline Leaf, a cognitive neuroscientist and communication pathologist with nearly four decades of experience, specializes in the intricate connection between thought, emotion, and brain health. Her book, *Cleaning Up Your Mental Mess*, delves into practical strategies for renewing the mind and achieving emotional and spiritual wholeness.[75] When she joined our podcast to discuss her work, Derek and I found ourselves hanging on every word, often with our jaws on the floor.

What resonated was how effortlessly Dr. Leaf's scientific insights wove into our understanding of identity and wholeness in Christ. This neuroscience was reclaiming who we truly are — beings wired for love.

---
75 Dr. Caroline Leaf, Cleaning Up Your Mental Mess: 5 Simple, Scientifically Proven Steps to Reduce Anxiety, Stress, and Toxic Thinking (Ada, MI: Baker Books, 2021).

"Our minds are made for optimism," Dr. Leaf declared, her South African accent giving her words an extra spark. "We are made for love." As she unpacked the science, the truth settled in—the brain's very structure, down to the cellular level, is designed to support love and optimism; it's hardwired into us. "We don't have structures for fear, anxiety, or depression in the brain," she explained. "Those are learned behaviors that disrupt our natural wiring."

That landed. If we are 'wired for love,' then renewing our minds isn't about becoming something new—it's about returning to who we've always been. It's about peeling back the layers of fear and lies that have accumulated over time and stepping into the wholeness that was always ours to begin with.

Talk about rethinking!

Dr. Leaf introduced the Neurocycle, a five-step process for mind management. "The ability to renew our minds is one of the most important things we can ever participate in," she emphasized. And this wasn't abstract theory—it was practical, daily work, a partnership with our divine design. "When you renew your mind, you're not eliminating your story," she said. "You're seeing it differently. That's reconceptualization."

She painted a vivid metaphor: "Imagine an old, broken-down house. You don't erase it from memory. You renovate it. You keep the photos of the moldy walls, but now you live in a beautiful new space. The past doesn't disappear; it's transformed." *That sounds kinda like how I view theological de and reconstruction*, I thought, but I didn't say it. I was too busy trying to keep up.

> ## WHOLENESS, THEN, ISN'T SOMETHING TO BE ACHIEVED; IT'S SOMETHING TO BE UNCOVERED.

Renewing our minds, as Dr. Leaf explained, isn't just about thinking positively. It's about aligning with our true identity. "Your brain is wired for love, and your mind is designed to operate in that truth," she said. "When we live out of fear or negativity, we're operating outside of our design."

One of the most liberating takeaways was this: "Renewing your mind isn't about slapping a Bible verse on your problems. It's about real, intentional work to bring every thought into captivity and align it with love."

Wholeness, then, isn't something to be achieved; it's something to be uncovered. It's already there, intricately woven into our neural pathways and spiritual DNA. We are created in Love's image and likeness. Thus, the process of renewing our minds is the journey back to wholeness, embracing our identity as beings wired for love.

"Life is experimental," Dr. Leaf said. "We have been given the ability to think, feel, and choose."[76] And in that choice lies our freedom—the freedom to return to who we were always meant to be.

Enter Dr. Jerome Lubbe.

DR. JEROME LUBBE: THE PATH TO WHOLENESS AND IDENTITY

"You were made whole," Brooke said. "Anything that says otherwise is a lie."

Brooke Waters, who started *Path to Wholeness*, guides people into well-being through spiritual insight, community support, and personal development. She has navigated deep traumas, particularly church-related wounds, shaping her compassionate approach to healing.

Brooke has become a close friend and an integral part of everything at *A Family Story*. From running our *Rethinking God with Tacos* Family Reunions to helping lead our Facebook community and occasionally co-hosting the podcast, her presence is invaluable. I can't express how grateful I am for her.

"It's not about becoming whole," Brooke said before our conversation with Dr. Jerome Lubbe. "It's about reconnecting with the wholeness that already exists within us. The wholeness that was never lost, only obscured by wounds and lies we've believed." This isn't just spiritual healing—it's identity restoration. When we see ourselves

---

[76] Jason Clark and Derek Turner, hosts, *Rethinking God with Tacos*, podcast, adapted excerpts from "Cleaning Up Your Mental Mess," May 4, 2021, https://www.youtube.com/watch?v=fWYuvDiVRsc.

as God sees us, we start living from that truth. There's a simplicity and childlike trust in this process, grounded in the transformative power of encountering the Trinity in a safe, loving way.

This framework of wholeness naturally flowed into our conversation with Dr. Jerome Lubbe, a functional neurologist based in Atlanta, GA. Known for his innovative work with the brain-based Enneagram and his holistic approach to healing, Jerome integrates body, personality, and spirituality. His insights into neuroplasticity and identity are profoundly transformative, offering a fresh, compassionate lens on personal growth and wholeness. His authenticity, vulnerability, and wisdom made this one of my favorite podcast conversations.

Jerome is a guide bridging the gap between science and soul. "I'm like a personal trainer for the brain," he said. "If you want your brain to work better, and you want to do it without drugs and surgery, and you're still above ground, we can do work."

His passion for healing the whole person—body, personality, and spirituality—was palpable.

One of the most profound rethinks in recent memory happened when Dr. Lubbe reintroduced the Enneagram. "You are not just one number," he said.

Exactly! I thought.

It quickly became clear that we weren't discussing the Enneagram as a personality typing tool. No, for Jerome, the Enneagram is a map, a dynamic, living framework that helps us understand not just what we do but why we do it.

He put it succinctly: "The Enneagram isn't about boxing you into a type; it's about revealing the whole spectrum of who you are."

I have to admit, I wasn't an Enneagram enthusiast before this conversation. It felt restrictive and limiting. *I am more than just a number*, I thought every time I engaged with the Enneagram. But Jerome's holistic approach was an aha moment that turned me into a fan. Through our conversation, I understood the Enneagram as a mirror that reveals nine distinct ways we've learned to navigate love, fear, and belonging, each offering a map of our defenses and a doorway into transformation.

Jerome introduced the "flight crew" concept, a metaphor illustrating how our personality traits interact. "Whatever your top numbers are, those are your pilots," he explained. "Your mid-range traits are the flight attendants, and the lowest traits are passengers."

This imagery of an airplane, with every part playing a role, resonated. It's not about silencing parts of ourselves but recognizing that all aspects contribute to our journey.

What struck me was how he connected this to our experiences of safety and trauma. "High Enneagram scores often develop from needing to survive unsafe experiences or reinforcing positive, life-giving encounters," he shared. Conversely, "low scores indicate areas where we've had few life-giving experiences or trauma, leading us to avoid engaging in those behaviors." It's not just about who we are on paper; it's about the stories behind those numbers, the experiences shaping our identity.

Perhaps the most powerful moment came when Jerome discussed the inner critic. "The lowest Enneagram number often represents the voice of your inner critic," he explained. "It influences self-perception and internal dialogue."

> **IT'S NOT ABOUT BEING LESS BROKEN. ... IT'S ABOUT BECOMING MORE WHOLE IN COMPARISON TO WHO YOU CURRENTLY ARE IN THIS MOMENT AND WHO YOU'VE BEEN IN THE PAST.**

And there it is—that dang self-perception that shapes everything. How often do we let that inner critic define us?

As Dr. Leaf pointed out, we are wired for love, and our foundation is wholeness. Yet, a false self-perception cuts us off from living whole.

But what if, before the foundations of the earth, we are one in Christ? What if we are created in Love's image and likeness?

Jerome's approach to healing is rooted in union—the union of our thoughts, emotions, and actions; the union of past experiences and present realities; the union of our fragmented selves into a cohesive whole; the union of our beloved Christ. "It's not about being less broken," he said.

"It's about becoming more whole compared to who you currently are in this moment and who you've been in the past."[77] There is such grace in that statement!

This journey toward wholeness is a return to our original design. It's participating in our I Am-ness. Wholeness isn't about perfection; it's about an authentic journey, an awakening to love, beholding, and becoming. And it starts with thinking differently, which is why our conversation with Bob Hamp is next.

BOB HAMP: THINK DIFFERENTLY, LIVE DIFFERENTLY

Brooke introduced me to Bob and co-hosted the conversation, which was one of my favorites. Yeah, that's how it works on the podcast.

Bob is a practical theologian with a rare ability to blend deep spiritual insights with tangible, real-world applications. His passion for rethinking faith, identity, and freedom is contagious, and his wisdom is grounding and liberating. Talking with Bob feels like sitting with a trusted guide—someone who doesn't just offer answers but travels with you into transformation.

"You had me at rethinking," Bob laughed early in our conversation, referencing how his books and our podcast share a title. For Bob, rethinking isn't about swapping out one set of ideas for another; it's about a complete shift in how we process reality. He broke it down like this: "There's the thoughts that we have, there's the thought processes

---

[77] Jason Clark and Brooke Waters, hosts, *Rethinking God with Tacos*, podcast, adapted excerpts from "Dr. Jerome Lubbe / The Brain-Based Enneagram: You Are Not a Number," August 14, 2024, https://www.youtube.com/watch?v=ECUjiJgFTIM.

that dictate that, and then there's the paradigms that dictate our thought processes." That's not just thinking different thoughts—that's thinking differently. And that's where metanoia comes in.

> **"FREEDOM IS NOT THE ABSENCE OF SOMETHING.... IT'S THE PRESENCE OF SOMEONE."**

That's Greek for rethinking . . . to be exact: "a change of mind" or "a transformative change of heart." I'm surprised I got this far in the book without providing that definition. Thanks, Bob.

"The word think differently is the literal meaning of the word metanoia," Bob explained. "Metanoia is translated in the New Testament as repent." But repentance isn't about feeling guilty or trying to fix our behavior. It's about changing the entire way we see God and ourselves. It's about transformation from the inside out.

That shift—from behavior to identity—was one of the most potent threads in our conversation. "Freedom is not the absence of something," Bob said. "It's the presence of someone." That's a game-changer. So often, we think of freedom as breaking habits, overcoming sin, or getting rid of negative patterns. But Bob invited us to see freedom as stepping into the fullness of who we already are in Christ.

"We've been convinced that we're supposed to live for God," Bob said, "and that's not in the Scripture. Scripture teaches we're supposed to live from God." That distinction—*from* versus *for*—is everything. Living for God keeps us in performance mode, always seeking His approval. But living from God means we're operating from a place of belonging, already loved and accepted. It's a life of overflow, not striving.

Bob explained with practical, brain-based insights. "There are two different ways to produce music," he said. "One is you memorize and recite. The other is you integrate and improvise." Most discipleship focused on identity and wholeness, Bob argues, has taught us to memorize and recite—to mimic behaviors and beliefs without truly integrating them into who we are. But true transformation comes when we're free to improvise, to live from the unique expression of God's image within us.

Bob continued. "The right brain can know things that it can't describe. The left brain can describe things that it can't experience," he said. That's why so much of discipleship feels incomplete. We've focused on left-brain learning—memorizing scriptures, understanding doctrines—but we've neglected the right-brain experiences that connect us deeply with God.

"Jesus didn't just teach facts," Bob said. "He told stories. He created experiences. He invited people to *live* the

Kingdom, not just understand it."[78] And that's the invitation for us today. To move beyond intellectual assent and step into a lived experience of God's love and presence.

What if wholeness isn't about knowing more or trying harder? What if it's about grace, metanoia, and transformation, and stepping into the freedom of the divine life?

What if wholeness is about awakening to our union—with God, ourselves, and each other? What if it's about living from the truth that we are deeply loved, inherently valuable, and beautifully designed? Well, that's a path worth treading.

---

78 Jason Clark and Brooke Waters, hosts, *Rethinking God with Tacos,* podcast, adapted excerpts from "Bob Hamp / Think Differently Live Differently," June 19, 2024, https://www.youtube.com/watch?v=xWqjpHH0-Rg&list=PLgimV9UoSbAIbXX447Gu_5-kGpLAO_eJO&index=35.

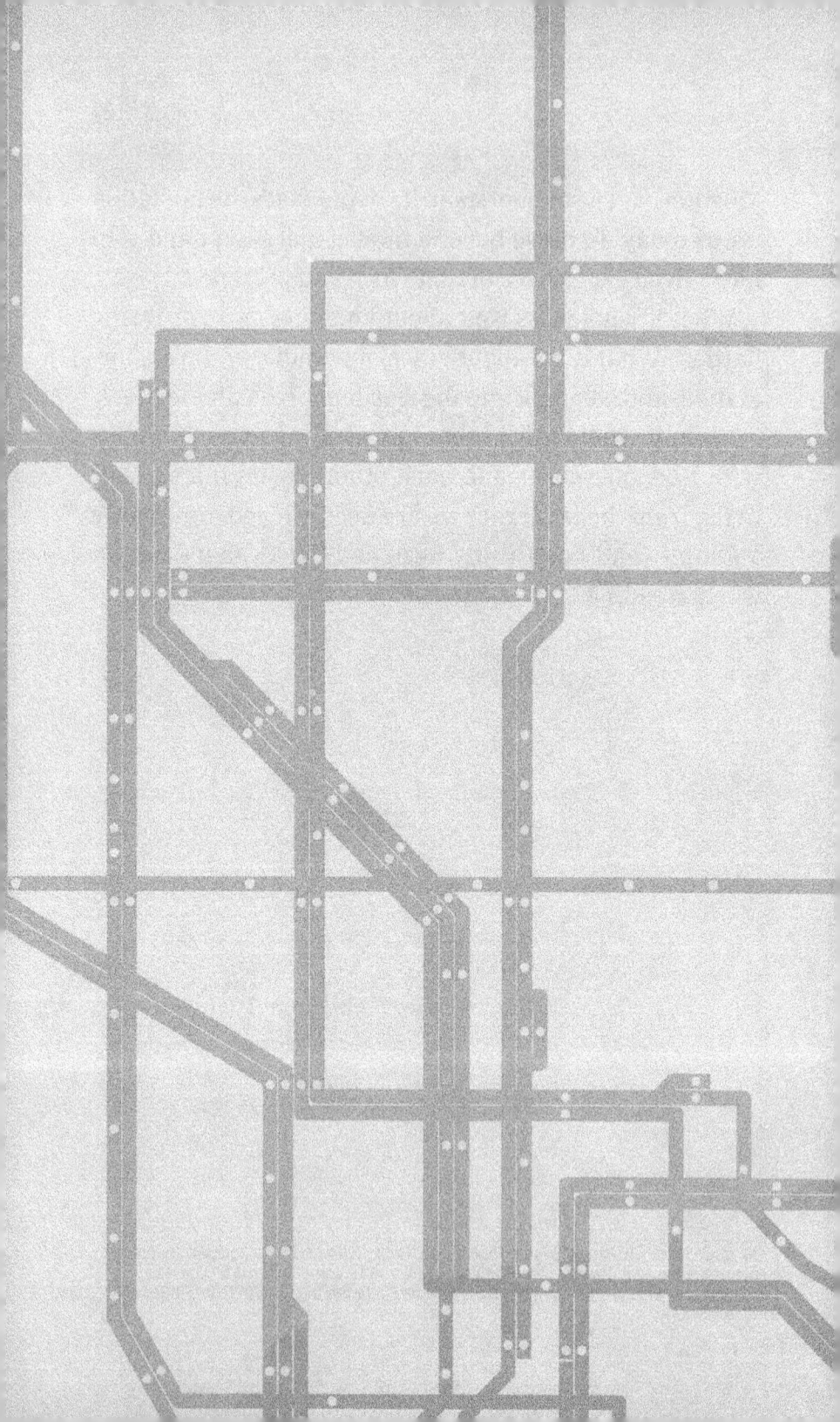

CHAPTER 11

THE CHURCH

We're in This Taco-gether

THE CHURCH I LOVE

I love the Church. She raised me. Most of my deepest friendships have been formed in the Church. I've experienced Her compassion, authenticity, kindness, generosity, wisdom, grace, desire for righteousness, wholeness, and innocence. I'm also thankful for Her various expressions.

I'm not writing about the religious institution. Rather, I'm writing about the people I've known and with whom I've grown through the vast expressions of the Church.

I've been sensitive with seekers, shaken with shakers, kneeled with kneelers, been lowly in high church, taken communion with robed Episcopalians, and fallen to the ground with 3,000 brothers and sisters after John Wimber prayed.

I've received benedictions with Catholics and confessed with a priest in Haiti just outside a children's hospital where he pours out his life for the least of these.

I've tasted God's goodness with the Methodist, raised a song with the Baptist, missionaried with the Alliance and The Assemblies, prayed in tongues with Pentecostals, and cried out in righteous hunger with friends from Lime, NY. I've become close with friends who are Eastern Orthodox and discovered the riches of the Anabaptists.

I've experienced the holiness of God in a home of the underground Church in China, danced with exuberant worshipers in South Africa, fellowshipped with hundreds of Filipinos who walked days to participate in revival, and laughed with loved and cared-for orphans in Nicaragua.

I've seen the impact of the Church, miracles large and small, more than a book could contain—broken marriages restored, the lonely put in family, the poor made rich, bodies made whole, and hearts, minds, and lives transformed.

THE CHURCH IS THE CITY ON A HILL, THE LIGHT THAT ILLUMINATES HIS RECONCILIATION FOR ALL CREATION.

I've seen addicts set free and imaginations restored. I've seen the poor receive care, the hungry fed, and the widow and orphan loved and protected.

I've been part of men's movements that swept the world, challenging us to live lives of character and kindness. I've been a part of equality movements for race and gender where faithful women and men of all colors confronted and led us as we repented for participating in prejudice, exclusivity, and hierarchy.

I could write a book on the history of how the Church has tended to every broken and unjust issue in this often cruel and punishing world, and it would barely scratch the surface of the heaven-to-earth impact the Church has had. Throughout history, the Church has been full of good, humble people whose lives became generous expressions of Greater Love. The world is infinitely richer because of the Church's authentic, other-centered kindness.

Greater Love is the hope for the world, and the Church is God's expression of it. The Church is God's idea, and His ideas are always brilliant.

The Church is the city on a hill, the light that illuminates His reconciliation for all creation. [79]

I love the Church. I wrote this book for Her. And it's because of my love for the Church that I confront our obsession with separation, our infatuation with retribution, and our hypocrisy of exclusion.

In my twenties, the early days of my deconstruction, long before anyone used that term, those post-Bible College years

---

79 Jason Clark, excerpts from *Leaving and Finding Jesus*.

when I reacted against the cruel and unkind hypocrisies within the institution, I often wondered if a baby was in the bath water.

In those early days, I thought the only hope for the Church was Jesus's return, and I occasionally thought about waiting for Him at home. But those days are so far behind me I hardly remember them.

You see, as I continue to rethink every Jesus that isn't reconciling, I also continue to rethink every idea of church that isn't built upon the Cornerstone of Greater Love. I've left every aspect of the church that practices us or them, in or out, for or against; and when I find I haven't, I repent.

I am discovering the Church Jesus described when He prayed that we would be one just as He was one with His Father. I am awakening to the inclusive Church Jesus revealed when He told His disciples, "On that day, you will realize that I am in my Father, and you are in me, and I am in you."

I love the Church!

DAVID HEWITT: A VISION OF PARTICIPATORY CHURCH

I love David Hewitt. He is a gatherer and a dreamer—someone who actively reimagines the Church in ways that feel both ancient and refreshingly new. His passion for authentic, participatory community resonates. I long to see it lived out in the world. David's a new friend but talking with him feels like a conversation with an old friend, the kind you trust to remind you why you fell in love with the Church in the first place.

David's book, Reconstructing Ecclesia: Is There *Any* Future for the Church?[80] is a heartfelt call to reimagine what the Church was meant to be. As we delved into the meaning of Ecclesia, David leaned forward, eyes bright with conviction.

"Ecclesia, as Jesus and Paul understood it," he began, "was about gathering. It wasn't about hierarchy or institutional power—it was about community. The Church was never meant to be a place where a few leaders dictate while everyone else sits passively. It was supposed to be a participatory space, where everyone contributes."

> **THE CHURCH HAS TO BE ABOUT LOVE—LOVE THAT MIRRORS THE TRINITY. WE'RE SUPPOSED TO REFLECT THE MUTUAL, SELF-GIVING LOVE OF FATHER, SON, AND SPIRIT.**

I could feel the resonance of that statement. Over the past thirty-some years, I've been rethinking church. Like David, I've experienced both the beauty and the frustration of the Western Evangelical model.

---

[80] David Hewitt, *Reconstructing Ecclesia: Is There Any Future for the Church?* (Wellsprings Community, 2023).

David's journey took him through various expressions of church life—high church, charismatic, and everything in between. But it's his experience in building Wellsprings Community in Edinburgh that has shaped much of his thinking. "We didn't even call it a church at first," he admitted, laughing softly. "We just knew we wanted something participatory, something authentic. The kind of church where people could bring their creativity, gifts, and lives, not just sit in pews."

It was this vision of church that captured my heart—a space where community isn't just about what happens on a Sunday morning but how we live together every day. David spoke passionately about the importance of relationships: "The Church has to be about love—love that mirrors the Trinity. We're supposed to reflect the mutual, self-giving love of Father, Son, and Spirit."

David's understanding of the ecclesia is deeply shaped by his personal journey. He's seen the good, the bad, and the ugly of church life. And through it all, he's remained hopeful. "I believe the Church has a future," he said firmly. "But it has to change. We need to rethink how we gather, how we worship, and how we live out Christ's love in the world."

I love David's emphasis on participation and think this is where the most significant change is already occurring. "The Church is meant to be a community where everyone is involved. We're a family—a body where every part matters," David concluded.[81]

Yes, and amen. And some Randall Worley.

RANDALL WORLEY: HOW GOD'S LOVE IS RESHAPING THE CHURCH

"Western Christianity thrives on certainty," Randall began, "But certainty has become a substitute for faith." I agreed. The Church's obsession with having all the answers has left little room for mystery, curiosity, or the dynamic relationship with God that faith requires. "Faith," I added, "is about living convinced of God's goodness in the mystery, not demanding certainty to feel secure."

This need for certainty, Randall suggested, has bled into how leadership operates in many Western churches. "We've made leadership about power and control rather than humility and servanthood," he said. Derek, who co-hosted, added to that thought, "True leadership in the Kingdom looks like Jesus washing the feet of His disciples, not standing in a pulpit declaring who's in and who's out."

Randall nodded and continued, "The Church was never meant to be a place where people come to be controlled. It's meant to be a place where they're liberated into the fullness of who God created them to be." I couldn't help but think about how often church leadership has conflated authority with dominance. *God's goodness isn't about enforcing rules;*

---

[81] Jason Clark and Derek Turner, hosts, *Rethinking God with Tacos*, podcast, adapted excerpts from "David Hewitt / Reconstructing Ecclesia," October 12, 2023, https://www.youtube.com/watch?v=6WNaAfWyf00&list=PLgimV9UoSbAIbXX447Gu_5-kGpLAO_eJO&index=69.

it's about revealing His heart, I thought as Derek shared. "If leadership doesn't point people to the radical love of God, then what's the point?"

When I asked Randall what God's love and goodness have to say about the Church's current state, his response was unwavering. "God's love doesn't tolerate us; it transforms us," he said. "And that's true for the Church as a whole. The love of God will dismantle anything that doesn't look like Jesus. It's not punitive—it's restorative."

He pointed to the Church's tendency to cling to tradition over transformation. "Tradition can be a beautiful thing," Randall admitted, "but when it becomes a fortress that keeps us from seeing God's new thing, it's no longer serving its purpose." His words reminded me of Isaiah's prophetic cry: "Behold, I am doing a new thing; now it springs forth, do you not perceive it?" (43:19, ESV)

> **IF CHURCH IS JUST SOMETHING TO BE CONSUMED RATHER THAN A PLACE TO BE TRANSFORMED—THEN NO WONDER PEOPLE ARE WALKING AWAY.**

Here's how I see it: we're in a moment. A reckoning. A reimagining. A waking up. And it's not just happening on the fringes—it's happening within the very core of the Church.

There's a shift not just in theology, but in methodology. If our understanding of God is expanding, doesn't it follow that the way we do church has to expand, too?

This is what Randall, Derek, and I kept circling back to. "When people begin to question so many different things under the broader umbrella of deconstruction," Randall said, "whether it be (our approach to) Scripture or the true nature of God, it also causes us to revisit and reevaluate our methodology as well." And this is good. It's what David Hewitt and so many others are investigating.

We are rethinking the Western, program-driven, personality-centered TED Talk church model. Not because that model is intrinsically wrong, but because, as we grow in this relational Trinitarian face-to-face understanding of the gospel, we are exploring a more relational way to connect.

Randall expounded on this idea. "(We are seeing) a methodology shift . . . more of a face-to-face, more of an intimate connection, more of an interaction of dialogue as opposed to a monologue."

That resonates. The lights, the fog machines, the finely tuned three-point sermons—that has and will likely continue to serve many. But there is a growing hunger for more. "How many questions does the average person have on a Sunday morning in a thirty to forty-five-minute message that goes unresolved?" Randall asked. The answer? A lot. A whole lot. And while there is often no space for those questions in the TED Talk model, there is a growing number who have left the model in search of a more holistic form of connection.

"What I'm finding," Randall told us, "is that something happens in more organic, relational, conversational-type settings that has far more indelible effect on people than listening to a monologue."

That word—indelible—stuck with me. That's what we're after? Not just engagement, but transformation? Not just attendance but awakening.

Listening to Randall, I was reminded that while the Church may feel fractured and faltering, God's goodness is the thread that holds it together. It's a call to embrace humility, prioritize love over dogma, and trust that even in the mess, God is at work—restoring, renewing, and transforming us into the image of Christ.

Perhaps the most poignant moment in our conversation came when Randall reflected on the Church's future. "I'm hopeful," he said with quiet confidence. "(God's) not done with the Church, not by a long shot. The love of God will dismantle anything that doesn't look like Jesus."[82]

And we're seeing this happen. And Scot McKnight has been writing about it.

SCOT MCKNIGHT: A CHURCH CALLED TOV

The Church is at a crossroads, a moment demanding we revisit what God intended it to be. Scot McKnight's

---

[82] Jason Clark and Derek Turner, hosts, *Rethinking God with Tacos*, podcast, adapted excerpts from Randall Worley / When The Church Was Young August 16, 2023, https://www.youtube.com/watch?v=fdXwY1U2cWA&list=PLgimV9UoSbAIbXX447Gu_5-kGpLAO_eJO&index=83

reflections on the Church and leadership point us back to the essence of what it means to embody God's goodness and love—a Tov culture.

Tov, the Hebrew word for goodness, echoes through the story of creation and God's heart for humanity. And Scot jumped into the conversation with both feet. "Everything God created is Tov." He said, "The Church, at its core, should reflect that goodness in every fiber of its being."

But too often, the Church has lost sight of Tov, trading it for something far less.

Scot McKnight is a prophetic voice for the Church, unafraid to name the dysfunction while relentlessly pointing us back to the goodness God intended. His work is deeply pastoral, a call to reshape church culture around empathy, truth, and Christlikeness. I admire his unwavering commitment to Tov, to seeing the Church not as a business or a stage for celebrity leaders but as a community of self-giving love, where the last are first and goodness is the standard.

"Tov is central to God's creation and character," Scot explained. "Everything God does is Tov—good. When the Church reflects Tov, it embodies empathy, grace, truth, and justice. It puts people first, resists narcissism, and rejects institutional self-preservation. Tov is what the gospel is all about—good news, rooted in God's goodness. In a Tov culture, we see Christlikeness, where leaders serve and prioritize others, not themselves… It's about nurturing what's right and healing what's broken. The

Church should always ask: Are we reflecting the goodness of God in all we do?"

Scot didn't mince words when discussing the crisis of leadership. "The pastorate," he says, "too often attracts narcissists—people seeking power and glory. The result is a culture of toxicity rather than one of service and Christlikeness." This kind of leadership misrepresents God's love, reducing the Church to an institution that prioritizes "success" over people. "Jesus never said, 'Come, become a leader,'" Scot reminded us. "He said, 'Come, follow me.' The Church's mission is to form followers of Christ, not build platforms for personalities."

> **"IN TOXIC CULTURES ... NARRATIVES ARE SPUN TO PROTECT THE INSTITUTION, BUT IN A TOV CULTURE, TRUTH IS NON-NEGOTIABLE."**

So, what does God's goodness have to say about leadership? It calls us to embody empathy, truth, and justice—qualities Scot sees as the antidote to toxicity. "A Tov church begins with empathy," he explained. "We listen to the marginalized, the victims, the powerless. We create space for their voices to be heard." In doing so, we reflect

God's heart, a heart that prioritizes people over institutional survival.

Scot's emphasis on truth-telling is also critical. "In toxic cultures," he said, "narratives are spun to protect the institution, but in a Tov culture, truth is non-negotiable." This commitment to honesty is an act of love, a way of saying the Church exists not to preserve itself but to reveal God's goodness.

And then there's justice. "Justice," Scot says, "isn't about rights or rules. It's about doing the right thing at the right time, as measured by Jesus." A church shaped by Tov doesn't exploit or marginalize—it restores, heals, and serves. It mirrors the self-giving love of Christ, a love that refuses to prioritize the institution over individuals.

Scot's challenge to the Church is both prophetic and hopeful. He believes in its potential to reflect God's goodness when it resists the pull of celebrity culture and embraces Christlikeness. "In a Tov church," he said, "the last are first, and leadership is marked by humility and service." This vision isn't just aspirational; it's essential. The Church's witness depends on its willingness to embody God's radical, reconciling love.

"We're not selling a product," Scot said. "We're creating disciples of Jesus."[83] And it's this simplicity—this return to Tov—that holds the power to transform the Church into

---

83 Jason Clark and Derek Turner, hosts, *Rethinking God with Tacos,* podcast, adapted excerpts from "Scot McKnight / A Church Called TOV," January 14, 2022, https://www.youtube.com/watch?v=6fD2ywsDr4I&list=PLgimV9UoSbAIbXX447Gu_5-kGpLAO_eJO&index=125.

what it was always meant to be: a beacon of God's goodness in a broken world.

FATHER KENNETH TANNER: TOGETHER AT THE TABLE

Father Kenneth Tanner is a wise and hopeful voice to close out these church conversations, and ours flowed naturally in that direction. "What does it mean to be a member of Christ's body?" This was the throughline of our conversation. And Kenneth's reflections were rich, weaving theology with personal experience in a way that brought ancient truths alive.

> **"CHRISTIAN WORSHIP IS A DINNER PARTY."**

"There's no perfect church because I'm a member of every church that might be good." That self-deprecating humor was his way of reminding us that the Church is made up of people on the same journey toward healing. But for Kenneth, that transformative and sometimes messy journey is no excuse for division. He spoke passionately about how the language of the New Testament is fundamentally communal: "Paul, every time he uses the word 'you,' almost every time, he's talking about the group—you all."

Kenneth explained that this collective identity shapes everything. He critiqued the individualism so prevalent in Western evangelicalism, calling it a distortion of the gospel. Being part of the body means living out a shared faith, one rooted in embodied practices.

"Christian worship is a dinner party," he said, describing the Eucharist as the central act of worship for centuries—a tangible, relational gathering around Christ. And for me, a guy who regularly rethinks with friends and tacos, he was preaching to the choir. Kenneth continued. "Pentecost teaches us this. It's about the family, the tribe, the nation—and eventually, for the whole world. . . .The Church is a mosaic," he continued, "Pieced together from diverse traditions, but it only forms the image of Jesus when united in love." [84]

Kenneth's words were the comma between the conversations represented in this chapter—a unified dialogue about what it means to be a family of faith. His reflections remind us that the Church, at its heart, is a family rooted in grace, love, and abundant life.

A FAMILY CALLED CHURCH

The Church is a place where you belong before you become, a sanctuary of mercy and forgiveness. It is where sins are not counted against us, and the lifeblood of honor flows freely. It is also a home in which we can be healed, delivered,

---

[84] Jason Clark and Derek Turner, hosts, *Rethinking God with Tacos*, podcast, adapted excerpts from "Fr. Kenneth Tanner / A Body of Which I Am a Member," August 28, 2024, https://www.youtube.com/watch?v=DQ5o9_Yuwpg&list=PLgimV9UoSbAIbXX447Gu_5-kGpLAO_eJO&index=163.

transformed, and restored. These values of family mirror the call to embody Tov, as Scot McKnight emphasized, to create a culture that reflects God's goodness in every fiber of its being.

> **JUST AS A FAMILY'S STRENGTH COMES FROM ITS UNITY AND SHARED PURPOSE, THE CHURCH'S STRENGTH LIES IN ITS ABILITY TO REFLECT THE MUTUAL, SELF-GIVING LOVE OF THE TRINITY.**

Randall's insights about living in humility and mystery resonate with the Church as a family that values presence over performance, intimacy over principles, and identity over behavior.

David's participatory vision adds another layer to this familial dynamic. The Church isn't a place of hierarchy but of shared gifts, creativity, and life. It is a family that thinks generationally, building for the future with love and intentionality.

Just as a family's strength comes from its unity and shared purpose, the Church's strength lies in its ability to reflect the mutual, self-giving love of the Trinity.

This is the invitation of Greater Love: to live as a family that overflows with joy, peace, and generosity. A family that believes in a measureless God, whose love and resources are not limited but abundant for all. A family that understands fullness is not when the cup is filled to the brim but when it overflows, spilling out to bless others.

When the Church lives as this kind of family, it includes rather than excludes, welcomes rather than repels. It becomes a beacon of hope and transformation, a true expression of God's idea of family—one where love never runs out and grace always abounds.

And through this family, the Kingdom is established on earth as it is in heaven.

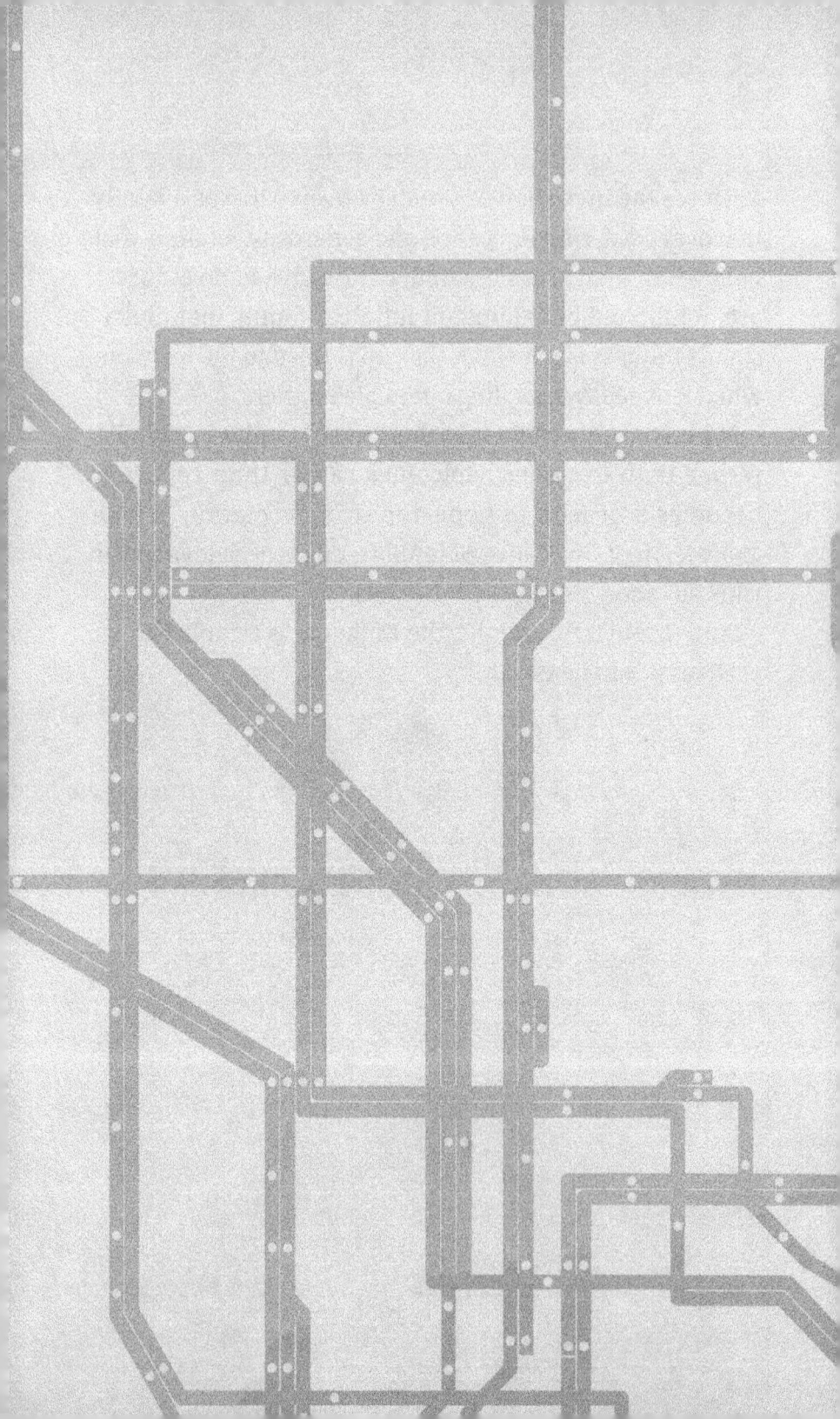

CHAPTER 12

THE KINGDOM

Righteousness, Peace, and Pico de Gallo

BEYOND THE MOAT: THE KINGDOM IS A FAMILY

My son has a framed work of art hanging on his bedroom wall that once graced the wall of my childhood bedroom. It is a colored pencil drawing of a castle with spires and battlements, a fortified tower, arrow slits, a drawbridge, a corresponding moat, and a gate.

It also features a soldier on guard duty standing tall, uniformed in royal blue trousers, a scarlet tunic, and a traditional English bearskin hat. His sword is unsheathed and held up in a salute—as if to let us know he maintains vigilant watch, eyes always scanning for signs of an enemy, ready to respond to any threat.

The soldier is disciplined, dedicated; he is steadfast, his loyalty to the King and Kingdom. He would die for the King.

How do I know? What qualifies me as an expert on this work of art?

I'm the artist.

Inspired by the castle mural painted on my Covenant Church third-grade classroom wall, I drew that solitary soldier and his kingdom. In my nine-year-old scrawl, above *my* castle, I wrote the phrase, *"The Kingdom God has prepared for us far exceeds any imagination."*

That phrase was inspired by 1 Corinthians 2:9 (BSB): "No eye has seen, no ear has heard, and no heart has imagined, what God has prepared for those who love Him."

Yeah, I grew up in the Church, and thus, I've been fascinated by the King and His Kingdom since before I can remember. The idea of Kings and Kingdoms permeated everything I knew about God, Scripture, and the way we Christians navigate all things. But the Kingdom I understood was a dichotomy—"a division into two parts":

The awe-inspired nine-year-old who drew that castle, grew up in a loving home, and knew a kind and loving King with a beautiful Kingdom that looked like family.

But that kid was also raised in the Church's dizzying obsession with good and evil and often compromised by a separation-based atonement theory. That innocent nine-year-old grew up in the Western Evangelical obsession with dominion by way of domination, sovereignty by way of control, justice by way of violent retribution, and power by way of hierarchies of exclusion.

While I knew the other-centered love of Jesus, I had to traverse the Church's literal application of violent Old

Testament delusions. The Kingdom was often presented as a militarized, politicized war machine leveraged by religious zealots and fork-tongued grifters for the purpose of control and exclusion.

Thus, as I entered adulthood, I began to believe that God's beautiful Kingdom was a *prepared* future heaven that could only be experienced if I survived the brutality of this present age.

Then, in my thirties, thanks to my Father's faithful love and those who've pioneered the goodness of God, I began to refocus my Kingdom definitions around what Jesus had to say about it.

Jesus talked about the Kingdom all the time. But never with a sword in His hand and always in the language of Greater Love and the context of family. Not once did Jesus call God "King;" He always called Him "Dad."

> **YOU COULD SAY IT THIS WAY: IF IT ISN'T FAMILY, IT ISN'T THE KINGDOM JESUS REVEALED.**

"When you pray, say Father," He instructed us in Luke 11:2, and he continued in Matthew 6:10. Dad, "Your Kingdom come . . . on earth as it is in heaven."

And boy did I pray—my nine-year-old earnest faith reignited in my thirty-something heart. I joined all creation in the age-old question; the one we've been asking since the lie of separation first entered the mind of Adam.

> *Some of the Pharisees asked Jesus, "When will the kingdom of God come?" Jesus answered, "God's kingdom is coming, but not in a way that you will be able to see with your eyes. People will not say, 'Look, here it is!' or, 'There it is!' because God's kingdom is within you." —Luke 17:20-21 (author paraphrase)*

Remember that castle-inspiring verse in Corinthians? "No eye has seen, no ear has heard, no heart has imagined, what God has prepared for those who love Him"—the very next verse reads, "But God has revealed it to us by the Spirit" (1 Corinthians 2:9-10, BSB).

It seems that Jesus believed the Kingdom wasn't a future heaven but a present Trinitarian revelation of the family relationship between Father, Son, and Holy Spirit established on earth through us.

Jesus reframed the Kingdom in the relational context of family. You could say it this way: if it isn't family, it isn't the Kingdom Jesus revealed. And that's pretty close to how my hero Bill Johnson says it. Thanks Bill.

> *The Kingdom is a Royal Family who co-reigns upon the Earth. . . . The heart of God in creating humanity is for family. His desire in the act of creation was not to expand His army but to give love through union and connection with Himself. . . . We were created for connection, oneness, and union with the Trinity.*

This is the first aspect of the Kingdom we need to see. The Kingdom is a family, and Father's heart is to expand that family.[85]

Those words are from my friend, Dubb Alexander. I'll introduce him soon. But they speak to that young fella who drew that castle.

You know, my Father loves that castle. He knew I saw myself in that soldier with the sharp military uniform and shiny sword and recognized my earnest salute—His eyes alive with laughter as, over the years, I've presented my vigilant watch.

He knew my warrior interpretation of His Kingdom would be transformed by His indwelling Spirit. He knew there would be fathers and mothers, brothers and sisters, heroes like Bill and friends like Dubb, who would come alongside me to re-present His Kingdom.

If I were to pick up the colored pencils today and let my imagination run wild, if I were to set about creating a work of art that represented the Kingdom, and if I were to hang that image on my wall, you most likely would see a family photo.

And I believe if you looked closely, you would see yourself in it. And it wouldn't be a distant future family. It would be the eternal life, ever-present, on earth as it is in heaven, family.

The Kingdom God has prepared for us far exceeds any imagination. And "God has revealed it to us by the Spirit."

---

[85] Dubb Alxander, Ryan Peña, Eunike Jonathan and Tony Robinson, *Kingdom Theology: Volume 1: The Kingdom* (School of Kingdom, 2024).

The Spirit who lives with us.

TOMMY MILLER: UNION, ADOPTION, AND THE KINGDOM AT HAND

In Luke 17:20-21, Jesus told us the Kingdom was near and then went further—the Kingdom is within us. As I grow ever sure in love, as I discover union over and again, these words continue to expand my heart. And that's pretty much the starting point of my conversation with Tommy Miller.

Tommy's whole message is that union is the foundation of everything. He challenges every false paradigm of separation with clarity, conviction, and contagious joy. I love the way he refuses to settle for theory—he lives what he preaches, and every conversation with him feels like an invitation to step deeper into the reality of oneness with Christ.

> **IN JESUS'S DEATH, THE VEIL WAS TORN. AND IN HIS RESURRECTION AND ASCENSION, WE DISCOVERED WHAT HAS ALWAYS BEEN TRUE: WE ARE ONE.**

"You can't have a gospel that starts with separation and ends with union," Tommy said. And yet, that's exactly what many of us were handed—an origin story that begins in distance from God and a redemption story where we slowly work our way back to Him. The problem is, as Tommy noted, "If the gospel starts with separation, it can never lead to union." But if we begin with oneness, then our Father's Kingdom is reframed through the lens of family, and suddenly, it's not just possible—it's inevitable.

Jesus didn't preach a message of getting closer to God, nor did He preach some future Kingdom. He preached a message of awareness—an awakening. He revealed a Kingdom at hand and more, a Kingdom within where separation is a lie, a veil. In Jesus's death, the veil was torn. And in His resurrection and ascension, we discover what has always been true: we are one.

Our conversation expanded on this thought: "If union is our starting place, then what does that mean for the Kingdom of God?" Tommy put it this way: "The goal of bringing heaven to earth includes superimposing that timeless realm onto this realm that's ruled by time." That means the Kingdom isn't about waiting, achieving, or revealing. It's about right now.

And it's about understanding our identity and with it, our authority.

When Adam lost sight of who he was, creation itself suffered. "It's proof positive that Adam kept his authority," Tommy explained, "because when he lost his identity (his sense of oneness), calamity set into creation." The world became a reflection of Adam's false belief in separation.

But Jesus came as the true Son, not to get back something Adam lost, but to reveal the truth that had never stopped being true—that we are one with the Father. This union is our inheritance. When we live from it, creation itself responds. "The Kingdom isn't about us becoming sons and daughters—it's about waking up to the fact that we already are," I said, and then asked Tommy to break down his thoughts on adoption.

> **IF WE SEE THE KINGDOM AS SOMETHING WE EXPERIENCE IN THE FUTURE, WE WILL DELAY TRANSFORMATION.**

Tommy nodded, noting the difference between our Western understanding and the Hebrew perspective. "Hebrew fathers adopt their biological children," he said. "Adoption wasn't about bringing an outsider into the family—it was about a son stepping into full authority."

Jesus's baptism was His adoption ceremony. Not because He wasn't already a son, but because the Father was publicly declaring it. That moment, when the heavens opened and God spoke, wasn't about inclusion—it was about maturity. "Now the Father trusts you with everything He has," Tommy explained. And if we are co-heirs with Christ, that means the Father trusts us in the same way.

And that's where we are invited to partner with our Father in living on earth as it is in heaven in the ever-present now. If we see the Kingdom as something we experience in the future, we will delay transformation. But if we see it as something present, the fruit of our union, we will expect that salvation, *sozo*, healing wholeness, abundant life—THE KINGDOM—will show up in our bodies, our relationships, and our communities.

That's the invitation of the Kingdom—not a future escape, but a present renewal. Not something we hope for, but something we participate in. "No one is going to heaven," Tommy said, "because no one ever left."[86]

Let that sink in. If the Kingdom is within us! If union is our starting place, then our focus isn't on leaving Earth for some distant future Kingdom of Heaven—it's about living Heaven on Earth in the ever-present now. It's about intimacy here and now. And there is no one better to speak to this reality than my new friend, Chris Gore.

CHRIS GORE: THE REVELATION OF FATHER AND THE KINGDOM AS REST

If union is the starting place, then the Kingdom isn't something we strive toward—it's something we wake up to. That's what Chris Gore has been preaching, living, and quietly embodying for years. When we spoke, it was like a conversation picked up midstream—like the current of union had already been flowing, and we just jumped in.

Chris is a gentle revolutionary. His revelation of the Father's love empowers us to discover a miraculous life. I'm thankful for his heart, humility, and how he lives what

---

[86] Jason Clark and Derek Turner, hosts, *Rethinking God with Tacos*, podcast, adapted excerpts from "Tommy Miller / Untethered from Love," December 11, 2024, https://www.youtube.com/watch?v=RehysCl3Rlc&list=PLgimV9UoSbAIbXX447Gu_5-kGpLAO_eJO&index=7.

he teaches. Chris carries a Kingdom insight where healing flows, not as something earned, but as the natural expression of presence, not from striving, but from rest.

"I discovered," Chris told me, "that desperation is not the prerequisite for your miracle."

"Come on!" I responded.

Growing up in the charismatic movement, I was taught that desperation was the high watermark of spiritual maturity. The more desperate I was for God, the holier I was. But that's a performance-based view of Christianity. And it's the antithesis of the truth that sets us free. There is no desperation in the hearts of those who know the measureless love of our Father. Spiritual maturity is connected to our confidence in His affection. "This is my son (or daughter), whom I love, and with whom I am well pleased." Those paraphrased words spoken by the Father over Jesus in Matthew 3:17 include us. They have always been true, and spiritual maturity is evidenced in the lives of those who believe them.

Chris knew my desperate experience well. He has had a similar journey—one that began with his daughter, born with severe disabilities, and him as a young father aching for healing.

"I was just a broken, hurting dad looking for a miracle," he said. "But what I found first was the heart of the Father."

And in that discovery, something shifted. The Kingdom isn't something far off, something to earn or storm the gates to attain. It's within. Around us. Moving through us. It is Greater Love, flowing from union.

"We've made the miraculous about our effort, but it's actually about intimacy," Chris said. "Miracles flow from resting (in our oneness), not from striving.... We're not trying to become healed—we're waking up to the healing that's already ours in Christ."

Chris lives this. He's seen radical healing—people standing out of wheelchairs, blind eyes opening, bodies restored. But his focus isn't on the fruit; it's on friendship, our oneness with Father, Son, and Holy Spirit.

"People say, 'You were healed, so now be healed.' But I say, you are healed—now live like it." Chris continued. "The Kingdom is already here. We're not pulling it down. We're remembering what's always been true."

Union isn't a future event—it's our origin story. When we live from that oneness, healing flows naturally, not as a disruption of reality, but as the unveiling of it. As Chris put it, "Jesus didn't go around teaching on healing. He just healed. And then He said, 'Now you go do the same.'"[87]

That's Kingdom. Not hype. Not hierarchy. Not hoop-jumping. Just sons and daughters living from love, confident in His good pleasure, moved by compassion, manifesting wholeness.

And just like that, the militarized metaphor of the Kingdom melts. The war horse gives way to a family table. The striving is silenced by the still small voice. The miraculous stops being proof and starts being presence. And the Kingdom stops being a far-off promise and starts being the air we breathe.

---

87 Jason Clark, host, *Rethinking God with Tacos*, podcast, adapted excerpts from "Chris Gore / Union & Miracles," September 11, 2024, https://www.youtube.com/watch?v=B6-KRK NPHvE&list=PLgimV9UoSbAIbXX447Gu_5-kGpLAO_eJO&index=25&t=11s.

This brings us to Dubb Alexander, a brother who's been exploring the right question for years: "What is the Kingdom?" His answer—like Chris's—starts with union.

DUBB ALEXANDER: UNION, LOVE, AND THE RESTORATION OF ALL THINGS

My favorite thing about the podcast is the friendships it creates. Dubb Alexander is someone I've gotten to know closely. I am thankful for his friendship and wisdom. He has mad skills with the tambourine and has expanded our understanding of God's Kingdom—not as a distant realm but as a present reality of love, restoration, and co-creation. I admire his boldness, his unwavering belief in God's goodness, and his passion to see heaven's solutions manifest on earth.

"What is the Kingdom? Holy Spirit began to wake me up every morning (with that question)," Dubb said. That question launched him on a journey from religious performance to prophetic authority, from separation to union, from fear-based faith to love-fueled co-creation.

"The Kingdom is familial in nature, governmental in structure," Dubb said. The Kingdom is not built on hierarchy, violence, or control. It's not an exclusive afterlife destination. It's about family, here and now!

And that's a thought that instantly realigns us—because if we get the family part wrong, the governmental part gets twisted. When we believe in a God who is distant, angry, and hard to please, we replicate that god in our structures. We build systems of domination instead of dominion. We enforce order through fear instead of empowering order through love.

For so long, the separation message has birthed fear, which has been the engine driving much of what we've called Christianity. When you build an entire system on fear, it inevitably leads to control. But as we awaken to union, as we start where Jesus starts, one with Father and Holy Spirit, we discover the Kingdom isn't about control; it's about relationship.

"Perfect love casts out all fear—including the fear of the Lord," Dubb said, and his words landed like lightning. I've known that kind of fear-based religion. I've seen how it warps the soul and poisons our understanding of the Father. But when fear is cast out, when the illusion of separation is dismantled, what remains is trust. And trust is the soil in which the Kingdom thrives.

> **MORE AND MORE PEOPLE ARE WAKING UP, REALIZING THAT THE GOSPEL ISN'T A FEAR-BASED TRANSACTION— IT'S A REVELATION OF UNION.**

"There is no hierarchy in the Kingdom, only an heir-archy. We are all co-heirs in Christ." Dubb grinned when he said it, but it wasn't just clever wordplay. It was the truth that resounds through the Trinitarian relationship—a truth that redefines power, authority, and identity.

"God has heavenly solutions for every earthly problem," Dubb said. And he's seen it! Dubb has worked with world leaders to help them implement strategies that reflect the goodness of God, even if they don't have the language for it yet. He has partnered with God to bring tangible solutions to nations.

"Love is the root from which all of heaven's solutions flow," Dubb continued. "If we want to see the Kingdom manifest on earth, it won't come through fear-based control. It'll come through perfect love."

Then Dubb dropped this line: "Religion is mankind's desperate attempt to meet God, whereas the Kingdom is the result of God meeting humanity in all of mankind's fallenness and brokenness, and then redeeming, reconciling, and establishing Him in his original place."

His original place? Union. No separation. No striving. No waiting for a rapture to rescue us from a doomed world. Union, the Kingdom—right here, right now.

Dubb got animated, "All of humanity is ready for an upgrade in a universal apprehension of truth and love." Dubb added, "The gospel is being restored." There's a shift happening. We can feel it. The Kingdom is not just coming. The Kingdom is here.[88]

Which brings us to Paul Golf. A teacher and practitioner who, like Dubb, refuses to settle for disembodied theology. Paul's vision of the Kingdom is Trinitarian, restorative, and

---

[88] Jason Clark and Derek Turner, hosts, *Rethinking God with Tacos*, podcast, adapted excerpts from "Dubb Alexander / The Kingdom," January 17, 2024, https://www.youtube.com/watch?v=nely6X0PSyc.

wildly incarnational. And like Dubb, he doesn't believe the Kingdom is a castle in the sky—it's Christ filling all in all.

PAUL GOLF: THE CHURCH AND THE KINGDOM

My Paul Golf conversation picked up where Dubb left off. "The Kingdom isn't a far-off dream," he explained. "It's Jesus filling everything in every way." This means God's Kingdom cannot be confined to the walls of a church. It's a living, breathing reality that permeates every sphere of life.

> **THE CHURCH'S JOB ISN'T TO CONTROL THE KINGDOM, IT'S TO WITNESS IT, REFLECT IT, AND CALL IT FORTH WHEREVER IT'S ALREADY BREAKING THROUGH.**

Paul Golf is another who has become a friend through the podcast. His passionate and deeply thoughtful voice in the conversation about God's Kingdom challenges long-held assumptions with a vision rooted in union and Trinitarian love. His ability to articulate complex theological ideas with clarity and conviction makes every conversation with him feel like stepping into a larger, more beautiful reality.

Paul's understanding of the Kingdom of God begins with union—our shared life with Christ that transforms how we see ourselves and the world. "Union isn't a theological concept," he said. "It's the heartbeat of the Kingdom. Jesus prayed, 'Your Kingdom come, your will be done, on earth as it is in heaven.' That wasn't wishful thinking; it was His reality." And it's our reality.

This vision of the Kingdom reframes the role of the Church. "The Church is the fullness of Him who fills everything in every way. It's not the whole Kingdom—it's the yeast in the dough." I love how Paul put it: "The Church's job isn't to control the Kingdom, it's to witness it, reflect it, and call it forth wherever it's already breaking through."

Paul acknowledged the challenges of this perspective, especially in a world where institutional Christianity is often met with skepticism. "We're in a season where Jesus is judging the Church," he said. "But it's not a judgment of wrath; it's one of mercy. He's exposing what doesn't reflect His heart, so we can move forward with what does."

I loved Paul's restorative perspective, which invites us to embrace the fluidity of the Kingdom without losing sight of its foundation in love and relationship. "The Kingdom is neither controlling nor coercive," he emphasized. The Spirit invites us to organize, yes, but never to manipulate or force."

This relational approach transforms how we, the Church, engage with the world. "When we operate from union with Christ, we don't need to convince people to join a religion," Paul said. "We bear witness to the love that's already drawing them in." He reminded us that the Kingdom is unshakable, rooted in the love of the Father, Son, and Spirit—a love that fills all things and invites all people.[89]

THE KINGDOM FAR EXCEEDS ANY IMAGINATION. . . .

As a kid, I saw glimpses of this Kingdom in the castle I drew, with its spires, battlements, and vigilant soldiers. Even then, I was stirred by the measureless nature of God's Kingdom: "No eye has seen, no ear has heard, no heart has imagined what God has prepared for those who love Him" (1 Corinthians 2:9, author paraphrase). This Kingdom, I thought, must be a place of wonder and belonging, far exceeding any dream I could conjure.

Today, I see the Kingdom as dynamic and transformative, not confined by walls or ruled by fear. It is a reflection of God's heart—a heart that longs for family, for union, for restoration. The image of the soldier I once drew, loyal and vigilant, now gives way to the image of a family gathered together, united by love. This Kingdom includes you and me, calling us to embody its values in every sphere of life. It is the extension of God's goodness, a living testament that His plans for us are infinitely greater than we could ever imagine.

This Kingdom far exceeds any imagination, revealing the heart of a Father who invites us into love, restoration, and co-creation. It is not a dream reserved for tomorrow; it is an invitation for today.

---

89 Jason Clark and Derek Turner, hosts, *Rethinking God with Tacos*, podcast, adapted excerpts from "Paul Golf / The Gospel 101 – Inexpressible & Glorious Joy," December 13, 2023, https://www.youtube.com/watch?v=zM—bxSyiAM.

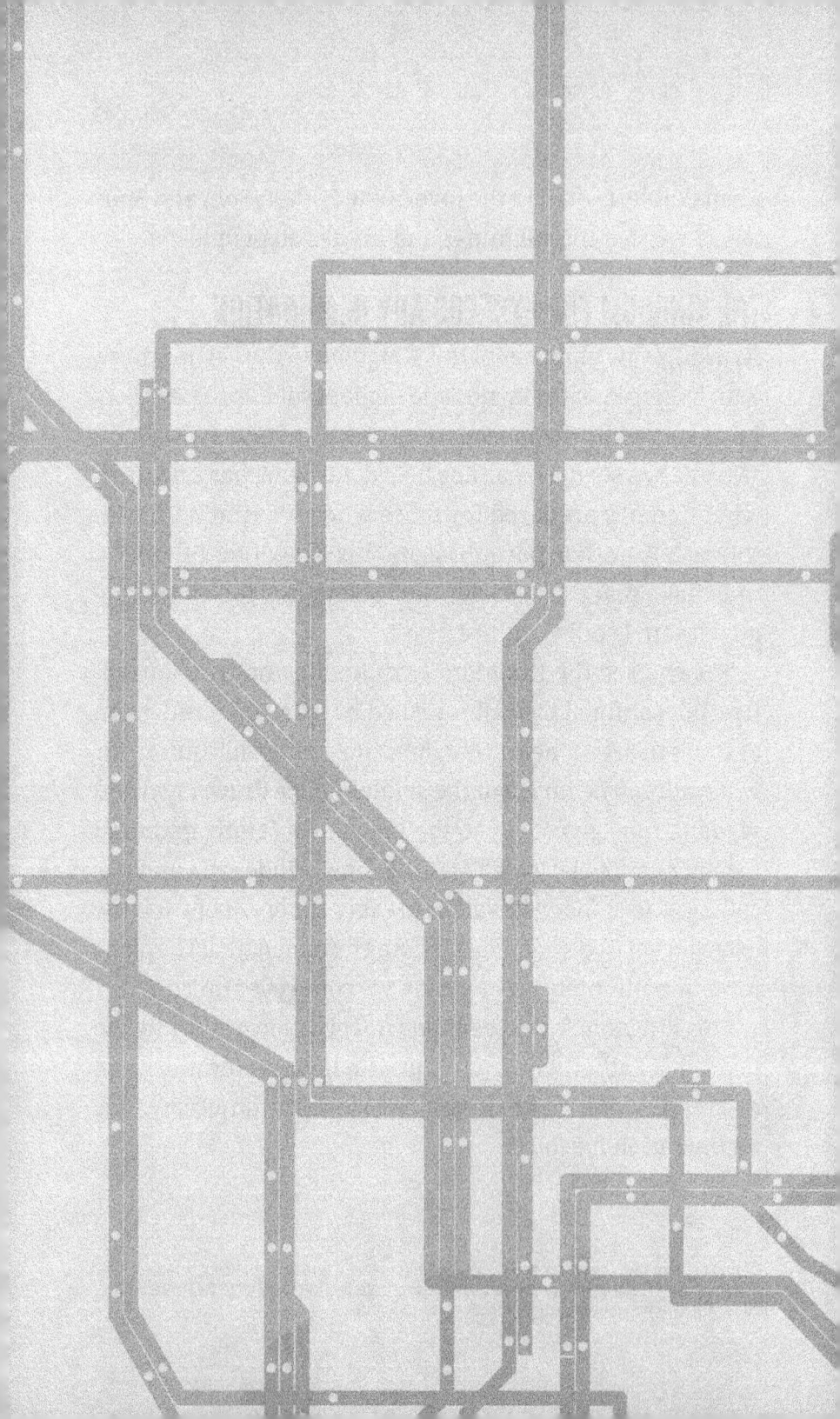

CHAPTER 13

GRACE

Bottomless Margaritas

UNBALANCED GRACE

If you want to read an amazing book on grace, I recommend "The Ragamuffin Gospel"[90] or anything by Brennan Manning. Brennan is a hero who faithfully banged the drum about God's love. He was also pretty good with a tambourine. He wrote about the beauty, freedom, and transforming power of grace. But my favorite thing about his writings is that he never felt compelled to balance grace.

I was hanging out with a friend the other day. He is in his mid-sixties and coming into such a wonderful revelation regarding our Father's love. He has lived most of his life enslaved to the harsh master known as *lack*. But he is beginning to discover an always good and loving Father. This beautiful revelation has entered his life in the form of Grace.

---

[90] Brennan Manning, *The Ragamuffin Gospel: Good News for the Bedraggled, Beat-Up, and Burnt Out* (Sisters, OR: Multnomah, 2008).

For twenty minutes, he spoke excitedly about how miraculously astonishing Grace is. As he shared, I wholeheartedly encouraged and agreed with him. When he told me about the incredible freedom he was discovering through amazing Grace, I laughed with him, reveling in the wonder. When he described how Grace was empowering him to live free of sins that had haunted him his whole life, I grinned and nodded enthusiastically and said, "Grace is good like that!"

> **GRACE IS A SCARY THING IF YOU LIVE WITH THE DELUSION THAT A GOOD FATHER CAN LOOK AWAY.**

He was well into praising how Grace was changing the way he saw the people in his life when it happened. It's understandable; I've done it. When raised at the trough of separation, you can't help but participate in the knowledge of good and evil. And that's what happened.

Suddenly, like a fist to the jaw, he balanced it.

While describing the most beautiful revelation, while speaking with more passion and freedom than I had encountered in my eighteen years of knowing the man, he paused mid-sentence and, at absolute odds with what he had been sharing, blurted, "I know you can abuse it, grace."

And there it was. Separation will have us measuring something that is measureless, it will burden us with counting sins against. . . .

I could almost hear his thoughts: *"Maybe I have gone too far; this grace thing is starting to sound too good to be true."* I understood what had happened. Grace is a scary thing if you live with the delusion that a good Father can look away.

In that separation paradigm, at some point, Grace is weighed, measured, and balanced.

That ugly faux grace has been taught by those who fear the world more than the revelation of the Kingdom of heaven; those who focus more on lack than Love, on not sinning instead of awakening to righteousness (See 2 Corinthians 5:21).

When distance and lack trump union and measureless love, grace is an after-school special, a cheap parlor trick—empty, powerless rhetoric.

Years ago, my dad made an amazing statement. "Jason, if you preach grace and the question from Romans 6:1-2 (NIV), 'shall we go on sinning so that grace may increase' isn't raised, you didn't preach grace right."

The rest of the scripture, by the way—"By no means! We are those who have died to sin; how can we live in it any longer?"

I am aware that abuses and brokenness have happened under a distorted view of grace. Jude 1:4 describes how men can pervert and change the message of grace into a license to sin. But that's not what I am writing about. I am addressing the nature, the person of Grace. The fact is, when you truly encounter Grace, you are transformed. When you truly know Grace, you don't want to sin.

Those who teach us that we can abuse grace don't know Grace. That teaching looks at Grace through the separation lens of distance and lack, the measurements of earth. It dumbs Grace down to a commodity that can be traded for freedom, or forgiveness, or favor.

GRACE IS NOT A TOOL TO HELP MONITOR BEHAVIOR.

The message of *balanced* grace is a lie birthed from separation that enslaves us to live in the limitations of lack. A balanced grace is simply another way to control. If Grace can be balanced, Her power is neutered, and a powerless Grace is a cruelty greater than no grace at all.

Grace won't be balanced! She is too perfect, too whole, too free, too just, too pure, too kind, too strong, too wild, too holy. Grace won't be belittled. She won't ever go bad or run out; She is the measureless in-dwelling good news—always.

After my friend attempted to balance it, there was a dark and brooding silence that threatened to ruin everything. For just a moment, we teetered on the brink of a faith crisis, but Grace would have none of it. Right there, on the verge of hopelessness, I told my friend the beautiful truth I am growing in: "You can't abuse Grace. Grace is not a tool to help monitor behavior; Grace is a revelation, an awakening, that empowers us to live free."

I told him that Grace isn't too good to be true, just the opposite—it's too good not to be true. Grace is unmerited favor discovered in union. We can't do anything to earn it, and we can't do anything to abuse it. Grace helps us to see ourselves from our Father's perspective and empowers us to live in agreement. He sees us as saints and sons and daughters and sisters and brothers and friends....[91]

DON KEATHLEY: GRACE

Sitting across from Don Keathley, I was struck by the depth and simplicity of his message about Grace. Don is a forerunner. He has been a walking revelation of Grace for decades, often taking hits for it, but his enthusiasm for the goodness of God remains as fresh as ever. Our conversation felt like a stream of living water, constantly flowing toward the heart of our Father.

For Don, Grace is the foundation of everything he teaches and lives. "Grace is a divine influence that produces effortless change as you rest in Him." Effortless change—what a contrast to the striving that often defines our spiritual journeys.

Most of us Westerners were raised to equate Grace with forgiveness, a divine eraser that cleans up our mistakes. But Grace is not just about wiping the slate

---
[91] Jason Clark, adapted from *Prone to Love*.

clean—it's about union. Yeah, the relational theologian is still banging on that drum.

Grace is not a transaction; it's the essence of God's love, the reality that we have always been one. Don put it perfectly: "The gospel is not an invitation to come and accept Jesus. It's a proclamation that He has already accepted you."

IF ADAM'S FALL AFFECTED EVERYONE, THEN WHY DO WE LIMIT CHRIST'S REDEMPTION?

Holiness isn't about moral perfection—it's about wholeness. When we discover our wholeness in Christ, our true identity, our behavior follows.

"Behavior follows identity." I said, and Don affirmed, then continued, "When we come into an understanding of divinity as identity—that we really are partakers of the divine nature—that just opens up the door to wholeness." That's the key. The moment we start seeing ourselves the way our Father sees us, our lives start aligning with that reality.

Many people get nervous when they hear the word "inclusion." But if we're serious about Grace, we have to deal with it. Was Jesus's work effective for all, or only for a select few? If Adam's fall affected everyone, then why do we limit Christ's redemption?

This topic is the focus of an upcoming chapter, but what Don shared is a good mouthful to start chewing on now.

"Everybody's a universalist when it comes to Adam," Don said. "But when it comes to Christ, all of a sudden, we have us and them, insiders and outsiders. If all died in Adam, then all have certainly been made alive in Christ." And just in case that sounds too good to be true, I'll give you chapter and verse. "For as in Adam all die, so in Christ all will be made alive" (1 Corinthians 15:22, NIV).

Don broke it down: "Paul said we were alienated and separated in our minds" (See Colossians 1:21). I emphasize "in our minds." Separation is a delusion, and Grace helps us see through it!

If all of this is true, then the next step isn't just knowing Grace—it's manifesting it. The world doesn't need more Christians who believe in Grace but live like it's fragile or needs to be balanced. All creation longs for sons and daughters who walk in the fullness of their union with Christ.

"As He is, so are we in this world," Don quoted from 1 John 4:17. He then added, "We've learned a lot, but I think the time is here when we are going to begin to demonstrate what it is that we now know. The sons will begin to manifest and shift our entire culture."

That sounds like Grace, I thought.

Grace empowers individual transformation but also cultural transformation.

GRACE ISN'T ABOUT FIXING WHAT'S BROKEN. IT'S ABOUT UNVEILING WHAT'S ALREADY WHOLE.

"We should have started before creation, where Ephesians 1:4 says that He chose us in Christ before the foundation of the world," Don reminded. "Rather than begin the message at a point of separation, maybe we should begin the message at a point of inclusion." And Grace is the language that reveals this!

Don noted how Grace transforms us in ways we don't always recognize in the moment. "People don't even realize they're changing," he said. They just look in the mirror one day and see they're different from what they were before."[92] It's a process that feels organic, not forced, as if Grace works from the inside out, reshaping us in quiet, miraculous ways—as if Grace is a person.

Que Steve McVey.

STEVE MCVEY: THE INEXHAUSTIBLE GIFT OF IDENTITY AND RESTORATION

Steve's ministry is named Grace Walk. So, while he will grace another chapter, I can't write a chapter on this subject without his thoughts.

---

92 Jason Clark and Derek Turner, hosts, *Rethinking God with Tacos*, podcast, adapted excerpts from "Don Keathley / A Grace Awakening!", June 26, 2024, https://www.youtube.com/watch?v=jUph-rswbQQ&list=PLgimV9UoSbAIbXX447Gu_5-kGpLAO_eJO&index=35.

Talking with Steve always feels like standing at the edge of an endless ocean—vast, breathtaking, and beyond comprehension. He has a way of illuminating deep-end thoughts about God in a way that's easy to understand.

"Grace," he explained, "is a person, and that person is Jesus Christ." He continued, "Grace is Jesus Himself, living and moving in us and through us.... Grace is not something separate from Christ. If you're talking about Grace, you're talking about Him. And if you're walking in Grace, you're walking in Him."

I agree, although these days, I've grown to know Grace's feminine nature through Holy Spirit. I believe you can also know Grace as our kind Father. Regardless, my heart burned as Steve incarnated Garce in Christ.

Steve continued, "Grace is a word that can more easily be described than it can be defined." He continued, "The Apostle Peter called it the manifold grace of God.

Manifold means multifaceted. It's like a cut diamond that you hold up and see its beauty, but then you slightly shift it, and the light catches a different facet. Suddenly, it's like you're looking at a different diamond altogether. That's Grace. You can't exhaust its beauty."

I grinned and added, "Grace is a measureless, fathomless revelation!"

Steve took it from there: "Paul says you'll never reach the bottom of it." Then he went further: "Grace is the divine enablement by the life of Christ in us to be all that He's created us to be and to do all that He's called us to do."

Of course, this understanding of Grace challenges many of the frameworks we've been given in the modern church. Steve addressed this head-on: "Anybody that says you need to balance grace, they might as well put a big banner on their head that says, 'I don't know what grace is.'"

He chuckled, but the point was serious. "You can't get out of balance with Grace. People who say, 'Be careful about hyper-grace,' don't understand what Grace really is. Grace empowers us to live righteously because it's Jesus empowering us."

> **"IF THE CHURCH WERE AS INTERESTED IN CHRIST AND HIS RIGHTEOUSNESS AS WE ARE IN SIN, WE'D GO A LONG WAY."**

This empowerment is key. Grace doesn't leave us where She finds us. She is transformative. As Steve put it, "The Grace of God has appeared, teaching us to deny ungodliness and worldly desires and to live soberly, righteously, and justly in this present age." Grace invites us into a deeper alignment with Christ, not through striving, but through surrender.

"If we're walking in Grace, we're not sinning," I said and continued. "Grace empowers us into righteousness because Grace is Christ's life being expressed uniquely through us."

Steve responded with a profound "yes, and."

"The word sin comes from the root meaning 'no structure,' a failure to understand your true form and identity. It's a case of mistaken identity. Grace comes to restore that identity, to remind us of who we really are in Christ."

It's this restoration that makes Grace so powerful. Steve reminded me of Paul's words: "Set your mind on the things of the Spirit, and you'll reap the things of the Spirit." He added, "If the Church were as interested in Christ and His righteousness as we are in sin, we'd go a long way."[93]

Que Matt Spinks.

MATT SPINKS: RESTING IN THE FINISHED WORK—AN INVITATION TO GRACE

One of the great joys of hosting Rethinking God with Tacos is the opportunity to sit down with people who radiate the love and joy of God. Matt Spinks is one of those people. His exuberance, his laughter, and his peace are contagious.

Matt describes Grace as "this unconditional embrace of God that allows us to rest in His love and joy without striving." Matt explained how this understanding reshaped his relationship with God:

"I grew up in the Church my whole life, but I never really felt the presence of God consistently. It wasn't until I encountered the overwhelming waves of peace, love, and joy in 2008 that everything shifted for me."

Matt's experience of Grace wasn't limited to an intellectual shift—it was an encounter that transformed his heart *and*

---

[93] Jason Clark and Derek Turner, hosts, *Rethinking God with Tacos*, podcast, excerpts from "Steve McVey / Beyond An Angry God" July 15, 2020, https://www.youtube.com/watch?v=dya9shtRii8&list=PLgimV9UoSbAIbXX447Gu_5-kGpLAO_eJO&index=170

mind. He realized Grace isn't just about getting a second chance or being forgiven; it's about living from the reality that everything we need has already been provided in Christ.

> **GRACE ISN'T ABOUT IGNORING SIN OR PRETENDING PROBLEMS DON'T EXIST. IT'S ABOUT RECOGNIZING THAT JESUS ALREADY ADDRESSED THEM.**

Of course, central to Matt's theology of Grace is union. Union is the starting point, not the finish line. He reminded us, "God is already in you. You're already united with Him. He's closer than the air you breathe."

This union is the natural result of the "finished work" of Christ—"Jesus didn't just forgive us or accept us; He actually accomplished something. He supplied us with everything we need for life and godliness."

Grace isn't about ignoring sin or pretending problems don't exist. It's about recognizing that Jesus already addressed them. "The finished work means we're not here to earn anything or fix ourselves. It's done. We get to live from that place of wholeness."

As we spoke, Matt's passion for the inclusive nature of God's Grace came through over and again. He spoke with awe about how the gospel tears down walls and invites everyone into the family of God. "Jesus didn't die for just a select few. He died for all of humanity. The finished work of the cross is for everyone, whether they realize it or not."

This inclusivity is deeply practical. Matt's ministry, whether through local community or international missions, reflects a heart that believes everyone is already embraced by God. "We've met people from all walks of life, and I keep seeing the same thing: God's Grace is for them. Every single one of them. It's not based on how they behave or what they believe—it's just who God is."

This radically inclusive Grace challenges many traditional theological assumptions. As Matt put it: "We've underestimated just how good God is. He's better than we ever imagined, and His love reaches further than we dare to believe."

One of the most beautiful takeaways from our conversation was how Matt connects Grace with joy. Joy is the natural outflow of walking in Grace. "When you realize God is happy, that He's pleased with you, it changes everything. You can't help but be joyful."

This isn't a superficial, performative joy but a deep, abiding bliss that sustains even through hard times. Matt shared, "Even in grief or challenges, there's this underlying bliss of union with God. It's not about pretending everything's fine—it's about knowing everything is held in His love."

Thus, "Grace isn't an escape from life's difficulties, but it is an invitation to rest. To rest in the truth that God has already done it all; and that we're loved more than we can imagine."[94]

---

94 Jason Clark and Derek Turner, hosts, *Rethinking God with Tacos,* podcast, adapted excerpts from "Matt Spinks / Ecstatic Joy!", December 20, 2023, https://www.youtube.com/watch?v=4nR9qemWwtw&list=PLgimV9UoSbAIbXX447Gu_5-kGpLAO_eJO&index=59.

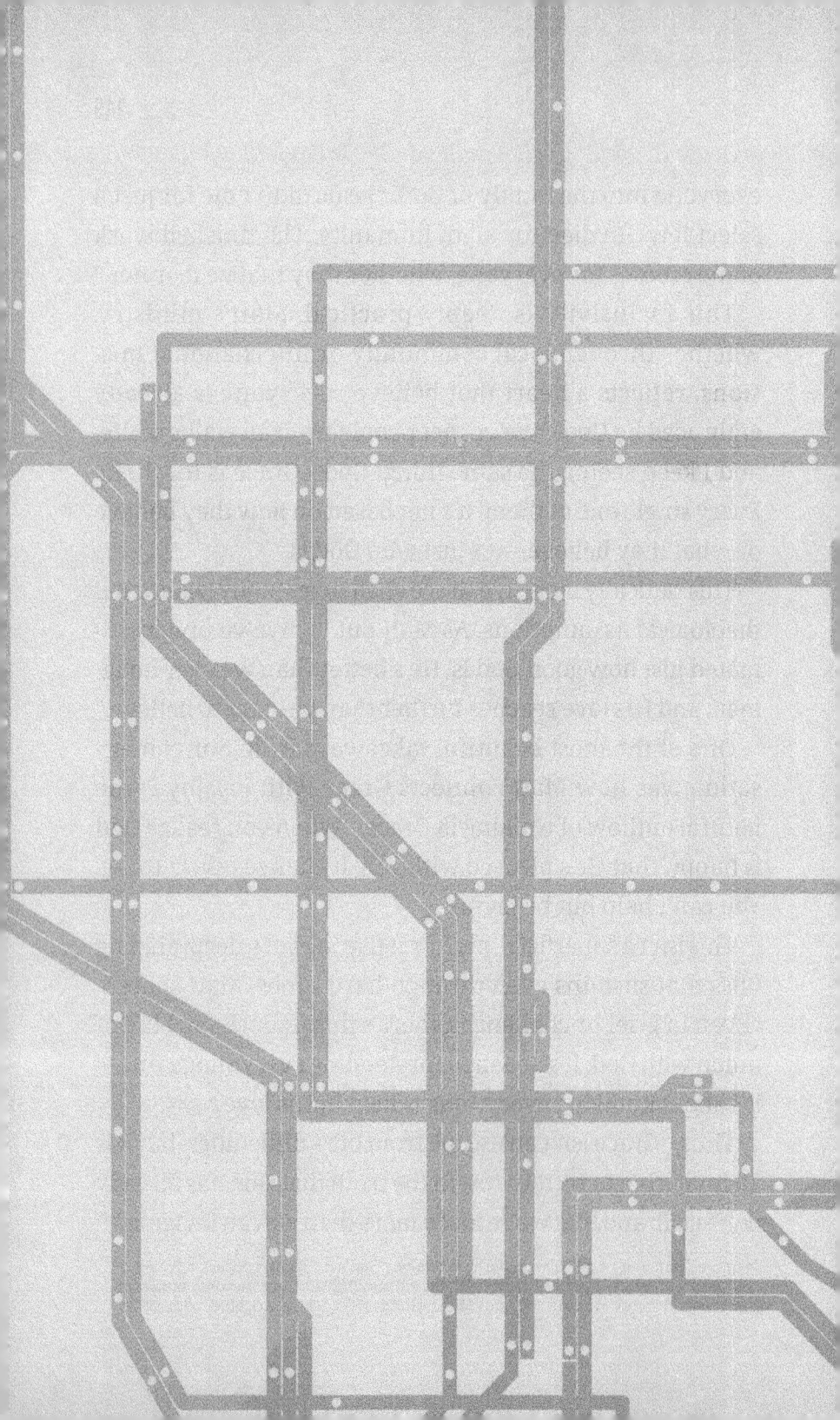

CHAPTER 14

INCLUSION

You Belong, Queso Closed

THE EARLY CHURCH

The early Church, led by Peter and a handful of others, was beautiful—and that's an understatement. From the moment Holy Spirit burst onto the scene in the upper room, as depicted in Acts 2, there was an evangelistic explosion. With *"many wonders and signs,"* folks were added to the Church daily, weekly, and monthly (See Acts 2:43; 5:2).

Unity marked this early Church. The phrases *"all together"* or *"of one accord"* can be found five times in the first five chapters of Acts. The power of God displayed by leadership was remarkable. Even Peter's shadow healed people (See Acts 5:15-16).

Miracles occurred at a rate the world had never seen. Yes, there was persecution, and yet the Church grew, and *"throughout all Judaea and Galilee and Samaria [they] had peace and richly increased in numbers"* (Acts 9:31, author paraphrase).

The presence of Holy Spirit manifested in every aspect of the Church. From Pentecost on, Holy Spirit was present and known to fall *"on all who heard the word"* (Acts 10:44, ESV).

In this beautiful Church, sons and daughters grew confident in the love of a good Father! This was a Church passionately releasing heaven on earth, the Kingdom within us; a Church where *"righteousness peace, and joy in the Holy Spirit"* (Romans 14:17, NIV) were deeply rooted in the soul and every aspect of life.

This was also a generous Church where the lost were found, the sick healed, the sinner forgiven and transformed, the lonely placed in family, all who were thirsty could come and drink, and where *"they sold property and possessions to give to anyone who had need"* (Acts 2:45, NIV).

All could be saved!

Except, well, anyone who wasn't Jewish.

So, not literally *all,* I guess. Just, well, the Jewish *all.*

In those first nine years or so of the early Church, when I write, *all could be saved,* what I mean is that a small exclusive group of people could be saved; all of the included *us,* but none of the excluded *them,* could be saved.

Just like today, the understanding of the Good News of Jesus within the Church and her leadership was limited but ever-expanding. In those beautifully formative early Church days, the limitation was that only Jews were *in.*

Imagine a Church stunning in fellowship—the Church Jesus referenced as *"the light of the world, a city set on a hill"* (Matthew 5:14, ESV). Imagine the revelation of *Greater Love* flowing through their veins. Imagine the power of their evangelism.

Now imagine, because of their tradition, culture, and limited understanding, they only shared this life-transforming Good News with a select few. Imagine a gospel message where most of humanity was excluded. That's the first nine years of the early Church.

The early Church and her leadership were authentic, sincere, and growing in revelation. At the same time, the early Church had a serious flaw in its God lens, the same dualistic hierarchical flaw the Church and her leadership continue to discover and repent of today.

Separation. Us or them. Insiders and outsiders.

The early Church was growing in the transformational Truth of a Greater Love that never leaves—union. They experienced the kindness that leads to repentance, and they followed a friend of Jesus who knew cruciform love and restoration like few others.

Peter and the early Church were daily awakening to the unconditional, reconciling love of God. Yet, even in the daily miraculous manifestation of His goodness, for the first nine years or so, the early Church seemed oblivious to the devastating us or them flaw in their theological lens—especially pertaining to Gentiles.

God didn't ignore their delusions nor condemn them for their exclusivity. He just walked beside them as He did on the Emmaus Road. He kept speaking to their burning hearts. Like that Farmer who went out to sow seed, Greater Love just kept sowing into every limitation of their understanding, every delusion, every hierarchy of exclusion, and every cruel and punishing missing of the mark.

> **THERE IS NO US OR THEM AT THE CROSS, NO FOR OR AGAINST AT THE CROSS, NO IN OR OUT AT THE CROSS.**

Exclusion is the fruit of separation, or a penal substitutionary atonement view of the cross—as though the Father looked away, as though Jesus only died to save some, as though Greater Love didn't reconcile *all* creation, as though what was lost in Adam wasn't fully restored in Christ, as though at the cross there was a delineation between Jew or Gentile, Black or White, lost or found, sinner or saint, gay or straight, Republican or Democrat, capitalist or socialist, Christian or Muslim . . . as though there is still a veil that separates some from His all-inclusive, measurelessly reconciling love.

Let's be clear. There is no *us* or *them* at the cross, no *for* or *against* at the cross, no *in* or *out* at the cross. God reconciled all creation at the cross.

It's why we call it the good news! And I am so thankful for the continual awakening to this glorious message. And for those walking two weeks ahead as expressions of this jingle jangle gospel of Grace, friends like Francois.[95]

FRANCOIS DU TOIT: THE RADICAL GOSPEL OF INCLUSION

"To see the gospel in any other light but in its all-inclusiveness would not be the gospel," Francois declared. He then recounted how some have warned him against using the term "inclusion," deeming it controversial. Yet, he's remained resolute: "What's left of the gospel if the next person isn't equally valued and equally loved?"

When Francois talks about this all-inclusive love, you can't help but become convinced. Why? Because Francois always speaks in the context of consent, the language of love.

"It's not about arm-wrestling someone with theological information," he shared. "It's about unveiling the Christ in them." His words carried the weight of transformative encounters and divine revelation, reminding us that the gospel's essence is about divine embrace—a love that already includes every person within the life of the Father, Son, and Spirit.

Francois's words were like a mirror—get it? The mirror reflecting back the reality of our union with God.

"We are never out of His thoughts. You cannot be abandoned. It's impossible for Father to abandon the human

---
95 Jason Clark, adapted excerpts from *Leaving and Finding Jesus*.

race."⁹⁶ This gospel Francois describes is pure, unfiltered inclusion—a story of union—a relentless, unyielding love that leaves no one out.

And I'm down for it.

And so was Peter.

GOD SHOWS NO PARTIALITY

Throughout history, God seems to believe His Greater Love is more powerfully inclusive than all our flawed and often exclusive understandings—and it is!

And it was. . . .

Ultimately, the early Church's *us* or *them* thinking began to change—often with Peter first. Then, one day, when the soil of Peter's heart could bear good fruit, our Father gave him an offensively good vision. You can read about it in Acts 10.

But the fruit of this vision is that it empowered and led Peter to visit the house of Cornelius, a Gentile, a heathen, an outsider, one of *them*. And on that day, Peter discovered a gospel so expansive as to include the whole world in the finished work of the cross—you see, God was present within the Gentiles.

Peter recognized, as Francois described it, "the Christ in them."

When Peter recognized this, he told Cornelius and his household, *"Truly I understand that God shows no partiality"* (Acts 10:34, ESV).

That's worth underlining.

---

96 Jason Clark, host, *Rethinking God with Tacos*, podcast, adapted excerpts from "Francois du Toit / Awakening to the I Am-ness of God.", https://afamilystory.org/2024/09/francois-lydia-du-toit-awakening-to-the-i-am-ness-of-god/

For nearly a decade, when it came to what the early Church believed, Gentiles were out. Then suddenly, Peter discovered what was always true, the Truth that set him free: there is no us or them, no in or out in the Trinity.

Peter discovered what Paul later wrote about in Galatians, *"There is neither Jew nor Gentile, neither slave nor free, nor is there male and female, for you are all one in Christ Jesus"* (Galatians 3:28, NIV).

Peter, realizing God shows no partiality, *"commanded them (Cornelius and his household) to be baptized in the name of Jesus Christ"* (Acts 2:38, author paraphrase and addition).

The same Peter, who years earlier swung a sword on behalf of separation, in defense of his punishing certainties about clean and unclean, Jew and Gentile, in and out, for and against, suddenly recognized and embraced the inclusive nature of reconciling love for the whole world.

Confronted by God's kindness, Peter repented of the long-standing exclusion on his ideological and theological lens. He changed his mind and aligned his thoughts and actions with Greater Love—and that's a big deal!

The willingness to face our offense and repent of our bias and exclusivity when confronted with the measureless nature of God's inclusive love is the birthplace of personal transformation and an absolute requirement for friends of Jesus, especially leaders who are feeding His sheep.[97]

Which is one of my favorite things about Brian Zahnd. He continues to rethink any *us or them* bias on the Christian lens.

---
[97] Jason Clark, excerpts adapted from *Leaving and Finding Jesus*.

BRIAN ZAHND: BREAKING DOWN THE WALLS OF DIVISION

"As long as we remain imprisoned in the reactive world of dualistic thinking, spiritual growth is impossible," Brian said as a call to abandon "in or out" thinking. "We must repent from us-versus-them thinking." Brian's words challenge the dualistic tree of the knowledge of good and evil mindset that fuels division and blocks spiritual growth.

Zahnd encouraged a shift from theoretical agreement to practical empathy. "We need to practice imagining ourselves in the place of others to truly understand and love them as Jesus taught," he said. This empathetic practice requires humility and vulnerability. By seeking to understand those we might label as "other," we begin dismantling the walls of division.

Zahnd illuminated how scapegoating—uniting against a perceived enemy—may feel unifying but is ultimately destructive. "The unholy spirit can feel so cathartic and produce such unity, but it's not the Holy Spirit," he cautioned.

Zahnd went on to illustrate how abandoning divisive thinking transformed his congregation. He shared about a community outreach program that paired volunteers with refugees. Initially, some church members resisted the idea, fearing cultural or religious differences. But as they got to know these families, their perspectives shifted. "True unity comes from recognizing our shared humanity and divine image."[98]

Which is the perfect setup for my friend Mark!

MARK APPLEYARD: DIGNITY AS THE FOUNDATION OF LOVE

Mark is one of my favorite people in the whole world. He's the OG "Yes. And . . ." guy. You know it—Mark is the friend I call when I have a thought about God that is so good I know it will offend people. "Hey, Mark, what if God is *this* inclusively good?" I'll say. Mark will nod uncomfortably, then grin, "Yes. And. What if He's even better. . . ."

Mark's resounding "Yes. And." invites exploration into the transformative possibilities discovered in the perfect love of God. His unwavering belief in God's goodness and the power of love has profoundly shaped my journey, offering both challenge and comfort in equal measure. I'm deeply grateful for Mark, not just for his wisdom, but for the way his life embodies the very dignity and inclusive love he speaks about—it's a gift to call him a friend.

Regarding this conversation, he has some profound thoughts about our image and likeness. And it starts with dignity.

---

[98] Jason Clark and Derek Turner, hosts, *Rethinking God with Tacos*, podcast, adapted excerpts from "Brian Zahnd / When Everything's on Fire," November 12, 2022, https://www.youtube.com/watch?v=d_j0sESZ4Vg.

> **WHEN YOU HONOR SOMEONE'S DIGNITY, YOU'RE SAYING, 'I SEE THE IMAGE OF GOD IN YOU, AND I'LL PROTECT IT WITH MY ACTIONS.'**

"Dignity is protecting the image of God in someone," he explained. For Mark, inclusion isn't optional; it's the foundation of authentic love. "True love doesn't divide people into categories of worthy and unworthy. If love isn't for everyone, then it's not love—it's something else entirely."

Mark's insights go beyond theory; they demand action and practical demonstration. He shared a powerful story of his ministry renting a house for a struggling woman and her daughter. This family had been caught in a cycle of hardship, with limited resources and no place to turn. "We believed she was worth it," Mark said. "It wasn't about fixing her or solving all her problems overnight. It was about protecting the image of God in her." This act of dignity led to a profound transformation. Over time, the woman began to rebuild her life, gain stability, and find hope for her future. Mark emphasized, "When people feel safe, they're able to open themselves to love—and love is what changes everything."

Mark's approach centers on creating environments where people can experience their inherent worth and value. He believes this isn't just an act of charity; it reflects the Kingdom of God. "Dignity is the spearhead of love," he said. "When you honor someone's dignity, you're saying, 'I see the image of God in you, and I'll protect it with my actions.'" He described this process as creating sacred spaces where love can flourish, unhindered by judgment or precondition.

Mark's theology that LOVE shows no partiality ties seamlessly into his focus on human flourishing. "A human fully alive," he said, "is the clearest revelation of God among us." This idea reframes how we understand our role in the lives of others. By nurturing dignity, we create the conditions for people to enter the fullness of who they were created to be. "That's the power of dignity—it restores and transforms."

Mark's focus on human flourishing also extends to how we see the Church's mission. "The gospel is about creating a world where everyone can flourish," Mark affirmed. "And that starts with seeing people the way God sees them. It's about stepping into the messiness of life, not to fix it but to reveal the beauty within it." He continued, "How often do we reduce people to their circumstances or their worst decisions?"

"Or how they identify," I added. Mark nodded.

"True love refuses to reduce people. It sees beyond and calls out the divine spark in everyone." Mark continued, "If we want to see God's Kingdom on earth, we need to start with the basics. Protect dignity. Love inclusively. And watch how human flourishing reveals the heart of God."[99]

Mark painted a compelling vision of Love's transformative power—one that begins with seeing and honoring the image of God in every person. And one that we, the Church, are continuing to awaken to. And I see that in how my friend, Shawn, pastors.

SHAWN HARNISH: LEADING WITH LOVE

Shawn Harnish is another of my oldest friends. He was a bandmate back when my hair was long, my ear pierced, and my voice given to rhythmic melodies. Shawn is brilliant and always up for better thoughts about God. He's been pastoring for decades now and embodies the kind of pastoral leadership that is rare and refreshing, rooted in humility, authenticity, and an unwavering commitment to love without conditions.

His ability to embrace the messiness of people's lives with compassion and without judgment inspires and reminds me of Jesus's inclusive heart. I admire Shawn not just for his boldness in challenging religious norms but also for the quiet, steadfast way he lives out the truth that no one is beyond the reach of Grace.

He leads a church in Dansville, New York, with a simple yet profound conviction: Jesus doesn't exclude. "It's not my

---

[99] Jason Clark and Derek Turner, hosts, *Rethinking God with Tacos*, podcast, adapted excerpts from "Mark Appleyard / Dignity: The Leading Edge of Love," June 21, 2023, https://www.youtube.com/watch?v=46xpYAMfo0c&list=PLgimV9UoSbAIbXX447Gu_5-kGpLAO_eJO&index=86.

job to decide who's in or out," Shawn shared. "It's my job to love them all."

One way Shawn lives out this conviction is through weddings. For him, they aren't just ceremonies; they're opportunities to reflect God's love. "People are going to get married anyway," he said. "But when they ask a minister, it means something. That's my chance to have a conversation about God's love." He shared a poignant story of officiating a wedding for a couple that many evangelical churches would have turned away. "I marry you before God," he explained. "That moment opened the door for deeper dialogue about faith and grace."

Shawn's approach also extends to funerals, where his focus shifts to those left behind. "Funerals are for the living," he emphasized. As a pastor, he's felt the pressure implicit in the separation paradigm to use the moment to preach an "in or out" message, one that leverages death's seeming finality to misrepresent the measureless infinite reconciling nature of Greater Love. But Shawn doesn't play in that paradigm. "My role is to comfort and love those who are grieving."

This sensitivity to human pain and joy is evident in every aspect of Shawn's ministry. "(I'm) pastoring the whole community," he said. "Love doesn't stop at the church building's walls."[100]

---

100 Jason Clark and Derek Turner, hosts, *Rethinking God with Tacos*, podcast, adapted excerpts from "Shawn Harnish / Unconditional Love," February 16, 2023, https://www.youtube.com/watch?v=-GBl8nDJTmQ&list=PLgimV9UoSbAIbXX447Gu_5-kGpLAO_eJO&index=101.

Shawn's words resonate with Mark's focus on dignity. Both leaders challenge us to see every individual as bearing the image of God, deserving of respect and love. I love Shawn's refusal to draw lines of exclusion and his invitation to reconsider how we live out the gospel in practice.

This sets the stage for my conversation with Eden Jersak and her journey toward inclusivity.

EDEN JERSAK: INCLUSION IN PRACTICE

There's something disarming about how Eden talks about God's measureless love. Listening to her, you get the sense she's lived her theology, not just studied it. She's pastored through the questions that make many uncomfortable and leaned into the tension rather than avoiding it.

Eden is a co-pastor, a relational theologian, and a trusted voice. Her wisdom runs deep, shaped by years of walking through the beauty and messiness of church life. When Eden speaks, I know I'm hearing the heart of someone transformed by the love she extends to others.

When she speaks about God's inclusive love, she's not theorizing; she's testifying.

"We dehumanize people when we put labels on them. When we call someone a sinner, an abomination, or anything less than human, we've already lost the plot. God's love is for every single one of us, no exceptions." I felt the weight of her words. How often have we, the Church, tried to define boundaries that God doesn't seem interested in drawing?

The fact is, God shows no partiality.

I brought up the story of the blind man in John's Gospel. Remember? The disciples asked Jesus, "Who sinned, this man or his parents, that he was born blind?" It's a classic case of dualistic thinking, where *we* are good and *they* are evil. But Jesus flips the script, and I love the Message Bible's interpretation. "You're asking the wrong question. You're looking for someone to blame. There is no such cause-and-effect here. Look instead for what God can do" (John 9:1-3).

"We, the Church, are often asking the wrong question," I said to Eden.

She nodded. "Exactly. We're so quick to measure, to sort people into in and out camps. But Jesus isn't asking those questions. He's not playing the blame game. He's showing us that sin isn't a tool to separate people; it's an opportunity for love to heal and restore."

Eden's church's journey to becoming inclusive and affirming wasn't easy. "I told our leadership team," she shared, 'This is the direction I'm leading (in). If you can't go there with me, I understand, but I'm not pretending to be someone I'm not.' It was a hard conversation, but I think it was necessary. You can't love people halfway."

She then explained how this shift wasn't about ignoring sin but about reframing it. "People ask, 'If we include everyone, are we diminishing God's standards?' But I've seen the opposite. The more we open the doors, the more expansive God's love becomes. It's not about lowering the bar; it's about realizing that God's grace has always been higher than we imagined."

> **WE'VE SPENT TOO MUCH TIME USING SIN AS A LITMUS TEST FOR BELONGING WHEN JESUS USED BELONGING AS THE ENTRY POINT FOR GRACE.**

I brought up the woman caught in adultery, another moment where Jesus upends expectations. The religious leaders were ready to stone her, eager to punish her for her sin. But Jesus? He knelt, wrote in the dust, and asked the crowd to examine themselves. *"Let any one of you who is without sin be the first to throw a stone"* (John 8:7, NIV).

Eden's eyes lit up. "That story is everything. Jesus didn't deny the law. He fulfilled it by showing mercy. He could've condemned her, but instead, He asked her where her accusers went. 'Neither do I condemn you. Go now and leave your life of sin.' He didn't sidestep sin, but He also didn't use it to shame her.

In fact, Jesus removed shame —*"Where are your accusers ... neither will I accuse you"*— before he ever addressed sin —*"now go and sin no more"* (vv. 10-11).

Love first. Always love. That's the ministry model of Jesus, the ministry that transforms.

I think Eden's right. We've spent too much time using sin as a litmus test for belonging when Jesus revealed belonging as an invitation to know Grace. Eden's approach to inclusion is deeply relational. It's about belonging before becoming.

She described the first time someone from the LGBTQ+ community asked to lead communion. "They told me, 'I haven't taken communion in years. I didn't think I was qualified.' That broke me. But sharing that moment with them? It was one of the holiest experiences of my life."

Eden's words linger: "Jesus doesn't need bouncers at the door. He's the one who told us not to pull the weeds because we'll end up uprooting the wheat, too. He's the Sower, scattering seed wildly on all soil, trusting it will be transformed by His unconditional love."

This is the gospel Eden lives out—a love without bounds, a Grace that keeps expanding. And in her words, "God's love isn't about erasing sin; it's about redeeming every part of us."[101] That's the kind of love that changes everything.

A TWENTY-FIRST CENTURY CHURCH

Many Christians who read about the early Church long to return, viewing those first handful of years as the high-water mark.

They weren't—not even close!

As beautifully transformative as She was, the early Church was even more beautifully transformative on the day Peter repented. It was more beautiful after She aligned with Greater Love and welcomed Cornelius, his family, your family, and my family!

---

[101] Jason Clark, hosts, *Rethinking God with Tacos,* podcast, adapted excerpts from "Eden Jersak / A Love That Includes Everyone," March 23, 2023, https://www.youtube.com/watch?v=ZKuV_bCp4Lo.

I'm thankful for Peter. I love how his leadership modeled a heart ever-expanding, and a mind ever open to rethinking, to deconstructing, and reconstructing on the Cornerstone of Greater Love.

Peter didn't always get it right, but oh boy, did he ever knock this moment out of the park! He was a man who repented; a leader whose authority was discovered in his friendship with Jesus.

And I'm encouraged these days because I'm meeting humble Christians, leaders like Peter, who are awakening to union and living as inclusive expressions in every area of their influence.

I believe the Church is amid another Cornelius revelation—a deeper understanding and agreement with what the early Church discovered in Cornelius' house: *there is no partiality in God,* no *us* or *them* in how our Father thinks, no *in* or *out* in His Kingdom, no *for* or *against* in family. Nothing separates us from His all-inclusive love.

As Bono sang, "One Love . . . one life."[102]

As Jesus prayed, *"that they will all be one, just as you and I are one—as you are in me, Father, and I am in you. And may they be in us so that the world will believe you sent me"* (John 17:21, NLT).

We are one, all creation, a family awakening to our union.

These are not the early Church days when only some could know this divine union life. These are twenty-first-century

---

[102] Bono, vocalist, "One" by Paul David Hewson, Adam Clayton, Larry Mullen, Dave Evans, November 18, 1991, track 3 on *Achtung Baby,* Island.

Church days where the measureless revelation that God *shows no partiality* has never been more available.

As it turns out, we're all insiders—every tribe and tongue, all humanity—welcomed sons and daughters, the whole world included in the friendship of the Trinity. As it turns out, the Good News is always more inclusive than we last imagined. [103]

---

103 Jason Clark, excerpts adapted from *Leaving and Finding Jesus*.

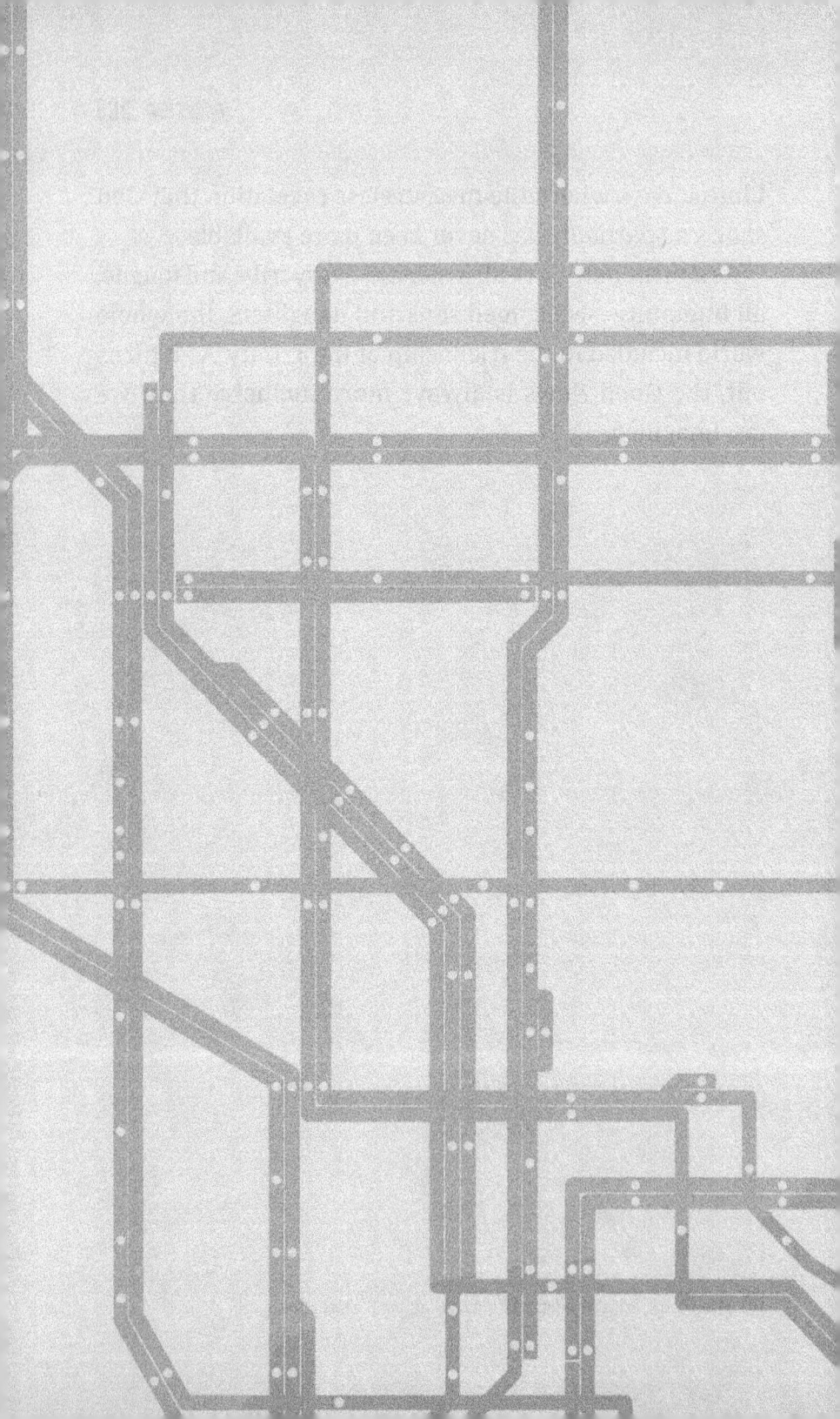

CHAPTER 15

RETHINKING UNIVERSALISM

Unlimited Chips and Salsa

A UNIVERSALIST?

In 2019, I wrote an article titled "Why I Am not a Universalist"[104] about the universal nature of God's love. The article noted how Universalism, as we Western evangelicals tend to think about it, perceives heaven and hell through a deterministic lens.

I wrote:

> To me, our Western mind perceives Universalism as empathetic Calvinism. Instead of predetermining hell, it predetermines heaven. Universalism, when viewed through this dualistic lens, perceives heaven and hell as reward and punishment.
>
> In my view, a conversation about Universalism in that context is pointless because the God Jesus

---
104 Jason Clark, "What I Am not a Universalist," unpublished article, 2019.

> *revealed doesn't do dualism or punishment. Such a conversation would be like two flat-earthers discussing where the earth ends—ultimately fruitless because the earth isn't flat.*
>
> *C.S. Lewis once suggested in his book, A Grief Observed, that many of our God questions are like asking, "How many hours are in a mile, or whether yellow is square or round? Probably half the questions we ask, half our great theological and metaphysical problems, are like that."*[105]

The article went on to note the universal reconciling nature of God's measureless love revealed through Jesus at the cross:

> *He died and rose. And when He did, all creation—all humanity—rose with Him. At the cross, Jesus exposed the lie of distance and separation. He revealed that He will never leave or forsake us. His love is measureless, always good, ultimately reconciling, doesn't deviate to the left or the right, and will never fail us, not in this life or the next."*[106]

Do you know what's so like a relational theologian?

In writing to reveal love, I never considered the "eternal" reward and punishment question my article might raise—at least, not until a young woman sincerely asked about it on Facebook.

"So, can we be saved after we die?" she queried.

---
105 C.S. Lewis, *A Grief Observed* (San Francisco, CA: HarperOne, 2009).
106 Jason Clark, "What I Am not a Universalist," unpublished article, 2019.

Since I had left a punishing God long ago, and maybe because I was still on my first cup of coffee, I responded to her question. But I didn't just respond. I went a step further. I naively posted my response as the weekly article on our online magazine at afamilystory.org under the eye-catching title my editor came up with, *Does Hell Exist?*[107]

Then, I went about my life as though nothing had changed. Two weeks later, because of that article, my family and I were kicked out of our church.

Rough, right? Don't worry, we're OK. That was years ago, around the time I started the podcast, actually. If you are curious about what happened, I wrote more in my book, *Leaving and Finding Jesus*,[108] but I note the experience here to acknowledge the price that's often paid to having better thoughts about God's love than the last best thoughts you've had. Not just the price my family and I've paid, but more so, the price paid by the voices I highlight in this book, and specifically this chapter. There are so many who have been willing to 'lay down their lives' for the glorious message of Greater Love and our face-to-face union with Father, Son, and Holy Spirit.

Even though this subject ruffles feathers—and that's putting it lightly—I'm grateful for those unwilling to live with the disparity of a universal conviction about our inclusion in Adam's fall that doesn't equally translate to our inclusion in Christ's resurrection.

---

[107] Jason Clark, "Does Hell Exist," *A Family Story*, October 30, 2019, https://afamilystory.org/2019/10/does-hell-exist/.
[108] Jason Clark, *Leaving and Finding Jesus*.

Let's be honest: every Christian is a universalist. We've been raised to believe that Adam's sin is a universal birthright while at the same time ignoring the universal reality that God in Christ reconciled the world (that's all of us) to Himself, not counting our sins against us.

We've lost the gospel of Jesus, the gospel of Grace.

But the good news is that Jesus is brilliant at restoration.[109]

DAVID ARTMAN: GRACE SAVES ALL

Talking with David Artman about Christian Universalism felt like stepping into a deeper understanding of Grace's unrelenting embrace. David is brilliantly articulate. He invites you into a deeper, more expansive understanding of God's love. His unwavering belief in the inclusive, restorative nature of grace resonates deeply, not just because of his theological insights but because of the authenticity and compassion he brings to every conversation. David is a Tambourine Man, and I walked away from our talk not only inspired by his conviction but grateful for the clarity and hope he offers in a world that desperately needs both.

David articulates so clearly that at the heart of Christian Universalism is union—the unbreakable, unconditional connection between God and all of creation. This message dismantles fear and reframes our faith not around exclusion or punishment but around an ever-expanding circle of divine love—the divine Trinitarian dance.

---

[109] Jason Clark, excerpts adapted from *Leaving and Finding Jesus*.

David doesn't mince words. "Grace that only potentially saves isn't Grace at all. If Grace saves, then it must save all, or else we're back to a transactional system that leaves some behind. I'm not interested in a Grace that can fail." That hit squarely.

> **IF WE CAN IMAGINE GOD DOING LESS, THEN WE'VE MISUNDERSTOOD THE HEART OF THE FATHER.**

Grace doesn't negotiate. It's not a contract—it's a covenant, one that God refuses to break.

At the center of Christian Universalism is the image of God as the ultimate loving parent. "I would never give up on one of my children, no matter what. And I refuse to believe I'm a better parent than God. If we can imagine God doing less, then we've misunderstood the heart of the Father." That's the kind of relational theology that confronts dualistic certainty with the Truth that sets us free—God is Love. And it just makes sense. So many have grown tired of doing mental gymnastics around what good means when it's simple— there is no shadow of turning in the love of our Father (see James 1:17).

David doesn't sidestep the tough stuff, like hell. But even here, union is the through-line. "If hell exists eternally, then evil has the last word, not Grace. I'm convinced the goodness of God will ultimately undo every sorrow, heal every wound, and bring every lost soul home."

For David, the idea of eternal separation doesn't hold up against the weight of God's goodness. It's not just a theological argument—it's a declaration of who God is: relentlessly good, endlessly loving, and unwavering in His pursuit of every heart.

David roots Christian Universalism in history. "This isn't some new idea. The earliest Church fathers spoke of universal reconciliation with hope and certainty. Somewhere along the way, we lost that voice—but I believe it's time to recover it." That recovery is about reawakening to the relational truth that we belong. All of us. We always have.

"Grace isn't transactional. It's not about what we do or don't do. Grace is inclusive by nature. It saves, and it saves everyone." David said, and my heart burned. *It's not Grace if it's selective. It's not love if it leaves anyone out.* I thought.

David drew a clear line between Christian Universalism and secular universalism, emphasizing the central role of Jesus in the former. "Christian Universalism isn't just a blanket statement that everyone gets in," David explained. "It's about the belief that God's love, as revealed in Jesus Christ, will ultimately reconcile all of creation."

While secular universalism suggests an impersonal, generalized inclusivity, Christian Universalism is rooted deeply in the relational nature of God. "The difference is that Christian Universalism sees Jesus at the center," he said. "It's not just that everyone is saved, it's that everyone is saved through Christ."

This Christ-centered focus distinguishes Christian Universalism from broader, more abstract notions of universal acceptance. "I'm not advocating for a vague, spiritual inclusivity," David clarified. "I'm talking about the transformative power of God's Grace through Jesus, which will ultimately bring every heart home." It's a hope anchored in both history and relationship, not just a generic optimism.

"Christian Universalism isn't about denying the need for salvation or judgment." David continued, "It's about recognizing that God's judgment is restorative, not punitive. It's about believing God's love will have the final word, bringing even the most lost home." It's not about erasing accountability; it's about redefining what God's justice looks like through the lens of love.

I loved how David kept coming back to the simplicity of Grace. "Grace isn't complicated. It's not a puzzle to solve or a riddle to crack. Grace is the unwavering, unrelenting love of God that refuses to let us go. That's the story I'm telling." And honestly, isn't that the story we all need to hear?

"Once we see God clearly, we're not losing our freedom by choosing Him. We're finally free to make the only choice that makes sense—to come home to love." That's the beauty of Christian Universalism. It's not about coercion. It's about clarity. *"We love because He first loved"* (1 John 4:19). Thus, the more we experience and know LOVE, the more we choose love. How could we choose anything else?

As we wrapped up, David left us with this: "If God's love is limitless and Grace is real, then no one is beyond redemption. That's the hope we carry."[110]

It's also the hope I carry—a hope that sees every person as part of the family, every story as part of the larger story of Grace, and every heart as already embraced by a God who is restoring all things.

JOHN CHAFFEE: THE RESTORATION OF ALL THINGS

John Chaffee is a thoughtful, deeply authentic voice in the evolving conversation about faith, spirituality, and the restoration of all things. I admire his vulnerability, willingness to wrestle with hard questions, and how his life radiates the hope and beauty of a gospel that's bigger and better than we've been told.

> **WE'VE BEEN HANDED A GOSPEL THAT'S TRIBAL AND EXCLUSIVE, BUT THE TRUTH IS, THE GOSPEL IS RADICALLY INCLUSIVE.**

---

110 Jason Clark and Derek Turner, hosts, *Rethinking God with Tacos*, podcast, adapted xcerpts from "David Artman / The Necessity of Christian Universalism," December 6, 2023, https://www.youtube.com/watch?v=Fv2QdR0DUrw&list=PLgimV9UoSbAIbXX447Gu_5-kGpLAO_eJO&index=61.

Talking with John Chaffee about *Apokatastasis*—the restoration of all things—is like taking a deep breath of fresh morning air.

The idea that God is actively, relentlessly working to reconcile and renew all creation, that He is in the business of restoring all things? I think it's the heartbeat of the gospel. And at the center of it all, of course, is *union*.

John didn't hesitate when I brought it up. "*Apokatastasis* is the belief that everything and everyone will be restored, reconciled, and renewed," he said. "It's not just about people—it's about all of creation. Nothing is left out."

John continued, "We've been handed a gospel that's tribal and exclusive, but the truth is, the gospel is radically inclusive. It's about the restoration of everyone, everywhere, from everything."

The word *all* is everywhere in Scripture, John noted. "Peter talks about the 'restoration of all things, and Paul says, 'In Christ, all will be made alive.'"

And it's not just Peter and Paul. John connected the dots to Church history, too. "Julian of Norwich said, 'All will be well, and all manner of things will be well.' The early Church fathers talked about the reconciliation of everything. This isn't some new idea—it's been here the whole time. We just forgot."[111]

What John was talking about—it's a lived reality. A gospel that refuses to leave anyone behind. A gospel that sees every

---

[111] Jason Clark and Derek Turner, hosts, *Rethinking God with Tacos,* podcast, adapted excerpts from "John Chaffee / The Restoration of All Things," September 6, 2023, https://www.youtube.com/watch?v=0B_xk4_0sKQ.

broken thing, every fractured relationship, and says, *"That, too, will be made whole."*

JOHN CROWDER AND BILL VANDERBUSH: REDISCOVERING INCLUSION

The conversation with John Crowder and Bill Vanderbush was nothing short of electric—not just because of their insights but also because of the undercurrent that ran through every word: union.

Universal reconciliation was the topic.

John jumped right in with his signature blend of humor and theological depth. "Look, we're not talking about some hippie free-for-all where anything goes. We're talking about the cosmic reality of what Jesus accomplished. He didn't come to give us a better religion. He came to reveal our union with the Father."

> **THE CALVINIST SAYS GOD CAN SAVE EVERYONE BUT DOESN'T WANT TO. THE ARMINIAN SAYS GOD WANTS TO SAVE EVERYONE BUT CAN'T. BOTH MISS THE MARK.**

Bill's approach was equally compelling but carried a pastoral tone. "Universalism speaks to the scope of the finished work, which I agree with. But reconciliation is about relationship. It's about sonship. It's about how we live in light of what's been done." This distinction sets the stage for a rich exploration of how universal reconciliation flows directly from our union with Christ.

John shared his journey candidly. "For years, I called myself a hopeful universalist. I wanted to believe in the reconciliation of all things, but I hesitated to fully embrace it because it felt like crossing a line from mystery to dogma." But the hesitation didn't last. "Eventually, I realized if God wants to save everyone and He's sovereign, then He will save everyone. To think otherwise is to question either His will or His power."

Bill reflected on his theological shifts. "I grew up Arminian. Then I explored Calvinism because, let's face it, they loved to argue, and I loved a good debate. But neither framework satisfied my growing awareness of God's relational nature." He paused, then added, "The Calvinist says God can save everyone but doesn't want to. The Arminian says God wants to save everyone but can't. Both miss the mark."

The conversation circled back to union. "In him, we live and move and have our being," John quoted from Acts 17:28 (NIV). "Humanity's inclusion in Christ is not conditional or partial. This isn't about a distant God deciding not to burn people. This is about a God who, through the incarnation, brought all of humanity into intimate relationship with Himself."

Bill echoed that sentiment but brought it to the personal level. "We've made salvation a commodity—something you have to earn or possess. But Jesus is salvation. He is the divine-human glue that holds all things together." That image—Jesus as the glue—that's the stuff.

John wasn't shy, which, if you know John, isn't surprising. He challenged the Western evangelical views of hell that we are familiar with. "As George McDonald wrote, 'Love loves unto purity.'[112] God's fire isn't punitive; it's purifying." John leaned in, "We're all salted with fire, but that fire is the love of God."

I finally got a word in. "The gospel isn't about a place; it's about a person. We've elevated the fall of Adam above the resurrection of Christ."

Bill nodded, "That's the real heresy." His words were a wake-up call, a reminder that the focus of our faith should always be on Jesus and His work.

GOD'S LOVE WILL OUTLAST OUR REBELLION. HE'S IN THIS FOR THE LONG HAUL.

---

[112] George MacDonald, *Unspoken Sermons* (CreateSpace Independent Publishing Platform, 2018).

As we dug into the historical roots of these ideas, John highlighted the early Church's understanding of salvation. "The first 500 years of Christianity were dominated by theologians who understood salvation as a cosmic victory. Gregory of Nyssa, Origen, Athanasius—these guys weren't preaching a God who needed blood to appease His wrath. They preached a God who, through Christ, reconciled all of creation."

Bill nodded again. "We're not inventing new theology here. We're rediscovering what was lost." That's the heart of it. This isn't some newfangled doctrine but a return to the roots of the faith, a recovery of truths that had been buried under layers of fear and misunderstanding.

This conversation was such a powerful invitation to the fullness of the gospel—a message that is as cosmic as it is personal, transformative, and inclusive. "The gospel is not about who gets in or out; it's about who we already are in Christ. This is the good news the world has been longing to hear."

Bill added, "God's love will outlast our rebellion. He's in this for the long haul."[113]

I grinned and closed the conversation with, "Love is the long game."

That phrase is a family saying, and the universal Truth I am daily growing sure in.

---

113 Jason Clark, host, *Rethinking God with Tacos*, podcast, adapted excerpts from "John Crowder / The Creator, Sustainer and Reconciler of ALL THINGS with Bill Vanderbush," February 11, 2025, https://www.youtube.com/watch?v=xDn5nCexvW0&list=PLgimV9UoSb AIbXX447Gu_5-kGpLAO_eJO&index=5.

THE LONG GAME OF LOVE

Years ago, my wife, Karen, and I visited with friends hosting a leader's weekend. At one point, the host pulled me aside to introduce me to his friend.

With a playful smile, he said, "Jason, I want to introduce you to my other universal reconciliationist friend."

I laughed. I thought I'd been more careful. Plus, that kinda label gets ya kicked out of churches.

Like Crowder, I called myself a hopeful universalist for years. I wanted to believe in the reconciliation of all things, but I hesitated to fully embrace it.

But when my friend used that term to introduce me, I suddenly realized it was true. I'd traveled too far into the measureless nature of Love not to embrace the joy and wonder of universal reconciliation fully.

I am growing ever more sure that God is Love, that the cosmic reality of Christ's work is union, and that universal reconciliation is the unveiling of humanity's union with God, rooted in Christ's finished work and discovered in the Trinity's relentless, transforming kindness.

Yep, the long game.

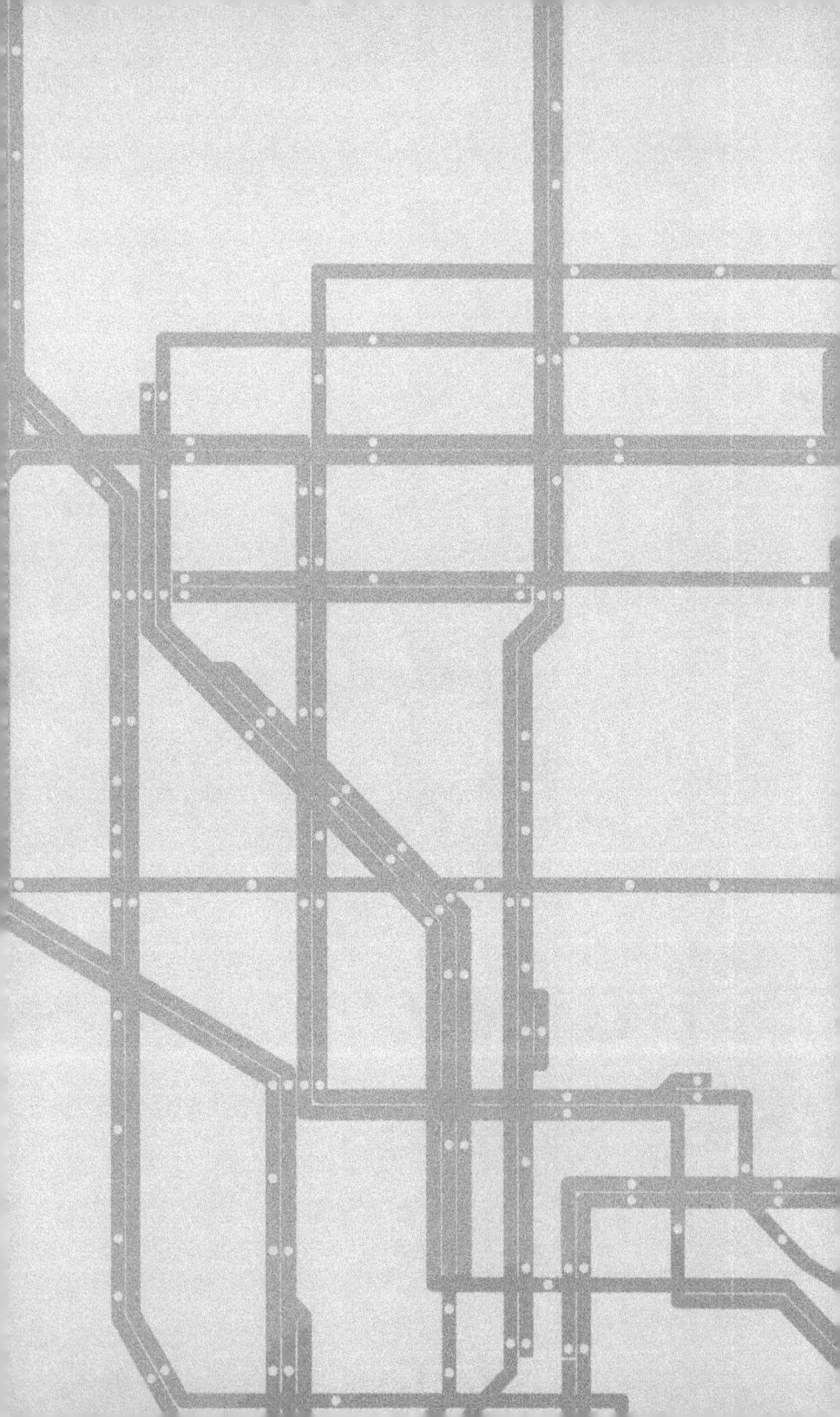

CHAPTER 16

RETHINKING HELL

Nacho Eternal Punishment

DAMON THOMPSON: THE REFORMATION OF THEOLOGY THROUGH UNION

If there's one thing I've learned in the last ten years, it's that questioning our Western understanding of hell makes many Christians mad. "That'll get you in trouble quick, won't it?" Damon Thompson said, laughing. "Yeah, it will," I responded, laughing as well. Damon continued, "But if we're serious about reformation in theology, if we're really committed to union, then we've got to be willing to go there."

Damon is a revelatory voice in this unfolding reformation, and I feel a deep kinship with him, like a long-lost brother in the same current of grace, carrying the same heart for union, goodness, and the undiluted gospel of Jesus. I was so encouraged by his friendship and the jingle-jangle insights in our podcast conversation.

"When you start to see God as pure light—when you realize that in Him there is no trace of darkness—it changes everything. Including how we view hell." Damon put it straight: "Whatever I don't allow the Holy Spirit to challenge is evidence to me that He's not Lord in that area." And that's where the real work begins. Are we brave enough to let Greater Love challenge the doctrines we've held sacred? Even the ones that feel untouchable?

> **CAN WE HOLD SPACE FOR MYSTERY, FOR QUESTIONS, FOR THE IDEA THAT MAYBE—JUST MAYBE—HELL ISN'T WHAT WE THOUGHT IT WAS?**

For both Damon and me, that journey started with rethinking the nature of God through the lens of Jesus. "I had learned of a retributive God," Damon said. "And I had preached a retributive God and been successful doing it." But success doesn't equal truth. When "beloved identity," or our oneness with Christ, becomes our God lens, we start to see the cracks in the old foundations. "We learned to torment people with fear of hell and then call that repentance, when only goodness can bring you to authentic rethinking."

Damon shared how he's got a book on his shelf with "four leading theologians that all have a different interpretation of what hell actually is." And the question he posed is the one that sticks: "Can you be okay with that?" Can we hold space for mystery, for questions, for the idea that maybe—just maybe—hell isn't what we thought it was?

"For the theology to change, there's going to have to be some flex in the doctrinal certitude." He continued. And that's the challenge. We were raised in systems that valued certainty over trust and control over mystery, but Greater Love doesn't work that way.

This union reformation isn't about getting all the answers right. It's about discovering the One who holds us in perfect love, even in our questions. "Anxiety serves as a witness that we've maintained a perverted relationship with time," Damon said. And in that same way, fear—especially fear of hell—reveals a perverted understanding of God's nature.

Damon continued by revealing the kindness of God that settles and transforms us. "I am the beloved of the Father, not just loved by the Father, but loved with the same measure of love that the Father has for His beloved Son Jesus."[114] My heart burst at this! This is the undiluted gospel— that we are loved and becoming love!

It's the *original* message that we have forgotten. Now, we're remembering. We're awakening.

We are growing sure in the truth that "God is pure light, and in Him there is no trace of darkness whatsoever" (1 John 1:5, author paraphrase). And we are shining that light into our theology, even into our thoughts about hell.

---

114 Jason Clark, host, *Rethinking God with Tacos,* podcast, adapted excerpts from "Damon Thompson / Awakening to Beloved Identity," February 3, 2025, https://www.youtube.com/watch?v=mCbyH9JHwq0&list=PLgimV9UoSbAIbXX447Gu_5-kGpLAO_eJO&index=6.

THOMAS JAY OORD AND KEITH GILES: HELL, RECONCILIATION, AND THE LOGIC OF LOVE

Derek and I loved our conversation with Thomas Jay Oord and Keith Giles, two brilliant fellas who've spent years dismantling the fiery retributive narratives many of us were handed about hell.

I've already introduced Tom, but Keith is no stranger. He is a rogue theologian with a knack for dismantling religious constructs, always circling back to the radical, self-giving love of Jesus. A former pastor who walked away from the pulpit to live out the gospel among the marginalized, he writes with a mix of sharp insight, deep compassion, and just the right amount of rebellious fire.

And let me tell you, this conversation had just the right amount of that fire. It was an invitation into something deeper, something more beautiful. As Tom puts it, "the logic of love!"

Our conversation focused on a book by Chad Bahl that Tom and Keith contributed to, *Deconstructing Hell*.[115] And that's what we did.

Growing up, hell was the backdrop of every altar call. It was the unspoken (or sometimes very spoken) reason we "accepted Jesus into our hearts." The idea of eternal conscious torment was baked into the very foundation of our faith structures.

Keith kicked things off by addressing a common misconception in the Church. "It was important to me to write a

---
115 Chad Bahl, *Deconstructing Hell: Open and Relational Responses to the Doctrine of Eternal Conscious Torment* (Fairview Shores, FL: SacraSage Press, 2023).

chapter where I could make the case that those who reject eternal conscious torment do so based on Scripture." Keith's chapter, "Constructing a Biblical Theology of Hell: The Case for Universal Restoration,"[116] dives into Scripture. "I found like seventy-six verses in support of universal reconciliation," he said. For instance, Philippians 2:10-11 (NIV): "That at the name of Jesus every knee should bow, in heaven and on earth and under the earth, and every tongue acknowledge that Jesus Christ is Lord, to the glory of God the Father." This passage suggests a willing and joyful confession rather than forced submission, pointing to a future where all are reconciled to God.

Then there's one of my favorites, 1 Corinthians 15:22 (NIV): "For as in Adam all die, so in Christ all will be made alive." Most of us were raised with a disingenuous universal perspective regarding that verse. We believed *all* are "in Adam." But completely ignored the word *all* when it came to being in Christ. If all humanity inherited death through Adam, then how much more will all experience life through Christ? This is the universal scope of reconciliation.

And this confronts the distorted retributive view of hell.

Tom's chapter, "God's Glory as Relentless Love," introduces a fourth view on hell, something he calls *relentless love*.[117] "The logic of love leads me to reject the idea that God condemns anyone to everlasting punishment," he said. And that's the heartbeat of this relational theology—love that

---

[116] Keith Giles, "Constructing a Biblical Theology of Hell: The Case for Universal Restoration," in *Deconstructing Hell: Open and Relational Responses to the Doctrine of Eternal Conscious Torment* (SacraSage Press, 2023).
[117] Tom Oord, "God's Glory as Relentless Love," in *Deconstructing Hell: Open and Relational Responses to the Doctrine of Eternal Conscious Torment* (SacraSage Press, 2023).

doesn't give up, love that pursues us even beyond death, a Greater Love that never turns away.

But here's where it gets really good. Both Keith and Tom agree that hell isn't about retributive justice. It's not about God getting His pound of flesh. Instead, they see hell—if you even want to call it that—as part of a restorative process. Keith put it this way: "Paul gives this beautiful analogy, that all are salted with fire, that all of us pass through the fire. It's a metaphor. It's not literal fire." He continued, "It's fire as a metaphor for purification, a cleansing, a healing, a restorative process."

This isn't about scaring people into heaven. It's about inviting us into union with God. Tom said it best: "There are natural negative consequences that come from sin. . . . but natural negative consequences are different from divine punishment." And that's a critical distinction. Sin has its own fallout, sure, but that's not the same as God actively inflicting suffering on His creation.

Now, let's address the elephant in the room—or maybe the Hitler in the room. Because every time you bring up universal reconciliation, someone inevitably asks, "Does Hitler go to heaven?" Keith tackled this head-on: "The historical doctrine of universal reconciliation doesn't teach that there's no hell. It actually teaches the opposite. It says that everybody goes through the fire." That includes Hitler, Mother Teresa, you, and me. But again: "The fire is a metaphor for purification, a cleansing . . . a restorative justice, not a retributive justice."

JESUS DOESN'T JUST SAVE US FROM SOMETHING—HE SAVES US FOR SOMETHING.

Tom chimed in, agreeing that transformation doesn't stop at death. "Hitler continues to engage God's love in the afterlife. And there'll be transformation that occurs *as* he cooperates with God's love."

What's heartbreaking is how deeply ingrained the fear of hell is in our religious psyche. Keith reflected, "For a very long time, this is pretty much how people joined the club—raise your hand if you don't want to burn in hell for eternity." But if that's the foundation of your faith, what happens when you start to question it? Keith didn't shy away from this: "If somebody begins to suggest that, well, there is no (retributive) hell, then it rattles the whole thing because we have built Christianity in America on the foundation that Jesus is pretty much only good for getting your butt out of hell."

But here's the truth we kept circling back to: Jesus didn't come to save us from a cosmic torture chamber. He came to restore us to union with God. Keith said, "Jesus doesn't just save us *from* something—He saves us *for* something. And that something is restoration, wholeness, and communion with God."

Tom summed it up perfectly: "If love took the lead, I could have an intellectually consistent view of God and how life seems to work." And that's what it all boils down to. Not fear. Not punishment. But love—relentless, restorative, and always awakening to union.

What I loved about this conversation is that it's being had worldwide. The Church is reimagining hell through a Christological lens, or as Tom says, "the logic of love," — what it means to be in relationship with God and with each other. This means hell is not seen as some punishing end, but as part of the journey toward healing, transformation, and the discovery of our union because, as Keith and Tom reminded us, LOVE always has the final word.

And this is where Jeff Turner enters the conversation. He is pretty good at communicating this final word.

JEFF TURNER: BEYOND HELL AND PENAL SUBSTITUTION

Sitting across from Jeff, you immediately sense his intensity—an earnestness born from wrestling through topics most avoid. Jeff is a theological explorer with the soul of a mystic, unafraid to question the structures that once defined his faith and brave enough to let them burn in pursuit of a truer, more beautiful gospel. He's a Tambourine Man through and through. I respect him deeply—not just for his intellect and insight but for his willingness to walk through the fire of deconstruction and come out the other side, trading fear for a faith rooted in love.

Our conversation ventured into the depths of hell, penal substitutionary atonement, and how these doctrines distort our image of God.

"I grew up in a tradition where hell was the ultimate leverage," Jeff began. "I could preach a hell message that would make Jonathan Edwards' *Sinners in the Hands of an Angry God*[118] look like a Mother's Day sermon." He laughed. I laughed too because I've read Jeff's book, *Saints in the Arms of a Happy God*[119], and the transformation is stark and beautiful.

> **WE WERE TOLD THAT THE CROSS CHANGED GOD'S MIND ABOUT US, BUT WHAT KIND OF LOVE REQUIRES BLOOD TO BE SATISFIED?**

Jeff described how his theology once tethered God's love to conditions. "Desperation was the hallmark of my spirituality," he admitted. "We were taught that being hungry and desperate for God was the pinnacle of faith, but it was like chasing a wisp of air. You never got there."

His unraveling began with questioning penal substitutionary atonement. "The idea that God required the violent

---
[118] Jonathan Edwards, *Sinners in the Hands of an Angry God* (New Kensington, PA: Whitaker House, 1997).
[119] Jeff Turner, *Saints in the Arms of a Happy God.*

death of His Son to forgive humanity? It never sat right with me," Jeff explained. "We were told that the cross changed God's mind about us, but what kind of love requires blood to be satisfied?"

This realization transformed Jeff's understanding. "The cross wasn't about changing God's disposition toward humanity; it was about revealing the unchanging nature of God's love. God wasn't punishing Jesus; He was in Christ, reconciling the world to Himself."

This revelation eventually led to Jeff rethinking how we, the Western Evangelical expression oof Christianity, have understood hell. "The God who needs hell to assert His justice is not the God revealed in Jesus," he said. "If love keeps no record of wrongs, as Paul says, then how can eternal torment be part of the equation?" Jeff realized that hell as he once understood it was a projection of fear, not the heart of the Father.

He shared a turning point: "I remember laying all my theology on the altar and saying, 'God, burn it up. If nothing remains, then none of it was worth keeping.' That's when love began to flood my life in ways I'd never known."

Jeff's analogy struck deep: "It's like the veil in the temple. When Jesus cried, 'My God, My God, why have You forsaken Me?' He wasn't declaring God's absence; He was exposing the gods we've made in our own image."

As our conversation closed, Jeff's parting thought resonated: "The gospel isn't about escaping hell or satisfying God's wrath. It's about unveiling the love that has been with us all along. The cross wasn't the price of admission; it was the revelation of our inclusion."[120]

And John Crowder may be the best at communicating this truth.

JOHN CROWDER: HELL REFRAMED

Hell, often, the elephant in the room of Western Christianity, is not about fear but love. John unpacked his thoughts regarding hell, offering a hopeful, restorative perspective that challenges Evangelical paradigms.

"The problem with the Western Church is this separation thinking," John began. "It's the root of the fall, this idea that we are separate from Jesus." This separation theology distorts our understanding of God's character. Hell, commonly framed as the ultimate separation, is thus a misconception. "Union is considered heresy today, while separation is twisted into orthodoxy," John explained.

> **HELL IS THE DISTORTION OF THE HUMAN CONDITION, NOT GOD SEPARATING HIMSELF FROM US.**

---

[120] Jason Clark, host, *Rethinking God with Tacos*, podcast, excerpts from "Jeff Turner / The Atheistic Theist," August 8, 2024, https://www.youtube.com/watch?v=MMDkyWsXcQY.

What if hell is not a place where God turns His back on sinners but a condition of the human heart? "We think of hell as this cosmic punishment chamber, but what we're really dealing with is the human condition." John reminded us that "The cross was not about divine abandonment but about restoration. "Jesus was healing the human race. He was curing our human condition, stepping into the depths of our depravity and pulling us out the other side as a new creation."

It's worth repeating. "Jesus wasn't healing God's view of humanity; He was healing humanity itself."

John continued, "Hell is the distortion of the human condition, not God separating Himself from us." Separation is an illusion. But if we participate in it, then, as John noted, "hell becomes our self-imposed exile—a refusal to embrace the union already established by God."[121]

And this sets up my friend, Jamie Englehart.

THE MYSTERY HIDDEN FROM THE AGES IS NOT CHRIST TO YOU; IT'S CHRIST IN YOU.

---

[121] Jason Clark, host, *Rethinking God with Tacos,* podcast, adapted excerpts from excerpts from "John Crowder / The Creator & Sustainer of All Things" February 11, 2025, https://www.youtube.com/watch?v=xDn5nCexvW0.

BISHOP JAMIE ENGLEHART: AWAKENING TO UNION

Jamie Englehart is a connector, and every conversation we have is the relational deep end. He is a brilliant communicator, theologically rich, thought-provoking, and he emphasizes the inclusive love of God. He personally knows Grace and Wisdom and has been "a tambourine and two weeks ahead for years." I love him and his thoughts on hell because they center on a profound reality of union with Christ—a truth that transforms our perception of darkness, separation, and redemption.

"The mystery hidden from the ages is not Christ to you; it's Christ in you," he explained. This mystery is not something that must be earned or even received—it is a reality that has always existed.

"Hell is rooted in unbelief." Jamie's statement echoed Crowder's thoughts. Hell is the self-imposed exile, where we reject the truth of our inclusion and union with God.

I jumped into the conversation with Jesus's words in Matthew 6:23 (NIV): "But if your eyes are unhealthy, your whole body will be full of darkness. If then the light within you is darkness, how great is that darkness!"

Whenever I quote that scripture, I follow up with the question, "Where is the Light?" This conversation was no different, but Jamie was way ahead of me and grinned. "Within you," he said before I could finish the question.

The Light has always been within you, even if how you perceived it has been distorted.

Yes! It seems our thoughts and perceptions don't change the nature of Light nor its inhabitation. Even if we perceive the Light within us as darkness, it remains Light and remains within us. That's because nothing separates us from the Love of God, or in this case, Light—and if there is no separation between God and humanity, then the question isn't, "Is the Light within us?" Rather, it's, "How do we perceive it?"

What if hell has nothing to do with getting the Light into us but everything to do with our perception of the finished work of the cross—His reconciling love? I shared as much with Jamie.

He took the ball and ran. "When Jesus said, 'It is finished,' all slavery to sin was dealt with," he emphasized. The cross was not about changing God's mind about humanity but about revealing humanity's identity in Christ. Yet many still live as though enslaved, bound by false narratives of separation and fear."

Jamie spoke to this with a striking analogy that compared awakening to the Light within us to the experience of slaves after the Emancipation Proclamation. "Many didn't know they were free, or they couldn't believe it because they'd lived as slaves for so long," he said. In the same way, many live as though separated from God, not realizing the freedom and union that has already been accomplished.

"When I see someone struggling, I no longer see them as distant from God. I see the Light in them, waiting to be unveiled." This perspective shifts the focus from judgment to restoration, from fear to love—on Earth as it is in Heaven!

For Jamie, the gospel invitation is not about getting people into heaven but about awakening them to the reality that heaven is already within them. "The Kingdom of God is within you," he said with conviction.

Jamie's closing thoughts encapsulated the heart of this union revelation: "Hell isn't the point; union is the reality. The gospel isn't about escaping darkness; it's about awakening to the light."[122] This awakening calls us to see beyond the illusions of separation and embrace the truth of Christ in us—a truth that transforms not only how we see God but how we live in the world. By reframing hell as a state of unbelief and union as the ultimate reality, Jamie offered a transformative perspective on the nature of divine Love and redemption.

BRYANT SPRATLIN: THE THIRD OPTION

Bryant Spratlin is a friend, a man of wisdom, humility, and relentless pursuit of God's goodness. He refuses to settle for easy answers and instead leans into the mystery of love and restoration. I love him, respect his journey, his courage to rethink, and how he embodies love.

Sitting with Bryant, you sense that every word he speaks is born from a place of deep reflection and lived experience. His perspective on hell, reframed through what he calls "the third option."

"The third option," Bryant began, "is union. It is God in Christ reconciling the world to himself." This phrase became a recurring motif, anchoring his theology and life philosophy. For Bryant, the traditional binary framework of

---

[122] Jason Clark, host, *Rethinking God with Tacos,* podcast, adapted excerpts from excerpts from "Bishop Jamie Englehart / Epignosis — A Deeper, More Personal, & Experiential Knowledge," April 3, 2024, https://www.youtube.com/watch?v=LstslzGfWYg.

heaven and hell as eternal destinations misses the deeper truth. "It's so easy to get trapped in this back-and-forth dualistic thing," he said. "We live in this dynamic of this either-or type of world."

Reflecting on the story of the woman caught in adultery, Bryant described how it encapsulates Jesus's wisdom and compassion. "It seems like Jesus is given two options: stone the woman and no longer be a friend of sinners, or say, 'Don't stone her,' and be looked at as a false teacher. But instead, he's brilliant—full of wisdom—and provides a third option." Bryant explained how Jesus, while disqualifying others from casting stones, uniquely qualified himself as sinless but chose not to throw one. "To me, it began this journey of, 'OK, there's always a third option, a (Christological) way of looking at things.'"

I agreed and added. "This third way is union, *and* it is always restorative."

"What is the purpose of hell? Is hell torment and eternal, or is hell redemptive and restorative?" Bryant asked and answered, "If everything that God does has to be redemptive, then I have to see hell—even if I can't understand it—as redemptive." At first, this realization, he admitted, wasn't easy. Only after he began to think relationally in the context of parenting did it truly begin to land.

Parenting is a surefire way to discover relational theology. I thought, smiling.

Being a dad became a profound lens through which Bryant experienced God's love. He recounted a pivotal moment with his young daughter: "She was angry at me because she believed a lie about me, something I absolutely had not done. I remember getting below her, on my knees, even lower than her eye level, and looking into her eyes. I apologized for how I hurt her, even knowing I'd done nothing wrong. That's what was needed in the moment to reestablish heart connection."

> **THE THIRD OPTION IS LITERALLY A PARADIGM SHIFT. IT'S AN INVITATION TO STEP AWAY FROM THE KNOWLEDGE OF GOOD AND EVIL AND INTO THE 'IT IS VERY GOOD' ORIGINAL DESIGN.**

This interaction transformed his understanding of how God relates to us. "If I would do that as a father, then why would I think God wouldn't do that? I see it throughout Scripture and my own life—God stooping even below us to lock eyes with us."

This makes my heart swell—it's the gospel.

The third option is an invitation to embrace grace and reject dualistic thinking. "The third option is literally a paradigm shift. It's an invitation to step away from the knowledge of good and evil and into the 'it is very good' original design."[123]

"Come on, man!" I said.

PETER HIETT: THE FIRE THAT RECONCILES

Peter is a bold and kind voice who has challenged the evangelical doctrines with a compelling vision of God's relentless, reconciling love. I deeply respect his courage, wisdom, and humor—his pastoral teaching is like a breath of fresh air, inviting us to see God as infinitely better than we ever imagined. And he has paid a high price to address our religious infatuation with a retributive perspective regarding hell.

> **AT THE END, DEATH AND HADES ARE THROWN INTO THE LAKE OF FIRE. DEATH IS NO MORE. THAT MEANS HADES COMES TO AN END."**

Derek was with me in this conversation, and we got right to the point. Hell is not the separation from God that many in the West imagine, but rather the failure to perceive His relentless presence and love. "Even if you make your bed in Sheol (death, the grave, hell), He's there," Peter asserted,

---
[123] Jason Clark, host, *Rethinking God with Tacos,* podcast, adapted excerpts from "Bryant Spratlin / The Third Option," May 27, 2024, https://www.youtube.com/watch?v=0CSICfvBWPA.

citing Psalm 139:8 (author paraphrase) to emphasize that God is never absent. Peter reiterated what I've noted from other conversations: that hell is not a physical place of torment but a relational experience—a self-imposed prison of the psyche where individuals struggle to see the divine presence within and surrounding them.

This interpretation of hell is deeply rooted in Scripture. Peter noted his exploration of Revelation, in particular. "The thing that rocked my world," he explained, "was years ago, preaching through Revelation and realizing that at the end, death and Hades are thrown into the lake of fire. Death is no more. That means Hades comes to an end." This realization can radically shift our framework, presenting hell not as an eternal state but as a temporary condition ultimately consumed by God's transformative love!

Peter reinterprets the Western imagery of the "lake of fire" to represent God's divine presence. "The word brimstone," Peter noted, "is the Greek word Theon, which can also mean divinity. The lake of fire and brimstone is not about torment; it's about the very substance of God. It's a fire that purifies, a divine presence that refines rather than destroys."

I agreed wholeheartedly. I am growing ever sure that Greater Love is a restorative fire illuminating darkness before the beginning and after the end, a relentless flame of Triune kindness that leads to rethinking until we discover our entire being as Love's mirror reflection. We are made in Love's image and likeness, and we are becoming as we truly behold.

For Peter, this restorative fire is inseparable from God's ultimate purpose of reconciliation. "God is saying, look, I'm giving you My life. I'm giving you a blood transfusion. You're watching Me create you with My very self. What I'm creating in you is My heart, so that you will love as I love," he explained. In this vision, the story of humanity is one of ongoing creation, where God's love actively transforms and redeems all things. The fire of God's presence, far from being destructive, becomes the mechanism through which all things are reconciled to Him.

Peter's views sharply critique Western evangelical notions of eternal conscious torment. "How do we arrange our theology so that God endlessly tortures people?" he asked pointedly. "I just don't think Scripture requires that. In fact, I think it eliminates that possibility at several points." Such views distort the character of God and undermine the heart of the gospel.

Peter's conviction regarding the love of God has not come without cost. He shared how he was defrocked for refusing to affirm doctrines of eternal torment. "They asked me to publicly confess that there was a group of people God could not save and that He delighted in their endless destruction. I just couldn't do it," he said. His refusal was born out of a deep conviction that the God revealed in Christ is better than we often dare to imagine. Peter is one of those Tambourine Men. I am thankful for his jingle jangle.

I love his reflections on hell and reconciliation. "God doesn't give up," he said. "He's not letting go. That's what the cross is about. . . . The cross isn't about satisfying God's anger," Peter declared. "It's about demonstrating the depth of God's commitment to His creation. It's a revelation of relentless, unyielding love." For Peter, this love is the fire that burns away all that is not love, leaving only reconciliation and renewal in its wake.

"I think the evil one has had us twist the beauty of the cross into a terrifying threat," he concluded. "But in reality, it is the revelation of the heart of God. The lake of fire is not the end; it's the beginning of restoration."[124]

A SPICY CONCLUSION

Rethinking hell, at its core, is a journey into the heart of the Trinity—a heart that is always love, always pursuing, always transforming, always restoring.

Hell, then, is not the absence of God, nor is it an eternal punishment inflicted by a wrathful deity. Rather, it is our flawed perception and participation in separation. And yet, love remains. Greater Love is relentlessly kind—a refining fire that purifies, an embrace that never lets go, an invitation that never ceases.

In the end, hell is not the final word. Love is. And LOVE never fails.

The friends in this chapter have invited us to see clearly and truly, beyond the retributive, fear-based narratives many of us inherited, so we might embrace a vision of a God whose justice is always redemptive, always restorative.

---

[124] Jason Clark and Derek Turner, hosts, *Rethinking God with Tacos,* podcast, adapted excerpts from "Peter Hiett / What About Hell?", March 2, 2022, https://www.youtube.com/watch?v=CffWzLLR04M.

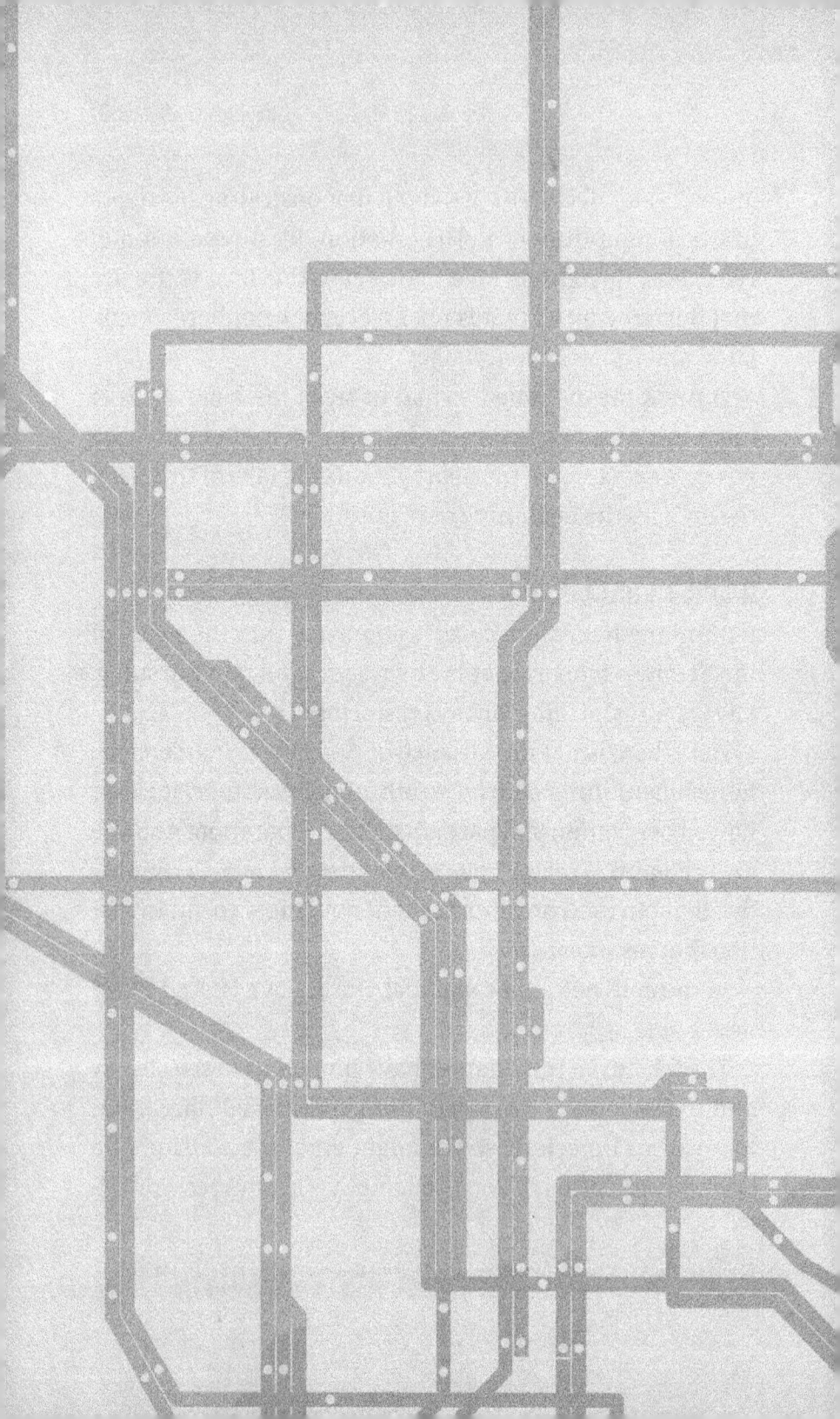

CHAPTER 17

JUSTICE

A Taco for a Taco

DANNY SILK: BREAKING UP WITH PUNISHMENT

Danny Silk has profound insight into love, honor, and restoration. His thoughts have shaped the way my wife and I lead, parent, and understand God's heart. I am thankful for him, especially for cracking the door open to the idea that God doesn't punish.

Danny's book Unpunishable dives into this paradigm shift as a practical lens for parenting, leadership, and relationships.[125] "God doesn't parent the way many of us were parented. He doesn't lead the way most of us have experienced leadership," he said. Danny's message is simple: God's goal is always connection, His leadership rooted in love, not fear.

---

[125] Danny Silk, *Unpunishable: Ending Our Love Affair with Punishment* (Loving on Purpose, 2019)

Danny opened with a striking truth: "God is not a God of punishment, but a God that restores, a God of love." It's a beautiful revelation—but not one most of us were raised with. Much of the Church clings to the image of a punitive God because, ironically, it gives us a sense of control. Even though it's a distortion, that false view of God can feel familiar, so letting go of it is both terrifying and liberating.

"The trigger point for human beings in the cycle of punishment has a lot to do with (how) addicted we are to self-preservation and control," Danny shared. We equate control with safety—in our relationships, churches, and parenting—and in doing so, we miss the invitation into a deeper trust rooted in love.

Fear fuels our desire for control—and when fear takes the wheel, punishment often follows. But what if God doesn't operate from a fear-based paradigm? What if fear and control were never effective to begin with?

Danny reflected on his years as a foster care social worker, during which time he witnessed firsthand how punishment-based parenting left deep emotional wounds. "Christian parents don't realize how much they rely on intimidation," he said. "Well, you cannot use those tools with foster children." That insight marked a turning point for Danny. It launched him on a journey to discover a better way—one grounded not in fear but in connection, honor, and love.

Honor kept surfacing in our conversation. Where punishment prioritizes control, honor esteems the person above their behavior. "Understanding that we are empowering people with our authority, not dominating people with our authority," Danny explained, "is the bedrock of a culture of honor." And this isn't just a parenting principle—it's a paradigm shift in understanding God.

OUR LOVE AFFAIR WITH PUNISHMENT ISN'T JUST ABOUT DISCIPLINE; IT'S ABOUT CONTROL.

If God empowers rather than controls, then every encounter with Him is an invitation into restoration, not retribution.

This shift is ultimately about freedom. "If you don't have self-control," Danny said, "that means something else controls you." We often confuse freedom with the absence of boundaries, but Danny reframed it as self-governance. "Self-control is what prevents something else from controlling me." In this light, God's restorative heart invites us into true freedom, where love, not fear, takes the lead.

By the end of our conversation, it was clear: our love affair with punishment is about control. But God's love isn't about control; it's about connection. "The goal is connection, not compliance."[126] And that's true in all our relationships.

God isn't in the business of keeping score or enforcing rules. He's restoring broken hearts, building trust, and empowering us to live in the fullness of who we were created to be. Once we see through the lens of *God in Christ reconciling the world to Himself, not counting our sins against us*, we can begin to define the true nature of justice.

AN EYE FOR AN EYE

"You have heard that it was said, 'Eye for eye....'" Jesus said in Matthew 5:38.

This phrase has long been a benchmark for justice, often interpreted through a punitive lens: If I take your eye, my eye is taken in retribution. But this approach perpetuates cycles of violence and offers no room for transformation.

Early Jewish and Christian traditions often saw "an eye for an eye" as restorative. If I take your eye, I become your eye—working to restore what I've harmed. This interpretation fosters repentance, transformation, and reconciliation. It mirrors Jesus's justice as He continues in Matthew 5:44, "But I say, love your enemies! Pray for those who persecute you!" (NLT).

Jesus redefined justice: "There is no greater love than to lay down one's life for one's friends" (John 15:13, NLT). Then, Greater Love laid His life down as the hermeneutic. Jesus's death and resurrection are the foundation of reconciliation

---

[126] Jason Clark & Thomas Floyd, hosts, *Rethinking God with Tacos*, podcast, adapted excerpts from "Danny Silk / Unpunishable," June 17, 2020, https://www.youtube.com/watch?v=DE1F4Cpgcbg.

and restoration, where forgiveness and love triumph over retribution.[127]

MAKO NAGASAWA: A JUSTICE THAT HEALS

Mako Nagasawa's insights on restorative justice are like finding a key to a door you've been banging on your whole life. Growing up in the West, we're steeped in the retributive framework—God as the angry judge, humanity as the guilty party, and Jesus as the one who took the hit. But Mako, with his calm, thoughtful tone, shared a lens that reframes everything.

"God's justice isn't about punishment; it's about restoration," Mako began. "When we talk about restorative justice, it's centered on healing what's been broken—relationships, communities, even ourselves. Contrast that with retributive justice, which focuses on making the offender suffer in proportion to their crime. They're fundamentally different frameworks."

Mako shared a personal story to illustrate. "When my daughter was in third grade," he said, "she wrote something inappropriate on the bathroom wall at school. The teachers could have punished her, suspended her even, but instead, they chose a restorative approach. She cleaned the wall, helped with classroom chores, and even baked brownies to apologize to the younger kids who felt scared by what she wrote. That process didn't just address the harm she caused; it helped her grow as a person."

---

127 Jason Clark, *Leaving and Finding Jesus.*

Mako's words brought us back to the cross, the ultimate act of justice. "He (Jesus) came to absorb the corruption in humanity. He kills the thing that's killing us. That's restorative justice."

I asked him to dig deeper into how this contrasts with the Western framework, and Mako didn't hold back. "In retributive justice," he said, "justice is centered on the offender. The idea is to make them suffer in proportion to their crime. But in restorative justice, the focus shifts to the victim. What does the victim need to heal? What (harm) does the offender need to repair to be restored to the community?"

"Restored" isn't about balancing scales; it's about repairing and renewing. "God's wrath," Mako added, "isn't directed at people. It's directed at the corruption within them. It's like a doctor hating cancer, not the patient. God's justice is about removing what doesn't belong, what's killing us, so we can thrive."

> **WRATH EMERGED ONLY WHEN SIN ENTERED THE PICTURE. AND EVEN THEN, IT'S NOT ABOUT PUNISHMENT; IT'S ABOUT HEALING.**

We pivoted to Scripture because, let's be honest, that's where most of us struggle to reconcile these ideas. "The early Church fathers," he said, "read Scripture with Jesus as the lens. They understood that God's justice is restorative because that's what they saw in Christ. Irenaeus called it 'recapitulation,' where Jesus redoes the story of humanity and heals it."

"So when you see God's wrath in Scripture," he continued, "look at the context. Fire, for example, is often a refining image. It's not about destruction but purification. Even in exile, God's 'punishment' is aimed at restoration, at undoing harm and rebuilding trust."

Mako didn't deny that these ideas clash with certain theological traditions. "There's a Western view," he said, "that sees God as having two faces: one of love and one of retributive justice. But the early Church didn't see it that way. They saw all of God's actions as flowing from love. Even His wrath is an expression of that love."

I was enthusiastic with my "come on" as Mako continued, "Before creation, there was no wrath in God—only love within the Trinity. Wrath emerged only when sin entered the picture. And even then, it's not about punishment; it's about healing."[128]

As the conversation wound down, Mako left us with a vision of what could be. "If we adopted God's restorative justice, our churches, families, and communities would look radically different," he said. "Justice wouldn't just be

---

[128] Jason Clark and Thomas Floyd, hosts, *Rethinking God with Tacos,* podcast, adapted excerpts from "Mako Nagasawa / A Restorative God," April 3, 2020, https://www.youtube.com/watch?v=xxUdIrwiB6I.

about retribution; it would be about reconciliation. It would reflect the cross, where Jesus takes on our brokenness to make us whole."

I absolutely loved Mako's call to embody the kind of justice that heals rather than harms. "It's the kind of truth that changes everything," he said as our conversation ended. I agreed and picked it back up with my friend Jared.

JARED NEUSCH: JUSTICE THAT LOOKS LIKE JESUS

"The cross is the great methodology of how evil is overcome," Jared Neusch shared with conviction during our conversation. "It's not just about forgiveness; it's a blueprint for how we're called to live." For Jared, Jesus's nonviolence and restorative justice are the very heart of the gospel.

Jared is a thoughtful, compassionate theologian whose gentle clarity and deep conviction continually inspire us to center our faith on the love of Jesus. I am thankful for his friendship. From the outset, Jared challenged our Western Evangelical understanding of justice. "If your God is violent," he explained, "you'll justify violence. But if your God looks like Jesus, everything changes." He emphasized how our perception of God directly shapes our actions and worldview. "A violent God leads to violent followers," Jared warned. "But Jesus's nonviolence is an invitation to a whole new way of being."

Our discussion naturally gravitated towards the Sermon on the Mount, which Jared referred to as "the Constitution of the Kingdom of God.... When Jesus tells us to love our enemies," he said, "He's laying out a practical roadmap for how to engage with the world." This roadmap culminates at the cross—the ultimate redefinition of justice. "The irony of the cross is that it's humanity's greatest act of violence," he explained. "And yet, through it, God brings about the ultimate act of justice. It's the ultimate act of restorative love."

Jared pointed to historical figures like Martin Luther King Jr. to illustrate how nonviolence can actively resist evil. "Christian pacifism isn't passivity," he stated. "Look at the Civil Rights Movement. It was active, creative, and subversive. It took the way of the cross and lived it out."

> **THE CROSS IS THE ONLY THING THAT OVERCOMES EVIL—NOT BY AVOIDING IT BUT BY ABSORBING IT WITH LOVE.**

Jared also spoke to the limitations of our collective imagination regarding justice. "We're stuck in a binary," he said. "We think it's either violence or nothing. But Jesus offers a third way—a way that's restorative, not destructive." He highlighted the disciples as examples of this third way. "They didn't just hear Jesus's teachings; they lived them. Not one of them retaliated, even in the face of death. They carried the way of the cross to the very end."

Jared's words were challenging but essential. "If we reject the way of the cross," he said, "we shouldn't be surprised when our solutions to evil don't work. The cross is the only thing that overcomes evil, not by avoiding it but by absorbing it with love."

Jared emphasized that this restorative approach could redefine justice in our personal lives. He described forgiveness not just as a personal virtue but as a revolutionary act against cycles of retribution. "To forgive isn't to excuse harm," he noted. "It's to refuse to perpetuate harm. It's to say that love and reconciliation will have the last word, not revenge."

As we wrapped up our conversation, Jared painted a compelling vision of justice rooted in Jesus's teachings. "Restorative justice isn't just about fixing the past; it's about shaping a future where love and reconciliation are the norm. It's about refusing to let violence have the last word."[129] His words lingered long after our conversation, echoing the call to embody this radical justice daily. Just as the cross serves as a divine blueprint, we are invited to create pathways of reconciliation in every relationship and community we touch.

This conversation became the seedbed for reflections I would later explore in my book, *Leaving and Finding Jesus.*[130] Here's a brief breakdown.

---

129 Jason Clark and Derek Turner, hosts, *Rethinking God with Tacos,* podcast, adapted excerpts from "Jared Neusch / A Christocentric Hermeneutic & a Non-violent God," June 19, 2023, https://www.youtube.com/watch?v=Wo5ngUlddnU.
130 Jason Clark, excerpts adapted from *Leaving and Finding Jesus.*

FATHER FORGIVE

Justice doesn't just heal; it transforms. This justice is revealed and experienced in Jesus's words and actions.

Punishment is never justice. In fact, punishment is hypocrisy for a Christian. It participates in the spirit of revenge, rooted in the knowledge of good and evil—and evil and evil and evil. But no matter how deeply we engage in retribution, God is like Jesus. His greater love defines His justice as restorative.

First Corinthians 13 is often quoted at weddings, a familiar chapter for many. It describes love as patient and kind and continues with attributes that mirror the nature of God. Nestled between "love isn't easily angered" and "love doesn't delight in evil" is a truth powerful enough to change the world:

"Love keeps no record of wrongs. . . ."

Jesus, Love in human form, hung on a cross between heaven and earth. His body battered, the lie of separation veiling His sense of the Father's affection. The myth of abandonment screamed through the iron nails that tore His flesh. Yet, amidst this suffering, Jesus reveals the power of a free will submitted to Love's sovereignty.

> **HIS JUSTICE DOESN'T COUNT SINS; IT RECONCILES AND RESTORES.**

Jesus—fully God, fully Man, one with the Father, intimate with the Holy Spirit—forgives. His forgiveness confronts the transactional, sin-counting, retributive justice system— "[What] seems right to a man" (Proverbs 14:12, ESV, author addition).

Casting back to before the beginning and forward to after the end, Jesus keeps no record of humanity's wrongs. "Father, forgive them, for they know not what they do" (Luke 23:34, ESV), He said. And the power of Greater Love saves the world.

Do you know what happened when Jesus kept no record of our wrongs?

He couldn't justify holding onto offense, and all creation was reborn in that powerful conclusion.

We've been invited to live in that same freedom and discover justice's transformative power!

All creation has been called to awaken to this reconciling, measureless revelation. Love doesn't count sins; He keeps no record of wrongs.

This paradigm dismantles the dualistic mindset of "us versus them" or "good versus evil." In the economy of grace, everyone is a beloved son or daughter being transformed into Love's likeness. Romans 3:23 tells us, "All have sinned," but Jesus doesn't leave us there. The next verse? ". . . . and all are justified freely by his grace through the redemption that came by Christ Jesus." His justice doesn't count sins; it reconciles and restores.

As we embrace this vision of justice, we step into the transformative power of a love that doesn't just heal wounds but makes all things new. Restorative justice is a call to live out the radical reconciliation embodied in Jesus's life, death, resurrection, and ascension. This is the justice that restores, the love that transforms, and the hope that saves the world.[131]

---

[131] Jason Clark, excerpts adapted from *Leaving and Finding Jesus*.

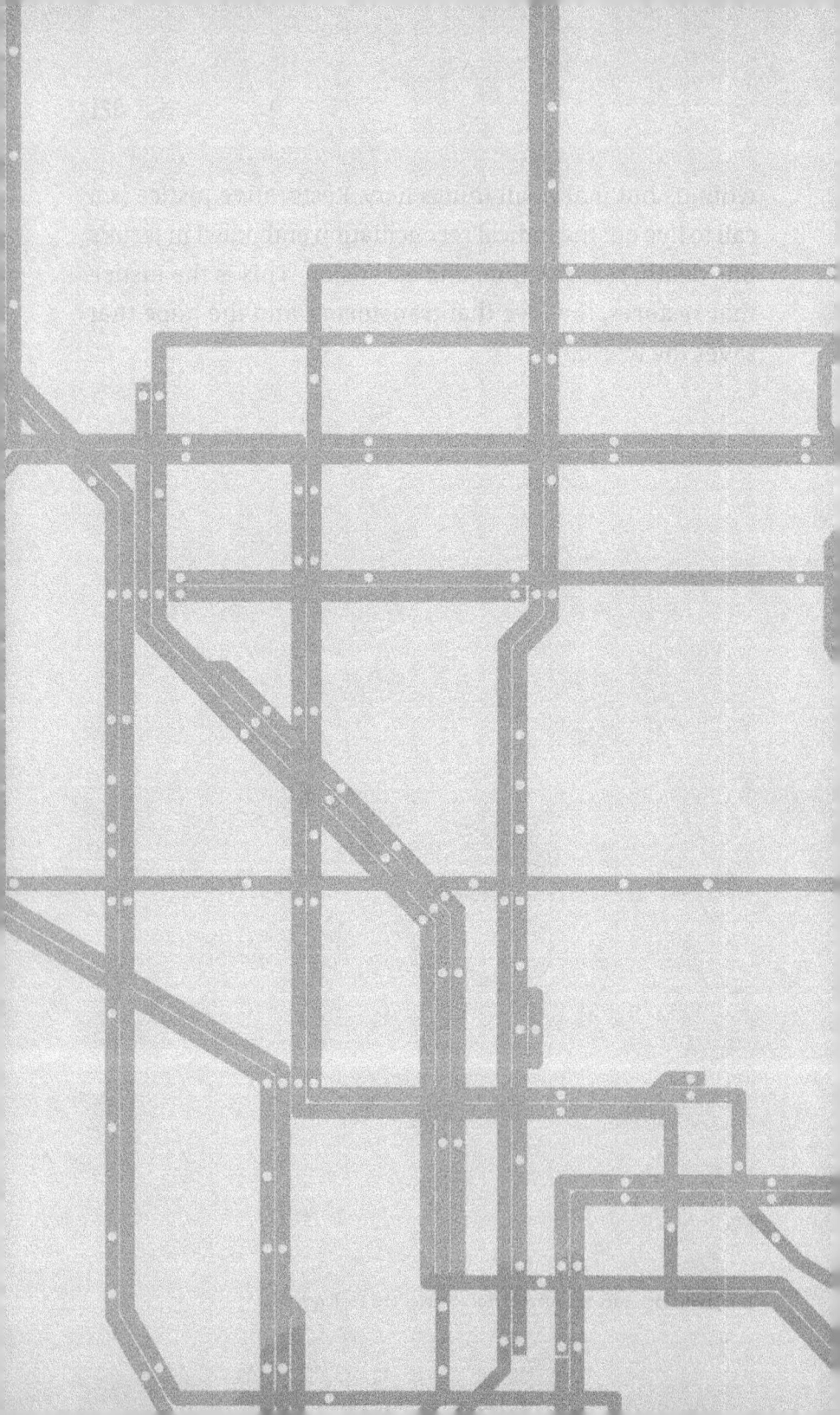

CHAPTER 18

THE LONG ARC OF LOVE
Slow-Cooked, Like Carnitas

BOB SWITZER: THE EPIC NARRATIVE

There's a moment in every great story where something shifts— the character suddenly sees with new eyes, where what was once rigid and certain cracks open, making room for something deeper, truer, more alive. That's what it felt like talking with Bob Switzer.

Bob is a fellow sojourner whose passion for Jesus and commitment to the long arc of God's love resonates deeply—I'm honored to call him a friend.

Bob is a storyteller who weaves narratives that reveal how our lives are stitched into the fabric of Scripture, wrapped in grace, and saturated with the goodness of God. "The Lord, He's so good, right?" Bob said early in our conversation. "He doesn't care where we start. He just always invites us to more." And that's the beauty of the long arc of love—the story God is telling, which forever invites us to follow Him into more.

Bob's story is an invitation to move from a rigid theological framework into the vast, wild, grace-drenched landscape of love. "I was so good at it," he told me, talking about his early years as a fundamentalist preacher. "I could make people come down the aisle. I was young and passionate. But the invitation kept coming. And every time the Lord invited me, it meant leaving where I was."

GOD ALWAYS INVITES US TO MORE.

That's the thing about love—it won't let us stay small. It keeps pulling us forward, even when it means letting go of what once felt certain. Bob experienced this profoundly when he was introduced to narrative preaching. "I had no idea it was a thing," he laughed. "I was trained in exegesis, three points, two illustrations, and definitely nothing about yourself—because it's not about you, it's about God. And I was so good at it. And yet . . . it wasn't me."

As love kept inviting him deeper, Bob began to realize it wasn't just about how he was preaching—it was about *Who* he was preaching. "Jesus is perfect theology," Bob said. "And always good!" I added. Bob nodded, then continued, "So, I started going back to Scripture (through a Christological lens) and saying, 'Alright, if something doesn't look like Jesus, I have to rethink it.'"

That's the work of love. It keeps reorienting us, asking us to look again, read again, see through Christ's lens, and then tell the world what we see—the story!

It's why storytelling matters—because it allows us to revisit, wrestle, discover, and participate with the long arc of Love. As Bob put it, "God always invites us to more."[132] And God's love story is still unfolding. It's "the long arc of love," I said, a quote from Baxter. And it's true. We are in a beautiful story where love is the beginning and the end.

Which is the perfect way to set up my friend and master storyteller, Malcolm Smith.

MALCOLM AND CHERYL SMITH: THE STORY WE'RE ALREADY IN

Malcolm is a forerunner of the unconditional love of God. His teaching has profoundly shaped our understanding of union. Cheryl is a radiant witness to the healing power of God's love. It was incredible to have them on the podcast. Oh, and Malcolm is a tambourine and *three* weeks ahead.

Malcolm tells stories the way a painter wields a brush—not to explain something, but to reveal what was always there. He doesn't analyze them from a distance. He steps inside them, breathes them in, and invites you to do the same. And if you accept the invitation, something shifts.

---

132 Jason Clark, host, *Rethinking God with Tacos*, podcast, adapted excerpts from "Bob Switzer / The Epic Narrative," March 13, 2024, https:/www.youtube.com/watch?v=t6EsuWy aLBQ&list=PLgimV9UoSbAlbXX447Gu_5-kGpLAO_eJO&index=49.

Suddenly, you're not just reading about love—you're encountering it.

That's the nature of the long arc of love. It's not linear, not easily mapped. It moves in mystery, in parables and presence, in glimpses that catch your breath and rearrange your theology. That's what happens the first time you hear Malcolm teach on the parable of the prodigal son.

"That parable is the war cry of the Prince of Peace," Malcolm said. "Jesus is throwing down the gauntlet to the religious leaders who have trapped people in fear. He's not just telling a nice story—He's exposing the lie of separation."

Separation. The great illusion. The original lie. But Jesus' story obliterates it. The son never stopped being a son. The father never wavered in his love. The whole crisis was in the son's mind—his belief he had forfeited his place.

"He came home rehearsing a speech about being a servant," Malcolm said, shaking his head. "He still didn't understand. He thought he had to earn his way back. But the father interrupted him. He didn't even let him finish his apology. Why? Because love doesn't keep score. It doesn't need an apology before it embraces. It just runs."

That moment—the father running, robes billowing, throwing dignity to the wind—wrecks me every time. In that moment, Jesus is storytelling in a way that reveals the heart of God. And once you see it, you can't unsee it. That's the long arc of love. It doesn't begin in judgment or end in exclusion. It begins and ends in the Father's embrace.

We live in a narrative where Love is the first and the final word. And it's the storytellers who help us see this. Jesus and

Malcolm bypass our devotion to good and evil with parables that reveal Life.

Truth isn't argued, it's recognized. And Malcolm describes it as an encounter with liquid love.

> # JESUS DIDN'T DIE FOR US—HE DIED AS US.

"I cannot explain myself apart from the Holy Spirit," he said. "The night I encountered Him; every ounce of fear I had been carrying since birth was sucked up and replaced with peace. That's what love does—it rewrites the story we've believed about ourselves."

And that's the long arc of love. Not a transaction. Not a contract. A story that's been unfolding since the beginning, with a single, unchanging through-line: God with us.

"Jesus didn't die for us—He died as us," Malcolm said. "He stepped inside our darkness, not to condemn, but to pull us out from within."[133]

That's why Malcolm doesn't teach theology—he tells stories. Stories that don't demand answers but awaken awareness. Stories that reveal union. Stories that invite us into the long arc of love already unfolding in our lives.

---

133 Jason Clark, host, *Rethinking God with Tacos*, podcast, adapted excerpts from "Malcolm & Cheryl Smith / The Storyteller," March 6, 2024, https://www.youtube.com/watch?v=7chgURZw7Lc&list=PLgimV9UoSbAIbXX447Gu_5-kGpLAO_eJO&index=50.

And that brings us to a storyteller of a different kind—one whose medium is quantum, but whose message echoes the same eternal love.

STEVE MCVEY: LIVING A QUANTUM LIFE

Love refuses to exist in isolation. It is expansive, connective, and relentless. It holds all things together, whether we recognize it or not. Steve McVey sees it everywhere.

"Quantum physics tells us what the Bible's been saying all along. Everything is connected. Nothing stands alone." Steve said this with quiet conviction, as one who has spent years dialoging with science and Scripture. And if that's the case—if everything is connected—then love isn't just an attribute of God. It's the fundamental nature of existence.

"I came across books on quantum mechanics by accident," Steve said. "But the more I read, the more I saw the same truths I had already discovered in Christ. It was like the circles overlapped until I couldn't separate them anymore."

I nodded, knowing what he meant. There comes a point when the language of faith and science begins to harmonize. "The old way of seeing the universe was mechanical—like a giant machine, where everything is separate and has to be controlled," Steve said. "But quantum physics shows us a different reality: one where everything exists in relationship."

It's the long arc of love again—bending everything toward wholeness and belonging. Quantum physics is simply a scientific way of describing it. It suggests every act of love ripples through existence in ways we can't begin to measure. "What we have referred to as miracles, scientists may begin to explain through quantum mechanics?" I asked.

Steve nodded, responding, "Miracles aren't supernatural interruptions. They're quantum expressions of the natural world—just as God designed it."

That alone is a cosmic shift. How often have we considered miracles as God stepping in to break the rules? But what if Love itself is the rule? What if healing, restoration, and transformation are built into the very design of the universe? And what if that is the long arc?

Steve continued, "Your DNA carries a song that God has written into existence. Scientists have actually mapped it."

> **IF OUR DNA IS SINGING, THEN OUR ROLE ISN'T TO FIND OUR SONG— IT'S TO STOP RESISTING THE ONE WE'VE ALREADY BEEN GIVEN.**

I leaned in. "You're saying my body is literally vibrating with a melody?"

Steve nodded. "Absolutely. And that melody is unique to you. It's God's song being sung through your life. You don't have to create it; you just have to live in tune with it." Steve continued, "The melody in your DNA? It's not just yours. It's God's song. And the world needs to hear it."

Beautiful, I thought. If love is the melody and resonance that binds us together, then every moment is sacred, every breath is holy. Another way to say it, in the quantum life: there is no striving, no proving—there is simply harmonizing with the love.

"You don't have to earn this love," Steve said. "You're already reconciled. You don't have to make something happen. You just wake up to what's already true."

Steve added, "The universe isn't random. It's infused with intention, love, and divine harmony." *We are in the long arc of love, where all things are being reconciled,* I thought and then expressed. This led to my favorite quote from the conversation.

"I often say this—that I am not a biblical universalist. The reason for that is because of my own perspective and understanding; there's just too much dialectical tension in Scripture. But you might call me a quantum universalist."[134]

That phrase lingered like a melody—quantum universalist. And it was in that resonance that we moved into the long arc frequency of Mike Popovich.

MIKE POPOVICH: THE FABRIC OF CREATION

For Mike, prayer isn't about hoping for change but acknowledging that the change already exists—it's about resonance. "Prayer isn't begging for something new; it's receiving

---

[134] Jason Clark and Derek Turner, hosts, *Rethinking God with Tacos,* podcast, adapted excerpts from "Steve McVey / Quantum Life," June 4, 2023, https://www.youtube.com/watch?v=5rjSjybuEXg&list=PLgimV9UoSbAIbXX447Gu_5-kGpLAO_eJO&index=88.

what's already yours," he said, drawing together faith, neuroscience, and quantum physics in one breath.

Everything he shared pointed to one truth: we are immersed in a love that's always been present. "The universe—all creation—responds to love and gratitude. It's wired that way because that's who God is," he explained.

Mike often parallels neuroscience with biblical principles. "Neuroscience is just Scripture with a brain scan," he said. "What you think and feel shapes your reality."

THE INVITATION ISN'T TO EARN IT. IT'S TO REMEMBER.

Divine connection, at its core, is love in motion. "Everything in the universe is responding to love because love is the very fabric of creation," he said. *It's the long arc,* I thought. *It's a living, pulsing energy— it moves, it transforms, it rewires, it is the essence of all that is.* Mike continued, "When we meditate on love, when we focus on gratitude, we're not just changing our mindset; we're reshaping our reality."

"Thus, the invitation isn't to earn it. It's to remember," I said. Mike nodded, "You don't have to earn love or chase it," Mike said. "You just have to wake up to the fact that it's already here, already holding you."[135]

Which sets up Baxter nicely.

BAXTER KRUGER: THE EMMAUS ROAD YES

"This is a long arc," Baxter said, his eyes lighting up as he described the story of redemption rooted in the eternal fellowship of Father, Son, and Spirit. "From before the foundations of the world, love was the plan, union the blueprint."

> **EVERY SINGLE PERSON ON THE PLANET IS HAVING AN EMMAUS ROAD EXPERIENCE; THEY JUST DON'T KNOW IT YET.**

Baxter leaned forward, his voice full of conviction. "Every single person on the planet is having an Emmaus Road experience; they just don't know it yet." I grinned. This is a conversation we've had many times. "God is walking with each one of us, even when we don't recognize Him," I said. "He is opening our eyes, breaking bread, speaking our names. He has been since before the foundations of the world and will be throughout eternity—our hearts are on

---

[135] Jason Clark and Thomas Floyd, hosts, *Rethinking God with Tacos,* podcast, adapted excerpts from "Mike Popovich / Prayer & Quantum Physics," April 3, 2020, https://www.youtube.com/watch?v=o7twPI5PEQw.

fire and we're ever awakening to the burning. That's the long arc of love."

Baxter nodded and said, "You need to have Bruce on (the podcast), he has been breaking down this long arc with me for years."[136]

And so, we conclude with Bruce.

BRUCE WAUCHOPE: LOVE AT THE BOTTOM

Bruce is a Tambourine Man. He is a firebrand of grace and a surgeon of the soul whose fierce tenderness and uncompromising revelation of union wrecked me in the best way—I'm honored to call him a brother and a new friend. My podcast conversation happened while I was wrapping up edits for this book. But by the time the conversation was over, I knew he was my closer.

"If you start with separation, you end up with the Western gospel," Bruce told me. "But if you start with union—if you start with the Father, Son, and Spirit already loving each other, already including us—then the whole thing shifts."

Bruce talked about the Christ who has descended into the very bottom of our humanity—the trauma, abuse, shame, and despair—and is sharing His life with us from that place. "God has descended into the abyss of human darkness and gone to the bottom," Bruce said. And from the bottom, He is sharing His love and life with you."

That's not a metaphor. That's the gospel. That's union.

---

[136] Jason Clark, *Rethinking God with Tacos,* adapted excerpts from "C. Baxter Kruger / Christ In You!"

"The Word became flesh and made his dwelling," Bruce paused. "The Greek doesn't say 'among us' (as most translations present it)—it says, 'in us. He made His dwelling *in* us!'"

He made His dwelling in us! That's the reality of the incarnation: Jesus in us, breaking our illusions of separation from the inside out.

As Bruce spoke, I could feel it—this is what the long arc of love looks like. It's not a line we follow upward toward God. It's a descent into our mess, pain, and fear, where we discover we've never been alone. "Underneath that," Bruce said, "are the everlasting arms holding you already. In you."

The implications are staggering.

EVEN IN THE MOST TORMENTED, DIFFICULT PERSON YOU MEET—AT THE BOTTOM OF THEM IS JESUS CHRIST.

If Jesus is in us—and we didn't put Him there—then we're not trying to get to God. We're waking up to God already here. "Jesus Christ is the death of human religion," Bruce said. And you know what? That's salvation. Not a theory. Not a system. But a person. A presence. A union that was never broken.

Then Bruce said something stunning: "There is no place deeper than where He's gone. So, there's nowhere you can go that's outside of His salvation."

That's the long arc of love. Not an escape plan. Not a contract. But a revelation. And that revelation always leads us home—to the Father who never left, the Spirit who never stopped whispering, the Son who took on our flesh to show us we were never forsaken.

This is the gospel of union. This is the long arc of love.

And it's not new. It's ancient. It's early Church. It's what the mystics saw. It's what the Orthodox preserved. It's what Bruce experienced in the middle of his darkest days, and what he now proclaims with fire and tenderness.

"You were forgiven before you were created," he said. "And even in the most tormented, difficult person you meet—at the bottom of them is Jesus Christ."[137]

That's union. That's the gospel. That's the love that never lets go.

It's the whole story. The beginning, the middle, the end, and everything after that.

The long arc of love throughout eternity.

---

137 Jason Clark, host, *Rethinking God with Tacos*, podcast, adapted excerpts from "Dr. Bruce Wauchope / Union: The Heart Of The Gospel," March 18, 2025 https://www.youtube.com/watch?v=OSbrvl9Vl10&t=3619s.

www.ingramcontent.com/pod-product-compliance
Lightning Source LLC
Chambersburg PA
CBHW050852160426
43194CB00011B/2127